Regime Change

Nijhoff Law Specials

VOLUME 84

The titles published in this series are listed at brill.com/nlsp

Regime Change

From Democratic Peace Theories to Forcible Regime Change

By

Rein Müllerson

MARTINUS NIJHOFF PUBLISHERS

LEIDEN · BOSTON
2013

Library of Congress Cataloging-in-Publication Data

Mullerson, R. A.
Regime change : from democratic peace theories to forcible regime change / by Rein Mullerson.
pages cm. -- (Nijhoff law specials ; v. 84)
Includes index.
ISBN 978-90-04-23230-3 (pbk. : alk. paper)
1. Regime change. 2. Democratization. I. Title.

JC489.M85 2013
321.09--dc23

2012046836

This publication has been typeset in the multilingual "Brill" typeface. With over 5,100 characters covering Latin, IPA, Greek, and Cyrillic, this typeface is especially suitable for use in the humanities. For more information, please see www.brill.com/brill-typeface.

ISSN 0924-4549
ISBN 978-90-04-23230-3 (paperback)
ISBN 978-90-04-23231-0 (e-book)

This book is printed on acid-free paper.

To the memory of my mother Erna Müllerson and to the future of Irina, Jan and George

I am most grateful to George Müllerson for his valuable comments and suggestions

CONTENTS

Introduction 1

I From an African Village to a Global Village 13
1. *Ex Uno Plures* in the Evolution of Humankind 15
2. Is *E Pluribus Unum* Replacing *Ex Uno Plures*? 21
3. Homogenisation of the World and Heterogenisation of Individual Societies 27
4. 'Oh, East is East, and West is West, and Never the Twain shall Meet, Till Earth and Sky Stand Presently at God's great Judgment Seat'? 29

II Whither goest thou, the World? 33
1. Universal History and Historical Determinism 33
2. Current Regime Changes: Socioeconomic and Political Problems 41
3. Problems of Liberal Democracy and Democratic Capitalism 56
4. Limits of Social Democratic Choice in a Globalised World 72
5. Any Viable Alternatives? 75

III On the Futility and Danger of External Attempts to 'Democratise' China 85
1. China's Rise and the Changing Balance of Power 86
2. Modernising China – a Democratic China? 88
3. A Small Diversion to Illustrate the Point: The Kyrgyz Tragedy of 2010 93
4. Back to China: Reforms, not Revolution 97
5. The World's Reaction to China's rise 104
6. From Westernisation to Sinification? 113

IV Regime Changes in Russia: Gorbachev, Yeltsin and Putin 119
1. Understanding Russia or Believing in Russia 119
2. Collapse of the USSR and the Emergence of Yeltsin's Russia 125

3. On Putin's Authoritarianism 134
4. Russia – Not Lost to Democracy 138
5. Russia – Too Big to Practice Bandwaggoning 140
6. Russia and its Close Neighbours 148
7. Russia – Part of Europe? 153

V Democratic Peace Theories and Regime change 161
1. Theory and Politics of Democratic Peace 161
2. Problems with Democratic Peace Theories 164
3. Immanuel Kant and the XXI Century World 173
4. On the War-Proneness of Some Democratising States 175

VI Humanitarian Intervention, Civil Wars and Regime Change 179
1. Use of Force and Humanitarian Concerns in 'Modern' and 'Post-Modern' International Societies 179
2. The Kosovo Case Revisited 187
3. Recognition of Kosovo, Abkhazia and South Ossetia 192
4. The Libya Case 194
5. The Syria Tragedy 199
6. Humanitarian Intervention and Regime Change: Some Generalisations 207
7. From Humanitarian Intervention to R2P or 'Old Wine in New Bottles'? 212
8. Intervention in Civil Wars or Internal Disturbances and Regime Change 223
9. Determinants of Success of External Interference: Efforts of Interveners or Characteristics of the Target Society? 225

Conclusions 233

Index 237

INTRODUCTION

The current series of regime changes in different parts of the world started with the transformation and collapse of the Soviet Union as the manifestation and guardian of communist ideology and totalitarian practices. This, in turn, released a chain of transformations in Eastern and Central Europe. These events and developments were seen as a triumph of liberal democracy over communist ideology and practices; and in a way it was exactly that, though the declarations concerning the 'end of history' or 'mission accomplished' were not only premature, but as it soon became clear, dead wrong. An aftershock, or rather series of after-tremors, to this epochal change, which can be justifiably defined as a world-wide social revolution, came slightly more than a decade later in several of the former Soviet republics (Georgia, Ukraine, Kyrgyzstan) in the form of the so-called 'colour revolutions' that combined in different degrees, *depending on the specific country* (sic!), expressions of popular discontent, external meddling, and opportunistic struggle for power; these were rather *coup d'états* than social revolutions.

Then, less than a decade later, came the 'Arab Spring' or the 'Arab Awakening', as it is also called, whose directions and meaning for these countries as well as for the world at large is still difficult to gauge. While these events have some common roots and similar features, as well as significant differences, often the former are exaggerated, and sometimes ignored. On the one hand, these events are all entwined by a general context, which is that of a globalising world with an almost instant flow of information. They are also a part of the general tendencies of different peoples, ethnicities, religions and other groups, which had hitherto been marginalised and disenfranchised, now demanding their say in deciding how to live, with whom to live and even where to live. In the eyes of many in the West, this is an accelerating run towards the 'end of history', a realisation of the idea of universal history. At the same time, the developments in all these societies, notwithstanding their quite obvious (often obvious because they are on the surface, i.e. relatively superficial), similarities are also very different. Even if the discontent of the Arab peoples has some significant common causes (repressive regimes that were mainly concerned with staying in power and enriching themselves, and more often than not serving the interests of foreign elites rather than their own people), their ethnic and religious compositions, demographic characteristics, levels of economic development, presence or absence of the 'oil curse', as well as their strategic alliances differ hugely. Equally, corruption, mismanagement and inter-ethnic tensions in the former Soviet republics of Georgia, Ukraine and Kyrgyzstan may have had many similar features and even causes, but there is no single uniform solution, their common history within the Czarist Empire and the Soviet Union notwithstanding. Happy countries, paraphrasing Tolstoy, may indeed look alike, but every unhappy country is unhappy very much in its own way. If this observation is correct, and below we will try to prove that it is, then countries that become happier, i.e. more prosperous, peaceful and free, will eventually indeed become in some important respects more similar to one another, though never, of course, becoming the same. However, as unhappy countries are all different, remedies that would make them happier are also different. Moreover, Tolstoy, though undoubtedly a brilliant writer, was not as great a philosopher as he wanted or even pretended to be, or as Isaiah Berlin put it, he was a fox who longed to be a hedgehog.[1] Today the world has too many aspiring hedgehogs in power, who – often sincerely – believe that the big picture of the world they hold is true for everybody. Foxes, in their view, are like those blind men who grope different parts of the elephant, and depending on the part they touch, imagine it either as a pillar or a tree or a rope. However, differently from the elephant – an organic integral system, where all parts are subordinated to and serve the system as a whole, the world is a much less integrated system and therefore foxes studying details, i.e. specific societies or issues, are after all not so blind. Even happy countries are not exactly the same, though there are some general features or principles, and ignoring them is problematic, if not impossible, in achieving happiness (peace, justice, prosperity and freedom). Yet, these are only the general features and principles that have to be adapted to cement conditions in any specific society. We, as individual human beings, are

---

[1] I. Berlin, *The Hedgehog and the Fox: An Essay on Tolstoy's View of History*, Ivan R Dee, 1993.

indeed quite the same. Even families (at least within the same civilization and culture) are quite similar. However, the bigger a social group, the more they differ from each other. China will never resemble Nauru, Sweden Iraq and the United States and Estonia will never be the same. History, culture, religion, geography and size – all matter even if, say, Iraq's per capita GDP were one day to surpass that of Sweden. So, a certain homogenisation of the world, whose important, controversial and topical aspect is the heterogenisation of individual societies, is a long-term tendency (which, like parallels in non-Euclidian geometry meet only in abstract theory or in cosmic practice, but in the tangible stay quite separate).

In this book it is argued that regime changes, which mark the turn of both the century and the millennium, take place in the general context of a globalising world that is characterised by a transformation of the balance of power and a crisis of dominant political and economic institutions. The still dominant West tries to channel justified popular discontent in many non-Western societies toward Western political and economic models that, however, are themselves in a state of crisis and in need of serious reforms. An ironic feature of the collapse of the communist system and the triumph of the West is the conclusion that these epochal events also revealed, though not immediately, the internal as well as external contradictions of the dominant and triumphant social, economic and political system, i.e. capitalist liberal democracy. It turned out to be only relatively triumphant, i.e. *vis-à-vis* its nemesis – the Soviet style communist system.

In the effort to channel the current social and political processes that are taking place in many countries towards one definitive model there are at least two dangers. First, most of these non-Western societies are not able to successfully and sustainably transform themselves into societies resembling Western models. In any case, even if they were to succeed, it would be in the long run and at the end of the day. Immediately, instead of democracy, there is a realistic potential of the emergence of anarchy *à la* Kyrgyzstan, of which more later, and instead of a market economy based on the rule of law, there would be a wild winner-takes-all type of capitalism *à la* Yeltsin's Russia, not to mention Afghanistan and Iraq which do not even remotely resemble the blueprints that were drawn up for these societies in Washington or Brussels. Secondly, even if some societies for various reasons may be able to implement Western models, this does not necessarily mean that they are following models that are the most appropriate for today's or even more appropriately for tomorrow's world. Current transformations concern not only societies that indeed were, so to say, on the 'wrong side of history', i.e. the former communist bloc countries. Their failure unleashed processes that revealed fundamental shortcomings in the triumphant – the Western liberal democracy – system. Today the whole world is groping the elephant in an attempt to make sense of a runaway world.

Regimes, whose changes we will analyse in this book, are of course political regimes. In following chapters (especially in the Chapter *Current Regime Changes: Socioeconomic and Political Problems*) we will discuss in detail different political regimes and, in particular, their interactions with other layers of society. We do not think that for our purposes it is necessary to go into the analysis of different definitions of the concept of 'political regime'. Nevertheless, it is preferable to have a working definition of the concept from the onset. There are some rather good ones, which we may, in principle, agree to accept. Guillermo O'Donnell and Philippe Schmitter, for example, write that by political regime they 'mean the ensemble of patterns, explicit or not, that determines the forms and channels of access to principal governmental positions, the characteristics of the actors who are admitted and excluded from such access, and the resources or strategies that they can use to gain access. This necessarily involves institutionalization, i.e., to be relevant, the patterns defining a given regime must be habitually known, practiced, and accepted.'[2] A shorter, and therefore more analogous to the law of parsimony or Occam's razor was given by Laurence Whitehead: 'The term "political regime" denotes a defined set of institutions and "rules of the game" that regulate access to, and the uses of, positions of public authority in a given society.'[3] For the purposes of this book,

---

[2] G. O'Donnell, P. Schmitter. *Transitions from Authoritarian Rule: Tentative Conclusions about Uncertain Democracies,* Baltimore, MD: The Johns Hopkins University Press, 1986, p. 73.

[3] L. Whitehead, 'Prospects for a 'Transition' from Authoritarian Rule in Mexico' in *The Politics of Economic Restructuring in Mexico: State-Society Relations and Regime Change in Mexico* (Maria Lorena Cook, Kevin Middlebrook, and Juan

using the wisdom of Plato, Aristotle, Immanuel Kant, Robert Dahl and many others, to whom references are made in appropriate places, we use the term political regime as a combination of rules, means, methods, techniques and forms of exercising political power in a given society. It obviously includes, and even starts from, formal constitutional institutional and territorial arrangements, but goes beyond them to include political ideology and most importantly practical, often informal and nowhere legally fixed, means and methods of the exercise of political power. As current regime changes take place in a world that is in the process of radical transformations and changing balances of power, it is necessary to analyse these regime changes in the context of these transformations, characterised by reflexivity and uncertainty.

In this book it is argued that notwithstanding globalisation and certain homogenisations within the world, the future of the humankind will be multipolar and diverse. The bigger a social system, the less uniform and more diverse it is. International society or the international system, encompassing all societies, is the widest possible social system and therefore it is, by definition, the most heterogeneous social system. Large empires, differently from so-called nation-states, as a rule let different parts of imperial space live their own lives, provided they comply with certain key requirements from the imperial centre – usually serving the security interests of the empire or paying tribute to it. Empires would not have survived had they tried to homogenize all of whole imperial space culturally, religiously or otherwise. These have been nation-states that have strived for ethnic, cultural or religious uniformity and homogenisation. It seems to us that one of the accelerators of the dissolution of some empires, e.g., of the Russian Empire, was their desire and attempts at the age of the formation of nation-states to become more like the nation-state. The policies of so-called 'Russification' within the Czarist Empire at the end of the nineteenth and the beginning of the twentieth century, not only did not prevent the dissolution of the Empire (though in a way, it continued in the form of the Soviet

---

Molinar Horcasitas, eds.), La Jolla, CA: Center for US-Mexican Studies/University of California, San Diego, 1994, p. 327.

Union; however, the latter could be called an empire, if the term is used in a rather loose way) but contributed to its demise. Once an empire, one cannot develop into a nation-state without losing or shedding off its imperial possessions.

Two chapters in the book are devoted to the processes of radical social, political and economic transformations in the two former communist giants – the People's Republic of China, the former USSR and the latter's continuation in today's Russia. We compare the reforms unleashed by Deng Xiaoping in China and by Michael Gorbachev in the Soviet Union, and their implications for these countries as well as for the world as a whole. More than thirty years after the initiation of reforms by Deng Xiaoping, and twenty five years since the start of Gorbachev's *perestroika* and *glasnost* policies, we may definitely conclude that China is doing much better than the USSR, which has ceased to exist, or its successor in the form of the Russian Federation. In these chapters we will try to give some answers to the question of why these two radical reform processes have led to such different outcomes. Even more importantly, we will try to discover whether there are any lessons to be learnt by others from the comparison of these two far-reaching transformations. We will also try to show that though Gorbachev's reforms, as they were intended to unfold (there really were not any thoroughly thought through blueprints of these reforms besides 'it is impossible to go on like that anymore') failed, Deng's version of the reforms that have succeeded in China and that have made of it the second biggest economy in the world, would not have worked in the case of the Soviet Union, though with hindsight we may conclude that Gorbachev could have done many things differently.[4] This comparison, among other things, shows that what may well work in one case,

---

[4] For example, Gorbachev and his advisers, and the author of this book among them, greatly underestimated and completely neglected the potential for inter-ethnic tension and the rise of suppressed nationalistic sentiments; erroneously believed that Swedish style socialism was closer to the Soviet style communism than wild west capitalism and naively thought that the short phase of the *Gorbymania* in the West would transform into a sustained era of the West, led by Washington, helping its former nemesis rise like Germany and Japan after the Second World War.

does not do so well, or is simply impossible, in a different situation. Often it may even lead to serious disasters.

Today, the liberal West, like the former communist giant – the Soviet Union, which believed in its mission to eventually make the whole world communist, is not content with non-western states simply following the Western lead – they have to also adopt the only correct way of doing things. Non-western societies have to become similar to Western societies, i.e. they have to become politically liberal democracies with a society-dominant free market economy. This is an expression of the Enlightenment's methodological legacy, common to both Marxism and liberal democracy, the expression of the idea of universal history working its way towards some specific end. In this book we will try to show that such a deterministic reading of history combined with voluntaristic attempts to accelerate historical processes towards certain goals determined either by 'laws of history', as Marxists used to put it, or by 'being on the right side of history', as liberal imperialists put it, not only causes conflicts and increases human suffering, but may also serve as an impediment for achieving progress in a gradual increase in global justice, freedom, democracy and prosperity. It is also contrary to the liberal principle of 'live and let live' in international relations.

In this book we will analyse the correlation between three layers of different societies – the economic system, the political system and civil society in the widest sense, including the history, traditions, religions and other societal institutions. We intend to show not only that they are interrelated and interdependent but also that the sequencing of the evolution of these layers and their institutions in Western Europe was unique and very different from the processes today taking place in many parts of the non-western world. Ignoring the interdependence between different societal layers as well as the experience of historical sequencing of reforms in the West that were quite unique, is not helpful when some non-western societies, either on their own volition and initiative or being prompted by external advisers, take up reforms.

As not all regime changes occur peacefully, and conceding that in many of them external factors play significant roles, we will analyse the respective roles of internal and external factors in social change, issues concerning the use of force for humanitarian purposes, and different forms of intervention in internal conflicts either on the side of the government or opposition. Of course, we analyse these phenomena only to the extent that they are related to problems of regime change. In this context we also critically analyse the so-called theories of democratic peace (DPT), not rejecting them entirely but showing their limits, contingencies and even the dangers stemming from unconditional reliance on them, or rather from their abuse. DPT may be considered as a part or aspect of a worldview that sees the world moving towards a certain uniform – liberal democratic and peaceful – end. These theories, even if academically quite rigorous, are open to doubt as to what extent they correspond to and reflect the complexities of the real world.

In comparing these theories, for example, with Realist theories of IR (international relations), it is possible to conclude that no internally coherent and non-controversial theory can comprehensively explain controversial and incoherent phenomena of international politics. As Bertrand Russell insightfully observed, 'No one has yet succeeded in inventing a philosophy at once credible and self-consistent. Locke aimed at credibility, and achieved it at the expense of consistency. Most of the great philosophers have done the opposite. A philosophy that is not self-consistent cannot be wholly true, but a philosophy, which is self-consistent, can very well be wholly false. The most fruitful philosophies have contained glaring inconsistencies, but for that very reason have been partially true'.[5] The same is true for the theories of international relations and law. That is why the study of international law and politics needs various theories, and there can hardly be a single grand theory attempting to explain equally well all the aspects of the phenomena under study. Rather, like a world-class tennis player, who combines a strong serve with excellent returns and uses, depending on circumstances, with equal skill both backhand and forehand, an international lawyer or a IR specialist (both as a practitioner and academic) ideally has to be ready to use, depending on the subject-matter and concrete tasks,

[5] B. Russell, *History of Western Philosophy and its Connection with Political and Social Circumstances from the Earliest Times to the Present Day*, George Allen and Unwin Ltd., 1946, p. 637.

different intellectual tools, that is to say, different theories and theoretical approaches. This, however, is rarely the case.

Inis Claude has aptly, albeit somewhat exaggeratedly, observed that 'most people are addicted to the overstatement of their favourite propositions, the exaggeration of the scope of their generalisations. We say "always" when we mean "sometimes", and "certainly" when we mean "perhaps"; we tend to convert conditional thoughts into absolute standards'.[6] Profound theorists are often men or women who passionately believe in the truthfulness of one big idea (they are hedgehogs, to use the famous comparison by Isaiah Berlin of hedgehogs and foxes). Such a passionate belief helps them to deepen their theories, to make them as detailed and rigorous as possible. Doubts in the truthfulness of one's views would hardly stimulate further development of these views. Without the belief (usually a passionate one) that their theory is not only the best theory but also the only true one, it would be difficult to develop profound and detailed theories. That is why theories that concentrate on only one aspect of a phenomenon under study (from the point of view of such a theorist, this may not be an aspect at all but the very essence of the phenomenon) are often more parsimonious, rigorous and logically less controversial than more comprehensive theories. Howard Williams, David Sullivan and Gwynn Matthews have observed that

> [I]n their view of history Marx and Engels are both monists and dogmatists. They are monists in that they believe that one principle can be seen as underlying human history, namely, material production, and they are dogmatists in believing that they solely give the correct outline of that principle. Marx's genius led him to an intellectual arrogance, an arrogance that he shared with Hegel. Neither is prepared to see their point of view as one possible interpretation of the world.[7]

John Ruggie has incisively observed that 'the strength of each approach is also the source of its major weakness'.[8] However, the converse may often also be true. Without some one-sidedness a

---

[6] I. Claude, 'The Tension between Principle and Pragmatism', 19 *Review of International Studies* (1993), p. 219.

[7] H. Williams, D. Sullivan, G. Matthews, *Francis Fukuyama and the End of History*, University of Wales Press, 1997, p. 55.

[8] J. Ruggie, *Construing the World Polity: Essays on International Institutionalization*, Routledge, 1998, p. 36.

genius is usually not a genius. Marx would not have been Marx had he not passionately believed in the truthfulness of his theory (e.g. that material production is the engine of progress and that social phenomena can be at the end of the day explained on the basis of class struggle). Not only the weakness, but more importantly, the strength of his theory lies in its, at least relative, one-sidedness. Limited (i.e. one-sided) theories, if those who use them understand their limits, may have more explanatory power than more comprehensive but looser and less rigorous theories. However, in such case they have to be complemented by theories that go deep into other aspects of the same phenomenon.

Different theories of international law and politics are like the petals of a flower, each one explains some aspects of the analysed reality, while in the centre of the flower there is not a grand 'theory of everything' (T.O.E.), but a relatively thin capitulum on which most theories or theoretical approaches can agree upon, thereby securing a necessary unity of research. At the same time, theories pretending to be general, and attempting to find a single most important factor that determines the outcome of certain wide and significant processes, like where the world is moving now, or what makes some societies rich and others poor, or will democracy flourish in the Middle East, may contain deep insights that are due, but one may be surprised at their one-sidedness. We believe that no single philosophy or theory can do justice to such multifaceted phenomena as world politics, economics or law. Every theoretical approach, quite naturally, strives to become internally more and more coherent, non-controversial and complete, that is to say, it strives to become academically more and more rigorous. This, in turn, tends to lead to the loss of the capacity to reflect reality, which is often controversial and volatile (i.e. non-rigorous), comprehensively. As Douglass North, a Nobel Prize winner in economics, has said, 'the price you pay for precision is inability to deal with real world questions'.[9]

The contemporary international system is certainly not a 'traditional' Westphalian international system where state sovereignty was considered absolute (of course it was more or less absolute only for those states that were strong enough to face challenges from

---

[9] *Wall Street Journal*, 29 July 1994, p. 1.

other states, i.e. it was near absolute for the European absolute monarchies) and whatever they did within their territory was no one else's concern. Today the principle of non-interference in internal affairs and even that of the non-use of force have to be balanced with the international law principle of respect for and observance of human rights and fundamental freedoms. However, it is not for the sake of dictators or authoritarian regimes that these traditional principles of international law prohibiting interference in internal affairs and use of force retain their validity, as some radical authors believe. These principles preserve their importance for various reasons; including the rationale that external interference in foreign countries, for even benevolent purposes is often incompetent, counterproductive and sometimes may amount to no more than to an expression of self-righteousness. This applies to different forms of interference, but most importantly it applies to military interventions. Moreover, the use of military force for the sake of justice is too blunt an instrument, and therefore should be used with extreme caution, though, as we will argue in this book, in extreme circumstances such as genocide or massive crimes against humanity it may be morally necessary and legally justifiable. And always, it is necessary to deconstruct lofty words and slogans, especially when expressed by the political leaders of powerful states. In that respect, democratically elected leaders are not in a different category from autocrats; sometimes politicians in democracies have even more reason than autocrats to conceal their real interests behind value-loaded slogans. In any case, it is always best to verify and not take at face value the declarations of political or military leaders. Words, be they concepts, doctrines or laws, may indeed reflect values that are universal, or which, at least in principle, may be universalisable, but they may also be used, either deliberately or mistakenly, to pass parochial ideas as universal values. Already in the 1920's, German philosopher and legal theoretician Carl Schmitt incisively wrote: 'When a state fights its political enemy in the name of humanity, it is not a war for the sake of humanity, but a war wherein a particular state seeks to usurp a universal concept against its military opponent. ... The concept of humanity is an especially useful ideological instrument of imperialist expansion, and in its ethical-humanitarian form it is a specific vehicle of economic imperialism.

Here one can be reminded of a somewhat modified expression of Proudhon's: whoever invokes humanity wants to cheat'.[10] Schmitt's controversial political affiliations and the fact that they were written almost a century ago do not diminish the topicality of his insights.

If this all sounds too Machiavellian, it is only due to the subject matter – politics, especially in its international dimension. Methods of study have to be chosen depending on the subject matter and the choice of theory depends on the problem that is being researched. As Alexander Wendt writes, 'the framing of problems and research strategies should be question-driven rather than method-driven'.[11] In world politics, Machiavellian questions and answers are preferable to Pollyannaish recipes because of the nature of the phenomena we are dealing with. It is difficult to disagree with Amitai Etzioni's analysis that the world, with some significant exceptions, is even today 'in a Hobbesian state and is not ready for a Lockean one.'[12] Pragmatism enlightened by idealism (or idealism moderated by pragmatism), which sees through hypocrisy and naivety, is the best tool for understanding our imperfect but somewhat perfectible world.

Finally, at the end of the book we return to where we started from and based on the preceding analysis sum up our understanding of where the world as a whole and various parts of it may be going. Of course, there is no preordained destiny and many possibilities (as well as impossibilities) exist. There are, paraphrasing the famous American military thinker Donald Rumsfeld, quite a few known unknowns and even many more unknown unknowns. The most plausible, most peaceful and most able to release human potential, as we try to explain, future would be multipolar and diverse. Attempts to make the world uniform – Western-centric, Sino-centric or Islamo-centric – are not only doomed to fail but they are also wrought with the danger of bloody conflicts.

---

[10] C. Schmitt, *The Concept of the Political*, University of Chicago Press, 1995, p. 54.

[11] A. Wendt, 'Anarchy Is What States Make of It: The Social Construction of Power Politics', 46 *International Organisation* (1992), p. 423.

[12] A. Etzioni, From Empire to Community: A New Approach to International Relations, Palgrave, 2004, p. 116.

Chapter One

FROM AN AFRICAN VILLAGE TO A GLOBAL VILLAGE

The dominant trend in western social and political philosophy, from Emmanuel Kant to John Rawls and many others both in-between and after, has been what one may call abstract (not necessarily in the negative meaning, though in a somewhat limited sense) philosophizing or theorizing, i.e. from some very general intuitive premises or axioms toward more concrete ideas and policy recommendations. What such an approach, notwithstanding the great insights of many original thinkers, lacks are historical and comparative analyses. Therefore, one may be tempted to agree with Raymond Geuss when he writes that '... political philosophy must be realist. That means, roughly speaking, that it must start from and be concerned in the first instance not how people ought to ideally (or ought "rationally") act, what they ought to desire, or value, the kind of people they ought to be, etc., but, rather, with the way social, economic, political, etc., institutions actually operate in some society at some given time, and what really moves human beings to act in given circumstances'.[1] Or as Francis Fukuyama writes: 'Putting the theory after the history constitutes what I regard as the correct approach to analysis: theories ought to be inferred from facts, and not the other way around. Of course, there is no such thing as pure confrontation with facts, devoid of prior theoretical constructs. Those who think they are empirical in that fashion are deluding themselves. But all too often social science begins with an elegant theory and then searches for facts that will confirm it'.[2] As most of these theories have been elaborated upon by Western thinkers, it is not at all surprising that practically all of them support, or have been used to support, some version of political arrangements based on western liberal democratic values.[3] Theoretical differences so far have been

---

1 R. Geuss, *Philosophy and Real Politics*, Princeton University Press, 2008.

2 F. Fukuyama, *The Origins of Political* Order From Prehuman Times to the French Revolution, Profile Books, 2011, p. 24.

3 Critique of ahistorical political theorizing see, e.g., Raymond Geuss, *Philosophy and Real Politics*, Princeton University Press, 2008 and *Political Philosophy versus*

mainly differences within the same, Western worldview (in a way, even the main twentieth century ideological contradiction between liberal-democratic and communist worldviews was an intra-Western ideological clash into which other peoples were dragged; this being not very dissimilar to the genesis of the two world wars), which has either ignored other worldviews or treated them with a certain condescension and dealt with the classics of Chinese, Indian and Islamic thought as only historically relevant. In order to avoid such theorizing without studying concrete societies which had previously existed or exist today, without the analysis of why some of them had become slave-owning societies while others had evolved into liberal-democracies, why somewhere a Idi Amin or a Saddam Hussein or another notorious strongman has ruled or still rules, while in different places democratically elected liberals fail to find solutions to today's challenges, it is necessary to take historical and comparative approaches to all these questions. Such approaches are even more necessary today at the turn of the XXI century, which seems to mark a turning point in the history of humankind. Among economic, political and other tangible factors bearing witness to this, of which more shall be discussed later in the book, is the increasing quantity (and often quality) of voluminous books that take the long historical view on today's and tomorrow's events, developments and perspectives. Ian Morris' *Why the West Rules – for Now* (going back about 14,000 years), Francis Fukuyama's *The Origins of Political Order from Prehuman Times to the French Revolution* (going back about more or less the same time-span), Steven Pinker's *The Better Angels of Our Nature: The Decline of Violence in History and its Causes* (10,000 years of history of violence) and some other similar works witness this tendency. Why do these and many other authors feel the need to take such a long run up to the discussion of today's problems? None of them is a professional historian; none of them specializes in ancient history. The most plausible answer seems to be that when history is drastically changing course – today's, and even more so tomorrow's problems and questions can only be answered when one looks at current tendencies through a longer historical

---

History: Contextualism and Real Politics in the Contemporary Political Thought (eds. J. Floyd, M. Stears), Cambridge University Press, 2011.

perspective. As famous Russian poet Sergei Yessenin wrote: 'When face to face/We cannot see the face/We should step back/ For better observation'. That is why we have chosen to carry out our study of the current regime changes in the context of a longer historical perspective. One of the problems of today's world (which, as we will discuss in detail in various parts of this book, should be taken account of when analysing current regime changes in different parts of the world) is the shifting balance between universalising or homogenising trends in the world on the one hand, and remaining and sometimes even increasing social diversity, on the other.

1. EX UNO PLURES *IN THE EVOLUTION OF HUMANKIND*

The issue of social diversity is a part of the problem of universal *versus* particular, which is not only a philosophical problem; it is also an important political and legal question concerning the world as a whole as well as many individual societies. In today's world, the Enlightenment's emphasis of universality based on the glorification of reason, and belief in science and progress as the most important common characteristics of humanity, is vying with the post-modern (and sometimes also pre-modern) emphasis on cultural relativism. For example, in the domain of human rights this contention is playing out in the form of a rivalry between the idea of the universality of all human rights (somewhat naively and/or hypocritically enshrined in a series of United Nations human rights documents) and the attempts of cultural relativists to prove (often self-servingly) the relative and contingent nature of all human rights. In order to better understand the current interplay of diversity and unity of humankind and existing contradictory trends in this interplay, it would be useful to look back at where we, i.e., the human race, started from and how we got from there to where we are now. How and why have we become so diverse while nonetheless retaining our fundamental unity as members of the same human species? A short historical excurse will serve as a necessary context for the following study of more concrete issues and tendencies of their evolution.

The motto *E Pluribus Unum* (out of many, one), enshrined in the Great Seal of the United States and written on the dollar bill, originally suggesting that out of many colonies or states emerges a single nation, has come to imply that out of many peoples, races, religions and ancestries has emerged a single people or nation—illustrating the melting pot concept of nation-building as in the United States of America. However, much earlier, when no one would have thought of using any Latin or hardly any other human language at all, there took place a process that one could call *Ex Uno Plures* (out of one, many). We have in mind not the Big Bang that around 13.7 billion years ago allegedly created our Universe, but the much more recent, though still ancient, process of the evolution of humankind during the previous tens of thousands of years, when somewhere in the East African Rift Valley region some members of either a single or a few communities of *Homo sapiens*—communities that were probably rather homogeneous—started to go their separate ways. In this process they acquired traits, both physical and cultural, that made these spreading and separating communities quite different from one another. Out of few emerged many; from a relatively homogeneous community emerged more and more diverse communities.

Luigi Luca Cavalli-Sforza observes that '[M]odern humans appear first in Africa, then move to Asia, and from this big continent they settled its three appendices: Oceania, Europe and America'.[4] In accordance with some estimates, he continues, 'the date of the human–chimps separations was estimated about five million years ago, and the separation of Africans from non-Africans gave a date of 143,000 years ago using mtDNA results',[5] while 'a number of recent independent genetic dates place the beginning of expansion from Africa close to 50,000 years ago.'[6] And though 'much remains to be learned about human evolution, but for now it is fairly widely agreed that modern humans evolved in Africa and that 60,000 years ago there was an expansion out of Africa of an initially small group of people. They may have spoken a single fully modern human language, which, together with technological advances, led to further population expansion and gradually more rapid migrations'.[7] Be that

[4] L. Luca Cavalli-Sforza, Genes, Peoples and Languages, Allen Lane, 2000, p. 81.
[5] Ibid., 131.
[6] Ibid.
[7] L. Stone, P. Lurquin and L. Luca Cavalli-Sforza, Genes, Culture, and Human Evolution: A Synthesis (Blackwell, 2007), p. 163.

as it may, for the purposes of our study it is sufficient to know that *Homo sapiens* moved out of Africa, out of either a single or few communities and gradually, over many millennia, a group or several groups of our ancestors, who looked very much the same and behaved in the same manner, spread all over the world, creating various social groups, tribes and communities, some of which for many centuries or even millennia became completely isolated from other groups. In the process of this proliferation, these social groups started to differ more and more from one another. The colour of their skin, the slant of their eyes and other physical parameters changed depending on the climate, other environmental and natural factors; they started not only to hunt for and domesticate different animals and beasts, but also began to sing dissimilar songs, pray to different gods and acquire differing marriage practices. Humankind was not born that diverse: we became so different during this long process of conquering the world. As Mark Pagel writes:

> The modern-human occupation of the world was now complete, all within a few tens of thousands of years after leaving Africa; and most of this within the first 20,000. It was an occupation that had begun back in Africa when as few as several hundred to several thousand people left that ancestral continent, so that today, remarkably, and in such a short period of time, all of us on Earth trace our ancestry back to this small and intrepid band. By the end of the Polynesian expansion, humans now inhabited deserts, savannah, prairies, marches, rain forests, and ice. ... They spoke thousands of distinct and mutually incomprehensible languages. They had evolved a variety of different mating practices such that sometimes men had more than one wife, other times women had more than one husband, and in other societies people practiced monogamy.[8]

Today, for an expanding world population of over 7 billion, all of the Planet Earth may have become smaller than eastern Africa was for the first groups of *Homo sapiens*; today, there are no hospitable, or even inhospitable, spaces and places without human traces.

Although in the process of this journey from Africa to all over the world the human race became gradually more and more diverse, it nevertheless remained the same human race, and its members have

[8] M. Pagel, *Wired for Culture: The Natural History of Human Cooperation*, Allen Lane, 2012 (Kindle version), loc., 608.

retained characteristics that are common to all humans; even the expanding human communities retained traits that are familiar to all societies. Most of the social groups that have ever existed in the world have, for long periods, been closely knit traditional communities and only recently have some of them, particularly in the West, become so individualistic that concerns have been raised over the weakening of societal bonds holding communities together.[9] This indicates that for long periods of human evolution communitarian ways of living have been, and for many societies still are, much more natural than the ways based on individualism, on rights and liberties of the individual *vis-à*-vis the community where they live. For millennia, *Homo sapiens* did not differentiate themselves as individuals, as personalities separate from social groups whose integral parts they were. Alexis de Tocqueville was right that 'the word "individualism", which we have coined for our own requirements, was unknown to our ancestors, for the good reason that in their days every individual necessarily belonged to a group and no one could regard himself as an isolated unit'.[10]

Universalists, i.e. proponents of a universal history of humankind – be they Marxists or liberal democrats, tend to underestimate, as we will discuss at length later, differences acquired in this process of the journey out of an African village. At the same time, cultural relativists, emphasizing the differences among societies (and they may be more or less right about the differences), fail to appreciate the commonalities that have existed in all or most of human communities, and that in a globalising world have the tendency to grow in importance. If differences are readily evident and immediately strike one's eye (for example, the colour of one's skin, the slant of one's eyes or how people are clad), commonalities more often than not have to be discovered in a process of close contact and communication. Our common humanity seems to be deeper, but therefore also more hidden than our differences, which are usually on the surface and therefore immediately visible. Marcel Granet, for example, wrote that 'attempts to express ancient Chinese thinking with English as

[9] See, for example, D. Selbourne, The Principle of Duty: An Essay on the Foundations of the Civic Order (University of Notre Dame Press, 2000).

[10] A. de Tocqueville, The Old Regime and the French Revolution (1856) (translated by Stewart Gilbert), Anchor Books, 1955, p. 96.

an instrument would be worth making, even if they did no more than demonstrate the disaccord between the two methods of thought and language'.[11] Adda Bozeman, equally, was of the opinion that '[I]deas, even under the best of auspices, are not transferable in their authenticity, and that reliable intercultural accords are therefore difficult to reach' and that 'in the final analysis cultures are different because they are associated with different modes of thought'.[12] The fact that most of us concentrate on differences, often exaggerating their significance, seems to indicate that we are still relatively primitive creatures, that we are unable to see below the surface to discover our common humanity.

Professional translators, as well as those who speak several languages, know well how difficult it is to convey in another language the exact meaning of the original, to say nothing of the translation of metaphoric utterances, humorous jokes or poetry. However, these difficulties should not be so surprising if we keep in mind that over thousands of years many languages and cultures developed in relative or sometimes even in complete isolation. What is really surprising is that languages that have for millennia evolved independently from each other have nevertheless so much in common that their bearers, if they make necessary efforts to learn languages of others, can communicate with each other. Therefore, it seems to be true, as Steven Pinker writes, that 'universal mental mechanisms can underlie superficial variations across cultures', and that 'all human languages can convey the same kinds of ideas'.[13] Anthropologists' latest research has shown that there are many traits in common between different cultures, even if these cultures have never had any significant post-African contacts with each other. Allow me to quote a lengthy passage from Steven Pinker:

> Some anthropologists have returned to an ethnographic record that used to trumpet differences among cultures and have found an astonishingly detailed set of aptitudes and tastes that all cultures have in common. This shared way of thinking, feeling and living makes us look like a single tribe, which the anthropologist Donald Brown has

---

[11] M. Granet, *La pensé Chinoise*, Paris, Editions Albin Michel,1934, p. 9.

[12] A. Bozeman, *The Future of Law in a Multicultural World*, Princeton University Press, 1971, p. 14.

[13] S. Pinker, *The Blank Slate*, Penguin Books, 2002, p. 37.

> called the Universal People, after Chomsky's Universal Grammar. Hundreds of traits, from fear of snakes to logical operations, from romantic love to humorous insults, from poetry to food taboos, from exchange of goods to mourning the dead, can be found in every society ever documented. It's not that every universal behaviour directly reflects a universal component of human nature—many arise from the interplay between universal properties of the mind, universal properties of the body, and universal properties of the world. Nonetheless, the sheer richness and detail in the rendering of the Universal People comes as a shock to any intuition that the mind is a blank slate or that cultures can vary without limit, and that there is something on the list to refute almost any theory growing out of those intuitions.[14]

In the appendix to his book (pp. 435–439), Pinker reproduces Donald Brown's list (five pages) of human universals that can be found in all cultures, even if these cultures have not had any interactions. To name but a few: dance, cooking, coyness, death rituals, distinguishing right and wrong, envy, fears, gossip, music, preference for own children and next of kin, taboos, conflicts, conflict resolution, etc. Since these are not simply groups of different species but rather human communities, there is much in common between various communities, even if contacts between them have been only sporadic or completely absent. As wolves remain wolves and wolf packs remain wolf packs notwithstanding whether they inhabit the Asian steppes or Alaskan mountains (having, of course, depending on the climate, landscape and available food, different hunting habits and even different sizes and fur colours[15]), humans remain humans and human communities remain human communities notwithstanding where they live and what different characteristics—genetic or cultural—they may have acquired in the process of their adaptation to the environment, or simply by chance. Differences between humans across various communal divides, especially if we exclude visible physical features such as the colour of the skin or the slant of the eyes, are rather superficial and insignificant. However,

---

[14] Ibid., 55.

[15] L. Stone and P. Lurquin observe that among the humans, "genetic variation inside a given population is greater than that between two distinct populations" and that diversity between wolf packs is considerably higher than between any two human populations (Stone, Lurquin, p. 145).

communities tend to impose their specific values, ethical norms and other cultural traits on their members who, as humans, as individuals, do not differ much from members of other communities. As Michael Walzer has aptly observed, '[E]very human society is universal because it is human, particular because it is a society.'[16] While our common humanity pulls us closer to each other, assures that our main needs and desires are very much the same notwithstanding where we live and how we look like, the traditions of our societies, acquired over millennia, often push us apart.

2. *IS* E PLURIBUS UNUM *REPLACING* EX UNO PLURES?

Tens of thousands of years long process of conquering the planet was paralleled by the process of dissimilation, i.e. we as individuals as well as human societies gradually became more and more different from one another. Therefore, this process of the expansion of Homo sapiens all over the world may also be called a process of dissimilation. If as individual human beings we became more or less superficially different, as members of distinct societies, our cultures, religions and ways of life in the widest sense have become much more substantially different. Today, when the world has virtually become a global village, a reverse process, though slow and painful (yet obviously not as slow as the processes of expansion and dissimilation), has set in, and may be called the process of contraction paralleled with a controversial process of assimilation.

Although we, the humans, retain most of the differences that we have acquired during this long process of spreading all over the world, in a new emerging global village practically all peoples interact closely, and in this process of interaction they exchange not only goods and technological know-how but also views and ideas, both the best and the worst of them. We see all over the world—wherever societies develop and do not stagnate—that people, besides trying to be innovative, also use the experiences of other countries by creatively (or sometimes not so creatively) copying what has worked in other societies. First of all, this applies to scientific and

[16] M. Walzer, *Thick and Thin: Moral Argument at Home and Abroad*, University of Notre Dame Press, 1994, p. 8.

technological innovations, but foreign experiences in the fields of social, economic and political relations have also served many societies well; indeed, often scientific-technological innovations cannot be successfully introduced without appropriate socio-economic changes. As Niall Ferguson writes, '[T]he Dutch Republic prevailed over the Habsburg Empire because having the world's first modern stock market was financially preferable to having the world's biggest silver mine.'[17] Today all respectable states have modern stock markets. Frances Fukuyama emphasizes that '[T]he process of economic rationalisation and development is an extremely powerful social force that compels societies to modernise along certain uniform lines'.[18] 'In this respect', he continues, 'there is clearly such a thing as "History" in the Marxist–Hegelian sense that homogenizes disparate cultures and pushes them in the direction of "modernity"'.[19] We remain unconvinced about the inevitable linear progress of humanity in either the Marxist–Hegelian or any other sense, and we are much more sceptical about the speed of the processes of homogenization, but borrowing from more successful societies is certainly not a new phenomenon and certain homogenization is without doubt taking place. Although cultural exchanges are, of course, slower than the spread of technological, economic or political novelties, cultures are not immutable either. Steven Pinker observes that

> Preserving cultural diversity is considered a supreme virtue today, but the members of diverse cultures don't always see it that way. People have wants and needs, and when cultures rub shoulders, people in one culture are bound to notice when their neighbours are satisfying those desires better than they are. When they do notice, history tells us, they shamelessly borrow whatever works best. Far from being self-preserving monoliths, cultures are porous and constantly in flux.[20]

Although the human world has been diverse for millennia, it has never before been so close and interconnected, and this is one of the most important novelties creating both opportunities and problems.

---

[17] N. Ferguson, *The Ascent of Money: A Financial History of the World*, Allen Lane, 2008, p. 3.

[18] F. Fukuyama, *Trust: The Social Virtues of the Creation of Prosperity*, Hamish Hamilton, 1995, p. 351.

[19] Ibid., 351–352.

[20] S. Pinker, The Blank Slate, p. 66.

Today, post-industrial (or, as they are often called, 'post-modern') and feudal or semi-feudal (or 'pre-modern') societies co-exist on the same planet, and they not only closely interact and influence each other, but they even interpenetrate. If centuries ago Europeans moved out to colonise (or civilise, as they believed) indigenous peoples, today communities from former colonies are already well established in many European societies. This inevitably creates strains and even conflicts: on the one hand, there is a trend towards greater homogeneity (especially in the economic and technological spheres) and interpenetration between different cultures but, on the other hand, we face a continuing, and in some cases even widening hiatus between the levels of development of different societies, or even communities within the same society. The interpenetration of cultures also leads, as a counter-reaction, to an even stronger search for identity in one's historical, cultural or religious roots (not in our common African past but in our more recent separate histories) and creates resistance to what is perceived as alien cultural penetration or challenge. This situation is a major challenge for many societies, for their traditions, and for human rights and international law as well. In his Nobel Peace Prize acceptance lecture, President Barak Obama said:

> As the world grows smaller, you might think it would be easier for human beings to recognize how similar we are; to understand that we're all basically seeking the same things; that we all hope for the chance to live out our lives with some measure of happiness and fulfilment for ourselves and our families. And yet somehow, given the dizzying pace of globalization, the cultural levelling of modernity, it perhaps comes as no surprise that people fear the loss of what they cherish in their particular identities – their race, their tribe, and perhaps most powerfully their religion. In some places, this fear has led to conflict. At times, it even feels like we're moving backwards. We see it in the Middle East, as the conflict between Arabs and Jews seems to harden. We see it in nations that are torn asunder by tribal lines.[21]

President Obama's thoughts reflects the two sides of the same coin—on the one hand, there is the need to recognise, notwithstanding all our religious, cultural, developmental and other

[21] The transcript of President Obama's speech at the Nobel Peace Prize ceremony in Oslo, *The International Herald Tribune* (10 December 2009).

differences, our commonality as humans, increasingly living in a smaller and smaller world, and on the other hand, the counter-tendency of hanging on to our past, glorifying and improving our history to serve particular ends.

Homo sapiens are not only a rational, but also a passionate and often quite illogical species; not always does reason succeed even at the end of the day. Therefore, a failure of some societies, or even humanity as a whole, cannot be completely ruled out. However, to avoid such failures, societies that are less successful in resolving their problems have to look at, and borrow from their neighbours those features, ideas and practices that have made the latter more successful. One need not be a social Darwinist to recognize that those who are healthier, wealthier and better educated do better than those who are sick, poor and illiterate. This means that a certain homogenization of humankind will probably be inevitable and even necessary if we want to become more prosperous, healthier and more peaceful, and if we do not want to exterminate each other over our differences. The important question, as we will discuss below, will be in which way, how fast, to what extent and how far this process will go. One of the main ideas developed in this book is the warning that an artificial acceleration of the processes of homogenization may be as dangerous as attempts to forestall them.

Human societies, in sharing and borrowing, have improved the quality of life for their members. Because of such interactions humankind has achieved a certain progress not only in the natural sciences, technology and wealth-creation but, we dare to say, in the domain of morals as well. Nicholas Wade observes:

> The vocabulary of evolutionary biology does not include the word progress, for evolution has no goal toward which progress might be made. But in the case of human evolution, this exclusion may not be entirely justified. People, after all, make choices. If these choices shape a society for generation after generation, and if they permit individuals of a certain character to have more children and propagate their genes, then the overall nature of society may come to be shaped, in part, by human choice. If the character in question is a tendency to cooperate with others, then such a society would become more cohesive internally and more conciliatory in its relations with neighbours. Other societies might become more aggressive in character, or more paranoid, or more adventurous. Yanomamo society, given

> that the *unokais* [those who have undergone a special ritual having killed somebody; they have on average 2.5 times as many wives as men who have not killed] have more children, has surely positioned to become more aggressive. But overall, despite many setbacks and reversions, human societies have made vast gains in peacefulness, complexity and cohesion in the last 15,000 years.[22]

Steven Pinker, in his *The Better Angels of Our Nature: The Decline of Violence in History and its Causes*,[23] shows how human societies, notwithstanding occasional lapses into barbarity, have in general curbed violence within as well as between societies.

The process of overcoming some of our differences does not necessarily mean that humankind will evolve towards any kind of uniformity; it means that human societies have to, and probably the more successful of them will, get rid of those elements in their ways of life, in their cultures, that either become hindrances for their development and competition with other societies, or cause conflicts between and within society; it means that alongside remaining cultural differences that enrich humankind there are also emerging more and more elements of common culture. Closeness and interpenetration of societies—a process which today is usually called globalisation—means not only that one can have Chinese noodles, McDonald's burgers or Scotch in most countries of the world; these processes also create a pull towards the universalisation of cultural features such as various normative values, including human rights, basic liberties and democratic procedures. In a world where some countries (and today, quite a lot) are mature and successful democracies with developed market economies, the ideas of democracy and human rights have become infectious. It was not so difficult for medieval kings and princes to rule with an iron fist, use torture as a legitimate and the surest way of extracting confessions, which could be used in courts of law, and bequeath their thrones to their offspring using the accepted rule of primogeniture. There were no legal or moral rules that would have required that things had to be done

---

22 N. Wade, *Before the Dawn: Recovering the Lost History of Our Ancestors*, The Penguin Press, 2007, pp. 177–178.

23 S. Pinker, *The Better Angels of Our Nature: The Decline of Violence in History and its Causes*, Allen Lane, 2011.

differently. Moreover, there were no examples of societies where things would have been done much differently. As Barry Buzan and Gerald Segal wrote, 'because the Europeans were the first to put together this mix of inventions and ideas, they had the unique privilege of finding their own path to modernity at a time when their dominance meant that they suffered little interference from the rest of the world—however much they interfered with each other'.[24] Today, prosperous and poor, free and authoritarian societies live side by side; they see, hear and take notice of each other. In such a world the absence of political and personal freedoms, corruption and a lack of economic reforms and opportunities in some societies, while other societies prosper, are among the factors that create conditions in which discontent, which cannot be channelled through legitimate institutions, may take violent forms. Immigration flows from less prosperous and more troubled regions to more prosperous and liberal societies have become a constant and probably permanent feature of globalisation. Today, some Western cities with their racial, linguistic and social mixes look like microcosms of the world as a whole. Equally, the widening gap between prosperous nations and poor nations[25] is also reproduced internally in many countries.

Sure, a new global village, even if the people living there were to shed some of the differences that cause inter- and intra-societal conflicts, cannot be a homogeneous entity such as the one in Africa, from where many millennia ago our ancestors started their exodus. Therefore, one of the important features that all communities ought to have in common is the acceptance of the inevitability of social diversity. We may call it universalisation of the need to recognise and respect diversity both in the world at large and even more importantly (since it is more difficult) within our own societies. Toleration, acceptance and even the welcoming of those differences that enrich humankind, while striving to get rid of those features

---

[24] B. Buzan and G. Segal, *Anticipating the Future: Twenty Millennia of Human Progress* (Simon & Schuster, 1998), p. 22.

[25] Although it is true that some of the formerly poor nations, such as China, India or Brazil, are today rapidly moving into the category of prosperous countries, and an important thing to note is that in this rapid process of change they are taking over quite a few things from more prosperous countries.

that cause conflicts or are obstacles for development, may indeed become a *conditio sine qua non* of the survival of human species. Today there are some societies which, to an extent, have developed such a capacity (in that respect I would single out the United States, though, as we will discuss further, in America the tolerance for diversity at home is not matched by a tolerance of diversity in the world), though none is close to an ideal, while others have not yet taken any steps in that direction.

3. HOMOGENISATION OF THE WORLD AND HETEROGENISATION OF INDIVIDUAL SOCIETIES

There are two contradictory, competing and sometimes in a way even cancelling each other out processes going on in today's world: the world as a whole is slowly becoming more and more homogeneous while most individual societies are increasingly becoming more heterogeneous. The very process of globalisation, especially some of its manifestations such as the increasing assimilation (homogenisation) of the world as a whole and increasing dissimilation (heterogenisation) of individual societies as well as the purposeful promotion of western-style liberal democracy and market economy, raise the question not only of the universality (unidirecionality) of humankind's history, but also that of values as professed as common for the whole humankind.

The relative homogenization of the world is not something completely new. Empires, both ancient and modern, contributed to this process, though they did not strive, as we have argued, to homogenise their imperial space as nation-states have tried to do. The end of the bi-polar international system, collapse of the USSR as a counterbalance to Western economic and political systems, and the opening up of China mark a new accelerating homogenization of the world. In many ways it is a spontaneous process. Interacting and interpenetrating societies borrow from each other what they believe works best; the flow of goods, ideas and practices across state boundaries make interacting societies in some important, as well as in some not so important respects more similar to one another.

The current migration waves, which are an aspect and result of the globalisation process, contribute to both of these – the assimilation of the world and the dissimilation of individual societies – tendencies. Until recently most migration waves have had predominantly economic explanations (through both push and pull factors), and armed conflicts that created refugee flows from conflict zones, as their main cause. However, we already see that environmental factors are starting to play a role in this too. Ian Morris warns that '[G]lobal warming threatens to make even the most lurid fears of anti-immigrant activists come true by the 2020s. Tens of millions of the world's hungriest, angriest, and most desperate people may be fleeing the Muslim world for Europe, and Latin America for the United States. The population movements could dwarf anything in history, reviving the kind of problems that the steppe highway [on which the hordes of Alexander the Great, the Huns, Chingiz Han, and others moved either to the West or to the East RM] used to present'.[26] Globalisation, and especially migration waves as one of its manifestations (being a source of homogenisation) leads to the heterogenisation of individual societies. In most societies all over the world, there are increasingly more goods, ideas, practices and people of foreign origin. If foreign material goods are, as a rule, accepted rather benevolently (though even here there are exceptions), foreign ideas, practices and especially the carriers of those ideas and practices tend to cause resistance from significant segments of the indigenous populations.

These controversial parallel processes of homogenization and heterogenisation have already created some serious problems. The world has become virtually one, interconnected, but also unmanageable. Everything is related to everything else, and more often than not our conscious and planned actions have unforeseen and unintended consequences. Negative events in one part of the world have an immediate impact on other parts. Economic and financial crises, terrorist attacks, environmental pollution and uncontrollable immigration waves are major negative consequences of globalization.

Although the democratization of Western European societies went in parallel with their homogenization and the latter supported

---

[26] I. Morris, *Why the West Rules – For Now: The Patterns of History and What They Reveal about Future*, Profile Books, 2011, p. 603.

the former, attempts at ethnic, cultural or religious homogenization are wrought with serious dangers, besides the obvious fact that today some techniques of homogenization that were practiced centuries ago are considered to be genocide, crimes against humanity or ethnic cleansing. An important point to note is also that, historically, it was not, say, the exclusion of ethnic or religious minorities or the expulsion of Jews or Huguenots that made some societies prosperous and dominant; on the contrary it was tolerance (often such tolerance was strategic, not humanitarian or humanistic) which helped societies such as the Empires of Rome or Genghis Khan, later the Dutch and the British Empires, and in the twentieth century the United States to prevail over other societies. Amy Chua has persuasively shown that "throughout history, no society based on racial purity, religious zealotry, or ethnic cleansing has ever become a world-dominant power".[27] If striving for ethnic or racial purity may lead to genetic diseases, the search for intellectual or ideological purity may be a cause of social schizophrenia. In any case, today in contradistinction to the Western Europe of the period of the formation of nation-states, the dominant tendency in most societies is the rise of diversity. Therefore, policies of ethnic, religious, cultural or linguistic homogenization will inevitably clash with this dominant trend and therefore will eventually fail, though before their failure becomes clear they will create trouble for societies that try to follow out-dated recipes, and cause pain on those individuals and groups who are the objects of this homogenization.

4. *'OH, EAST IS EAST, AND WEST IS WEST, AND NEVER THE TWAIN SHALL MEET, TILL EARTH AND SKY STAND PRESENTLY AT GOD'S GREAT JUDGMENT SEAT'?*

In the West it is usually accepted that the East (or the South, for that matter), in order to succeed, has to copy many things from the West (starting with the principles of market economy and finishing with human rights and IT technology) and become more similar to the

---

[27] A.Chua, *Day of Empire. How Hyperpowers Rise to Global Dominance – and Why They Fall* (Doubleday, 2007), p. XXV.

West. Barry Buzan and Gerald Segal, rejecting such views as simplistic, nevertheless write of the emergence of a 'Westernistic' era that, in contradistinction to the prevailing Western domination, is 'defined by the interplay between the spread of Western ideas around the globe on the one hand, and the reassertion of non-Western cultures on the other'.[28] There is some truth to this, but it is certainly not the whole truth. There is a lot in the East that the West can ignore only to its own detriment, and it is not only in the past that the West benefited by borrowing quite heavily from the East. The compass, papermaking, gunpowder, printing and many other discoveries originated in China. However, even today, for example, the Eastern emphasis on the importance of societal bonds and discipline may be among the features that the West could learn from the East. Buzan and Segal themselves recognise that '[T]he old West may well have to re-learn from Asia some of its ideas about how to sustain a community rather than just a collection of individuals'.[29] The non-adversarial approach to conflict resolution as a characteristic of many Eastern societies also stands quite favourably in comparison with the individualistic, litigation-ridden Western, and especially American, social practices. The Confucian preference for mediation instead of litigation means not only that the rule of law in China will always be different from that in the United States or in Western Europe, but it may also mean that the West may learn from the East in that respect as well. The West is justifiably proud of its regular free elections. However, constant electoral processes have led, in many Western countries, to political and economic 'short-termism'. Martin Jacques, speaking of East Asian States, notes that their leaders 'are not hemmed in and constrained in the same manner as Western leaders. In some ways East Asian political leaders are also more accessible and more approachable because they view their accountability to society in a more holistic way and people take a similar attitude towards them. Their greater all-round authority, rooted in the symbiotic relationship between paternalism and dependency, can also enable them to take a longer-term attitude

---

[28] B. Buzan and G. Segal, *Anticipating the Future: Twenty Millennia of Human Progress* (Simon & Schuster, 1998), p. XIV.
[29] Ibid., 186.

towards society and its needs'.[30] Finally, nobody could deny that Easterners can not only cook and heal well, but their cars and TV sets are among the best in the world.

Kishore Mahbubani, in writing about the rise of Asia in today's world, insightfully observes that the rapid progress in many Asian countries, especially in China and India, is to a great extent due to their pragmatic, non-ideological use of the best created and tested in the West, though the latter is not celebrating this triumph of its achievements in non-Western countries. Why, asks Mahbubani, does the West not 'celebrate the clear presence of Western values in the rise of Asia?'[31] His answer is: because the use of these borrowed practices has led to a relative loss in another key area—power. Is not this one of the reasons why many in the West see only the problems with China and Russia, while ignoring their potential and progress? If an open-minded observer were to compare today's China not with a twenty-first century Sweden or Germany, but with a China, say, thirty years back, they would see huge progress, not only in the material well-being of the majority of Chinese people, which is naturally the most tangible achievement for any society (especially for poorer societies), they would also see progress in terms of personal freedoms that the Chinese people enjoy today. Daniel Deudney and John Ikenberry are right that '[C]ompared to where these countries [China and Russia] were several decades ago, they have made remarkable progress in throwing off centuries of accumulated economic and political backwardness, and by the yardstick of world historical change, they have moved and are moving in directions consistent with the liberal modernization narrative. China and Russia are not liberal democracies, but they are much more liberal and democratic than they have ever been – and many of the crucial foundations for sustainable liberal democracy are emerging'.[32] There is no way of knowing whether the Western liberal-democratic model, or any other socio-political model, will triumph at the end of the day

30 M. Jacques, When China Rules the World. The Rise of the Middle Kingdom and the End of the Western World (Allen Lane, 2009), p. 186.

31 K. Mahbubani, *The New Asian Hemisphere: The Irresistible Shift of Global Power to the East* (Public Affairs, 2008), p. 102.

32 D. Deudney and G. John Ikenberry, 'The Myth of the Autocratic Revival. Why Liberal Democracy Will Prevail', *Foreign Affairs*, January– February 2009, p. 57.

(one thing seems to be clear: there will not be any final destinations or ends for history). We cannot be certain even about short- or medium-term predictions. However, borrowing from each other, and as a result a certain convergence of different societies, which are using each other's 'best practices', seems to be a common trend.

Chapter Two

WHITHER GOEST THOU, THE WORLD?

1. UNIVERSAL HISTORY AND HISTORICAL DETERMINISM

Besides a spontaneous homogenization of the world, there have been many conscious attempts to make it more homogeneous. Monotheistic religions such as Christianity and Islam have both, either through conquest or missionary activities, tried to make the world the same in terms of faith. The ideas of the Enlightenment, based on a belief in the universality of reason and its eventual triumph over emotions, spontaneity and irrationality, have been a powerful source of attempts to remake the world in accordance with elaborate blueprints. The Enlightenment's legacy, whose main elements are individual autonomy, reason and universality,[1] is on the basis of human progress, and as we showed above, this progress is not restricted to the field of natural sciences. It is difficult to tell what have been more in negative effects (or rather side-effects) of some of the emancipatory ideals of the Enlightenment: were they abuses of those ideals, their distortions, or perhaps it is simply that all great ideas contain not only a potential for good but for evil as well. For example, the current process of the promotion of democracy has, like its predecessor – the *mission civilisatrice* or the white man's burden of the nineteenth century, though in different degrees and forms, two aspects – idealistic and humanitarian on the one hand, and hypocritical and domineering on the other. Both of these aspects have their roots in the Enlightenment's dual legacy: a desire for freedom and a tendency for domination. On the European continent, Enlightenment ideas served, to a great extent, a liberating purpose, while at the same time creating conditions, material as well as intellectual and psychological, for colonial domination outside Europe. Dan Hind observes that

---

[1] See, e.g., T. Todorov, *In Defence of the Enlightenment*, Atlantic Books, 2009, pp. 4–5.

> [W]e can certainly trace one history of Enlightenment from Bacon to the British Empire and to the modern global administration. The insurgent European powers of the period after 1700 depended heavily on the "enlightened" institutions for a technological base that in turn empowered global domination. The desire for total knowledge, in the service of total power, which we find in the Department of Defence and the Ministry of Defence is an expression of Enlightenment. But this history must ignore the sense of Enlightenment as freedom of inquiry and freedom to publish. For the Enlightenment could not be contained within those institutions and their equivalents in Soviet Russia and Nazi Germany. Enlightenment informed the movements of national and social liberation within and outside Europe as surely as it informed the colonial powers' war-making technology.[2]

Swedish writer Per Olov Enquist observes that 'if the Enlightenment has rational and hard face, which is the belief in reason and empiricism within mathematics, physics and astronomy, it has also a soft face, which is the Enlightenment as freedom of thought, tolerance and liberty'.[3] This 'hard face', which is morally neutral, has indeed been used not only for the liberation of men and women from political oppression, economic hardships and from a dependence on the blind forces of nature, but also for the purposes of domination of other individuals and societies.

Marxism was certainly the most prominent emanation of the Enlightenment that planned to consciously redesign the world according to 'societal laws' that Karl Marx and Marxists had, allegedly, scientifically discovered. In this endeavour, historical determinism and voluntarism joined forces. Having discovered 'iron laws' that would inevitably and through identical stages lead all societies towards the full emancipation of humankind in a communist formation, Marxists' task was to facilitate the birth pangs of this new world, to play the role of midwife. Erik Olin Wright is right in claiming that 'Marx proposed a highly deterministic theory of the demise of capitalism'.[4] However, what is more intriguing is that, as he adds, Marx also offered 'a relatively voluntaristic theory of the construction of its [capitalism's] alternative'.[5] It is even more important to note that

[2] D. Hind, *The Threat to Reason*, Verso, 2007, p. 104.
[3] P.O. Enqwist, *The Visit of the Royal Physician*, Vintage, 2004, p. 92.
[4] E.O. Wright, *Envisioning Real Utopias*, Verso, 2010, p.98.
[5] Ibid.

it is not only Marxism that is guilty of such a confusion of these phenomena (historical determinism and voluntarism) which at first glance are complete opposites and seem to offer contradictory and irreconcilable explanations of social processes; both of these 'irreconcilable reconcilables', if we may say so, have their roots in the Judeo-Christian worldview and Enlightenment's legacy.

The dominant liberal democratic vision of the world is methodologically close to, and almost indistinguishable from, Marxist 'scientific' revelations, though ontologically they point at opposite directions. It should not be surprising since they both are heirs of the Enlightenment, and they are both also based upon linear visions of a historical evolution of human societies. Like Marxism, the liberal democratic mental picture of the world's evolution is also a combination of deterministic and voluntaristic elements. Being certain that eventually all societies necessarily evolve towards free market liberal democracy, many liberal-democrats also believe that it is their duty to help those societies that are not yet liberal democracies to quicker reach their final destiny. This belief, and acting upon it, has been especially strong among Anglo-Saxon societies. Walter Russell Mead speaks of it as '...the "Whig" narrative – a theory of history that sees the slow and gradual march of progress in a free society as the dominant force not only in Anglo-American history but in the wider world as well'.[6] He observes that first Great Britain and later the United States, as sea powers, having established the liberal maritime international order, use 'the strategic flexibility of an offshore power, protected to some degree from the rivalries and hostilities of land powers surrounded by powerful neighbours, to build power strategies that other countries cannot counter. It means using command of the seas to plant colonies whose wealth and success reinforce the mother country. It involves developing a global system that is relatively easy to establish and which, once developed, proves extremely difficult to dislodge'.[7] The gist of such a view is that the world is almost inevitably not only dominated and led by the Anglo-Saxon countries, but for other societies not to be thrown, using the

---

[6] W. Russell Mead, *God and Gold. Britain, America, and the Making of the Modern World*, Atlantic Books, 2007, p. 15

[7] Ibid., p. 95.

Marxist lexicon, into the dustbin of history, they have to become *volens nolens* more and more similar to Anglo-Saxon countries. At the same time, the Anglo-Saxon societies, together with those who are already converted to their ways, using, *inter alia*, their strategic position as offshore powers, help other societies, by force if necessary, join this progressive march of history. This is, quite obviously, a deterministic interpretation of history.

John Gray, for example, explains that former British Prime Minister Tony Blair's vision of the world was a simplistic unilinear vision, where the world was moving towards a specific final destination since he 'never doubted that globalisation was creating a worldwide market economy that must eventually be complemented by global democracy'.[8] Therefore, Blair also believed in the ability of military force to ensure the triumph of good.[9] Gray is right when he warns against the dangers of utopian visionaries who have acquired political power. The Bush-Blair axis did indeed lead to some disasters, among which the Iraqi invasion of 2003 and its consequences should stand as a warning for future generations. However, Gray, like his great predecessor at the London School of Economics and Political Science (LSE) Karl Popper, who introduced the concept of 'piecemeal engineering' into the philosophy of politics, is himself too absolutist when he denies any positive role for social utopias and visionary policies and politicians. Gray is also overly harsh towards the Enlightenment's legacy, seeing it as a monolithic whole, and mostly in a negative light. However, as an example, the so-called 'war on terror' has not been so much a war of reason (i.e. Enlightenment's concept) against religiously justified violence (i.e. an irrational and therefore non-Enlightenment, pre-modern, concept) as it is a war of one faith against another. It is the unconditional faith in the supremacy of Western values, including free market, globalisation and democracy, against the faith in the ability of Islam to bring justice and wellbeing to all of mankind. Both are, in a sense, religious faiths as far as faith is a religious concept. As Alastair Crooke observes, the Islamist faith is 'no more the savagery of "divine violence" than the

---

[8] J. Gray, *Black Mass. Apocalyptic Religion and the Death of Utopia*, Allen Lane, 2007, p. 97.

[9] Ibid.

systemic violence, practiced as "legitimate force", that has been embraced by the West in pursuit of its articles of faith: both have roots in religious insights.'[10] It is not by chance that Tony Blair was one of the most, if not the most, religious British Prime Ministers for many decades, and former President George W. Bush was not only a born again Christian; he was also very close to American religious conservatives, many of whom believe in a literal interpretation of the Bible. In his second inaugural address, President Bush stated that 'America's vital interests and our deepest beliefs are now one .... So it is the policy of the United States to seek and support the growth of democratic movements and institutions in every nation and culture'.[11] One may have ample reasons for believing that the Western style of liberal democracy is preferable to an Islamic Caliphate, if not for any philosophical or theoretical reason then at least, as Richard Rorty wrote, because 'it is theocracies who lose refugees to us, and not vice versa'.[12] And though you or I may well agree with Rorty, this does not mean that everybody everywhere is of the same opinion, or that those peoples who are not organised as in Western societies are able and willing to transform themselves into liberal democracies.

Many of those who have promoted liberal democracy or are doing so today also believe, while not usually openly recognizing it, that in their evolution all societies move in the same direction, and it is only due to the unreasonable and selfish leaders of some states who prevent their peoples from reaching the Promised Land, that there is not yet world-wide liberal democracy. For example, already a century ago, American Baptists, desirous to civilize Russia before the Bolshevik revolution of 1917, believed that 'for Russia, sooner or later, there will be Runnymede and a Magna Charta, if not a Bunker Hill and Yorktown'.[13] Hence, they foresaw for Russia if not the American way of development, then at least the British one, i.e. the same linear, Anglo-Saxon, historical path. Things haven't changed much

---

10 A. Crooke, *Resistance: The Essence of the Islamist Revolution,* Pluto Press, 2009, p. 238.

11 George W. Bush, "President Bush's Second Inaugural Address", January 20, 2005, http://www.npr.org/templates/story/story-php?storyID=4460172.

12 S. Blackburn, 'Portrait: Richard Rorty', 85 *Prospect Magazine* (2003).

13 D.S. Foglesong, *The American Mission and the 'Evil Empire'*, Cambridge University Press, 2007, p. 38.

since. Francis Fukuyama's *The End of History and the Last Man* may be seen today as a bit of a caricature of liberal democratic triumphalist visions of the future, but more moderate and therefore less prominent versions of the same vision are as influential as ever. In their otherwise interesting, balanced and forward-looking article Daniel Deudney and G. John Ikenberry observe that '[J]ust as the Nazis envisioned a "new order" for Europe and the Soviet Union designed an interstate economic and political order, so, too, did the liberal West'. This is a correct observation. However, using the same method that Marxists had used, these two American professors come to the optimistic conclusion that '[T]he foreign policy of the liberal states should continue to be based on the broad assumption that there is ultimately *one path to modernity* [emphasis added RM]– and that it is essentially liberal in character' and that '[L]iberal states should not assume that history has ended, but they can still be certain that it is on their side'.[14] This is only a slightly modified and moderated version of the deterministic, unilinear explanation of history. Even Fukuyama, at the end of the 1980s, did not believe that history had ended in a literal sense. He also thought that history was on the side of liberal democracy and therefore, sooner or later, all societies would eventually arrive in the Promised Land.

And here, once again, voluntarism, feeding on its opposite – determinism, steps in. It is human agents, who are on the 'right side of history', who realize humankind's destiny. Political regimes, as well as economic systems that are on the 'wrong side of history', have to go, and better sooner rather than later. Therefore, Slavoj Žižek is right when observing that 'it is easy to make fun of Fukuyama's notion of the "End of History", but most people today are Fukuyamean, accepting liberal-democratic capitalism as the finally found formula of the best possible society, such that all one can do is to try to make it more just, more tolerant, and so on'.[15]

Such triumphant historical unidirecionality is not only simplistic and wrong, as is any social theory based on historical determinism; acting upon it may be also extremely dangerous. The thousands of

---

[14] D. Deudney and G. John Ikenberry, 'The Myth of the Autocratic Revival. Why Liberal Democracy Will Prevail', Foreign Affairs, January-February 2009.

[15] S. Žižek, First as Tragedy, Then as Farce, Verso, 2009, p. 88.

years history of humankind testifies that there is no final form of social, political or economic arrangement of societies, and that no domination is eternal. Therefore, Žižek is right that 'we should thus ruthlessly abandon the prejudice that the linear time of evolution is "on our side", that History is "working for us".[16] It becomes known *ex post facto*, and usually long after the fact, where history is leading us. We, the contemporaries, can only make educated short-term and medium-term conjectures that we should be ready to constantly revise.

If many liberal democrats, who sincerely believe in the ultimate triumph of their ideology and practices in all societies, consider that the best way to promote liberal democracy is by way of example and in assisting those societies that have chosen to follow the example of liberal democracies, there are also liberal interventionists who believe in the necessity of actively enlarging the circle of liberal democracies (liberal preachers and liberal warriors). In the United States, liberal interventionists such as Samantha Power and Anne-Marie Slaughter have joined forces with neo-conservatives like Paul Wolfowitz, Robert Kagan or Randy Scheunemann, though the reasons for their coming together on similar policy conclusions are quite different. Richard Burt and Dimitri Simes make an interesting observation: 'Strangely, it is precisely in this area that the two leading foreign-policy schools—liberal interventionism and neoconservative unilateralism—converge. For example, Princeton professor Anne-Marie Slaughter and *Washington Post* columnist Charles Krauthammer often agree on the need for U.S. intervention abroad. And anyone who follows the media closely knows that when these two groups align, America is headed for an unnecessary war—or at least for serious trouble'.[17]

If for neo-conservatives interventionist policies are primarily dictated by pragmatic American interests (oil, gas, strategic benefits), though wrapped in declarations about universal values, liberal interventionists seem to sincerely believe in their mission to make the world a better place for all the peoples (though in many cases these

---

16 Ibid., p. 149.

17 R. Burt, D. Simes, 'Morality Play Instead of Policy', The National Interest, 22 August 2012.

two mutually exclusive political motivations may peacefully coexist in the mind of the same person). Most people tend to sincerely believe in the universal acceptability of their views as dictated by their particular interests. In such a case, those particular interests become expressed and justified as universal values.

It is obvious that history is not an impersonal *perpetuum mobile* but is made by men (and today also by women). Using Marx's words, '[M]en make their own history, but they do not make it as they please; they do not make it under self-selected circumstances, but under circumstances existing already, given and transmitted from the past'.[18] Or as Ian Morris, having carried out a comparative study of social development both the East and West during the last 14,000 years, concludes, '[S]ocial development is not a gift or curse laid on humanity ...; it is something we make ourselves, just not in ways of our own choosing'.[19] What studies taking a longer historical perspective show is that it is necessary to plan for the future, and that past and present trends are of some assistance in this endeavour. However, our plans will never be realised exactly as intended and therefore we have to be ready to constantly correct them. Most importantly, history doesn't move to any specific end. History seems to be a combination or confluence of three categories of factors: deterministic (not everything is possible and some things are really impossible, at least for the time being); voluntaristic (quite a few things indeed depend on our purposeful choices and efforts) and chance (many things just happen and they depend neither on our rational or irrational choices nor are they predetermined by any discernable pre-existing causes). Cambridge Professor Philip Allott has given the best, in our opinion, answer to the dilemma of voluntarism *versus* determinism in social spheres, and therefore allow us to quote him in some length:

> It is as if an ingenious and inquisitive Creator had chosen to conduct an experiment in one small corner of the universe – an experiment in which a piece of matter would be given a certain measure of control over its changing States, a living organism would be given a special kind of choice over its own life. But two possibilities of control and

[18] K. Marx, *The Eighteenth Brumaire of Louis Bonaparte*, Arc Manor, 2008, p. 15.
[19] I. Morris, op.cit., p. 194.

> choice would be withheld – the possibility of simply submitting entirely to the necessary order of the physical universe and the possibility of acting entirely independently of the necessary order of the physical universe.[20]

As the freedom of choice is relative, so are the constraints both of the physical universe and of the existing social order. People are able, but only to an extent, and sometimes with catastrophic side effects (e.g., environmental disasters), to change the order of the physical universe. People are also able to transform the existing social order, but have many constraints that they neglect, as we will discuss in this book, at their own peril.

2. *CURRENT REGIME CHANGES: SOCIOECONOMIC AND POLITICAL PROBLEMS*

Contemporary societies are practically all organized in the form of so-called nation-states (today, it would be more accurate to call them simply *de jure* sovereign states), consisting of three main interconnected layers: the political system, economic system and civil society. The latter includes not only civil society organizations or NGOs (non-governmental organizations) as it is sometimes assumed. It also comprises of historical traditions, religious norms and organizations, culture, family structures and similar institutions. Jürgen Habermas, explaining his theory of communicative action and deliberative democracy, writes of the lifeworld, i.e. the world in which life is experienced by individuals individually and collectively, as the 'background' environment of competences, practices, and attitudes represented in terms of one's cognitive horizon. Habermas explains: 'The lifeworld is constituted from a network of communicative actions that branch out through social space and historical time, and these live off sources of cultural tradition and legitimate orders no less than they depend on the identities of socialized individuals'.[21] Speaking of the role of law in society, he adds: 'But the legal code not only keeps one foot in the medium of ordinary language, through which everyday communication

---

[20] P. Allott, *Eunomia*, Oxford University Press, 1990, p. 55.
[21] J. Habermas, *Between Facts and Norms*, Polity Press, 2004, p. 80.

achieves social integration in the lifeworld; it also accepts messages that originate there and puts these into a form comprehensible to the special codes of the power-steering administration and the money-steering economy'.[22] So, according to Jürgen Habermas, there is the lifeworld, consisting of its societal component, including law as experienced by people as individuals and collectively, culture and personality structures, as well as the power-steered administration and money-steered economy, i.e. there are the same three layers of society. These layers are interlinked, interdependent and integral parts of society as a whole.

The relative interconnectedness, interdependence and impact of these three layers on each other differ from society to society. Ideally, none of them should dominate the other two. In dictatorships, such as Saddam Hussein's Iraq or Colonel Gadaffi's Libya, or like in the former USSR or today's North Korea and Turkmenistan, civil society has been virtually absent. In democracies with neo-liberal tendencies, especially in the United States, the free market economic system enjoys the commanding position. There, the call for a 'smaller state' is central to such a vision and practice. However, such a call is not aimed at increasing the role of civil society, enlarging democracy or individual liberties; its main purpose is to further unbridle market forces. Tariq Ramadan, who is right in asserting that it is impossible to analyse and 'evaluate the uprisings that together make up the Arab awakening without taking time to develop a critical analysis of the state of contemporary democracies',[23] continues: 'First, it must be acknowledged that today's states and democratically elected governments find themselves, structurally, in a position of virtual subservience to the economic sphere, which possesses it own imperatives, its institutions and multinationals where egalitarian, democratic and/or transparent administrative practices are not enforced. The doctrine of free markets appears to be assuming the form of a new religion in the very heart of the secularized order,' and that 'the economy, finance and media, which wield such power – and on occasion new authority – over state entities that

---

22 Ibid., p. 81.

23 T. Ramadan, *The Arab Awakening: Islam and the New Middle East,* Allen Lane, 2012, p. 119.

they threaten to undermine the very foundations of democracy that they need and claim to defend'.[24] Certainly, those who struggle for more democracy in fledgling democracies, aspire or fight for democracy under authoritarian regimes do not want to lose their gains to unbridled market forces. It would be to change the direct and more visible domination by authoritarian state apparatus for the less direct and therefore also less visible domination by uncontrolled (uncontrolled by democratically elected governments) markets, which mostly benefit the upper 1% of the population.[25]

There is nowhere in the world a society where the civil society layer would dominate the other two; therefore the increase of its relative role would probably be one of the indicators of that society's progressive development. In a case where the political system, i.e. first of all the state, either actually dominates or has a tendency to increase its control over the other two societal layers, we either have a full-fledged dictatorship or the threat of the emergence of an authoritarian political regime, while in the case of the economic system's domination there is a danger that society may move towards a winner-takes-all kind of neo-liberal entity, or is already there. And though in practice there is nowhere in the world a civil-society-dominant country, it may happen that in underdeveloped countries, attempts to weaken the role of the state and a simultaneous encouragement of the development of a free market economy and civil society may, instead of increasing the liberties of individuals and contributing to their well-being, lead to anarchy and chaos. In advanced liberal-democracies this would not necessarily increase the role of civil society; instead, market forces using state apparatus would increase their supremacy over civil society.

The central aspect of any political system is the state, while political parties, other political movements and lobby groups serve as conveyer belts relating the state to other layers of society. According to traditional Marxist social theory, society's political system was considered to be a part of the superstructure while its basis, which eventually determined the nature of the superstructure, was society's economic structure, i.e. its 'productive relations'. Although

---

24 Ibid.
25 J. Stiglitz, 'Of the 1 %, by the 1%, for the 1%', *Vanity Fair*, May 2011.

critics of Marx have often oversimplified Karl Marx's views when accusing him of economic determinism, there is no doubt that Marx and Engels, and even more so the so-called 'official' Marxism, though not denying the relative autonomy of the superstructure, believed that economic relations, at least at the end of the day, constituted a determinative effect on the other two layers of society. Although it may sound ironic today, and primarily in the liberal democratic West, this Marxist proposition is increasingly becoming true; capitalism is indeed a social arrangement where the market tends to dominate and uses the state for that purpose.

It is often reiterated by many experts that as the Chinese economy develops, China's political system will either change in order to correspond to the needs of the economy, or in case it doesn't change (i.e. if it doesn't become more like the Western liberal-democratic system), China's political system will increasingly serve as a brake on the country's economic development. For example, *Time Magazine* in a study devoted to China emphasises: 'Excessive state control is creating potentially lethal distortions in the economy. ... State firms are crowding out the entrepreneurial private sector. The hard truth is that China needs a new growth model, driven more by the market than the state and more balanced, open and fair. Otherwise the consequences would be severe'.[26] This is an interesting comment in several respects. First, as a general proposition this statement is true in the sense that it expresses the view that there has to be some congruence between the different layers of a society; in this case between its economic and political systems. Secondly, the statement is true in the sense that China obviously needs indeed less state control over and interference with the economy; in China the political system still dominates the economic system. And thirdly, by reversing the accents of this statement, it would be possible to say that markets in some Western societies and the global financial market have run out of any control, which has led (and not potentially but actually) to lethal distortions, with severe consequences for many societies and millions of individuals.

However, for the purposes of our study, there is the question of the extent to which political and economic systems, as well as civil

[26] M. Schuman, 'Why China Must Push Reset', *Time*, 18 June 2012, p. 36.

society are dependent on each other, have to correspond to each other and whether it is possible to radically change the political system, i.e. to carry out a regime change, without transforming the other two layers of society. Finally, it is also about sequencing the transformation of these layers. In that respect, the third layer, civil society, is not less important than the other two. Often it is even more vital in the sense that in comparison with the first two layers, civil society layer is the most conservative and less amenable to change. But without changing it, transformations in the political and economic layers become either impossible or distorted or unsustainable.

Current attempts at regime changes in Asia, Northern Africa and the Middle East are often attempts to export Western political (liberal democracy) and economic (free market capitalism) systems to societies where civil society have been absent, severely suppressed or very different from those existing in the West. That is why such exports very often end up in chaos and anarchy instead of democracy; instead of Western style capitalist markets based on the principles of the rule of law, feudal markets evolve, where all lucrative businesses are controlled by central and local strongmen. These examples demonstrate that the three societal layers are closely interrelated and interdependent. They also show that while it is relatively easy to implant the formal features of Western political (e.g., elections) and economic (e.g., privatisation and deregulation) systems in non-Western societies, these implants acquire, in the absence of adequately responsive civil societies, distorted forms.

The study of history and sequence of evolution in the Western world of institutions belonging to these three societal layers highlights the problem that the borrowed or exported Western models of development in the non-Western world often do not work as intended because there, the proverbial cart is in front of the horse. Francis Fukuyama, for example, makes an important point observing that '[T]he sequencing of political development in Western Europe was highly unusual when compared to other parts of the world. Individualism on a social level appeared centuries before the rise of either modern states or capitalism; the rule of law existed before political power was concentrated in the hands of centralized governments; and institutions of accountability arouse because modern, centralized states were unable to completely defeat of eliminate ancient feudal institutions like representative assemblies',[27] and that the extreme fragmentation of power in Europe 'led to an unusual situation in which rule of law became imbedded in European society even before the advent not just of democracy and accountable government but also the modern state-building process itself'.[28] This observation, mentioned also by some other authors, is true. Daron Acemoglu and James Robinson, for example, describe how in England in 1724, a certain John Huntridge, a local resident, while outside a deer park belonging to then Secretary of State (Prime Minister) Sir Robert Walpole, was accused of aiding deer stealers and abetting so-called Blacks, who stole and destroyed the property of the rich, while painting their faces black. Both crimes were punishable by hanging. Walpole took the keenest interest in the trial both for personal as well as political reasons. The conviction of John Huntridge ought to have been a foregone conclusion. However, after eight or nine hours of trial the jury acquitted the man, partly on procedural grounds.[29] This example well illustrates that in England, already by the first half of the eighteenth century, certain personal rights were rather well guaranteed and protected, even while democracy was still in its infancy. The rule of law and certain personal liberties, like the *habeas corpus* rule and elements of fair trial, had evolved well ahead of the development of democracy. As we will discuss below, proponents of democratic peace theory do not count the 1812 war between Britain and the United States as a war between two democracies, since they do not consider the Britain of 1812 as democracy.[30] Although they may have excluded the Britain of 1812 from the camp of democracies mainly for the self-serving reason of trying to prove that democracies do not fight each other, there is certainly some truth in their observation. Britain was a democracy by few and for a few; at the same time it had already become a 'rule of

---

27 F. Fukuyama, *The Origins of Political Order. From Prehuman Times to the French Revolution*, Profile Books, 2011, p. 22.

28 Ibid., p. 288.

29 D. Acemoglu, J. Robinson, *Why Nations Fail: The Origins of Power, Prosperity and Poverty*, Profile Books, 2012, p. 305.

30 See, e.g., B. Russett, *Grasping the Democratic Peace: Principles for a Post-Cold War World*, Princeton University Press, 1993, p. 16.

law' state for many. Acemoglu and Robinson appropriately entitle the chapter, following the discussion of this and other similar cases that had taken place in the first half of the eighteenth century and that testify to the existence at that time of the rule of law in Britain, *The Slow March of Democracy*.[31] Even the 1832 reforms in Great Britain, doubling the voting franchise from eight percent to sixteen percent, included only the adult male (sic!) population. 'What is more', emphasise Acemoglu and Robinson, 'the principle of the rule of law opens the door for greater participation in the political process and greater inclusivity, as it powerfully introduces the idea that people should be equal not only before the law but also in the political system. This was one of the principles that made it difficult for the British political system to resist the forceful calls for greater democracy throughout the nineteenth century, opening the way to the gradual extension of the franchise to all adults'.[32] What we see today in many countries is that the immediate introduction of a general franchise to the adult population does not lead to the emergence, immediate or otherwise, of the rule of law; there is no slow march from democracy towards a 'rule of law' state. The problem is not only in sequencing, though it certainly plays a role, but more in the truth that while democracy is a relatively more formal institution, more tangible and therefore easier to establish and laud (and therefore also easier to lose), the rule of law is a more fundamental institution, much closer to and more strongly rooted in the fabric of society, and more dependent on its history and traditions. Therefore, once established, it is also more sustainable and able to guarantee the slow march towards a genuinely inclusive political system.

Therefore, it is amazing that notwithstanding Fukuyama's correct statement that 'the sequencing of political development in Western Europe was highly unusual when compared to other parts of the world', and the fact that the whole of Fukuyama's book *The Origins of Political Order. From Prehuman Times to the French Revolution* shows that, depending on differing cultures and traditions, the political histories of societies have taken different forms, he writes that 'one of the great mistakes of early modernization theory, beyond the

31 Acemoglu, Robinson, Op. Cit., p. 309.
32 Ibid., p. 333.

error in thinking that politics, economics, and culture had to be congruent with one another, was to think that transitions between the "stages" of history were clean and irreversible'.[33] It is easy to agree with Fukuyama's point on the transitions between the 'stages' of history that indeed are rarely, if ever, clean and irreversible, but his own analysis of the political history of many countries over long periods (from pre-human times until the French revolution, as the title and the content of the book say) pays tribute to the view that a certain congruence between, and sequencing of, the evolution of economic and political systems as well as civil society are historical facts. An important difference between the evolution of the Western and non-Western world is also in the fact that while the former evolved on their own, without much, if any, interference or impact from the outside, using the trial and error method, other societies have felt in their evolution the heavy impact of Western civilization. In their evolution this natural congruence and sequencing, which emerged in the West through trial and error and in that respect, we may say, more naturally, has been absent in many other parts of the world. And this has created serious problems, especially but not only for, the former colonies of European empires. As Ian Morris observes:

> When we look at reactions to Western rule within a longer time frame, we in fact see two striking correlations. The first is that those regions that had relatively high social development before the Western rule, like the Eastern core, tended to industrialize themselves faster than those that had relatively low development scores; the second, that those regions that avoided direct European colonization tended to industrialize faster than those that did become colonies. Japan had high social development before 1853 and was not colonized; its modernization took off in the 1870s. China had high development and was partly colonized; its modernization took off in the 1950s. India had moderate development and was fully colonized; its modernization did not take off until the 1990s. Sub-Saharan Africa had low development and full colonization, and is only now starting to catch up.[34]

Besides their deterministic-voluntaristic unidirectional approach to history, there is one more common methodological element between the Soviet brand of Marxism and contemporary liberal democracies.

---

33 Ibid., p. 77–78.

34 I. Morris, *Why the West Rules – For Now. The Patterns of History and What They Reveal about the Future*, Profile Books, 2011, p. 522.

During the Cold War, when the Soviet Union was vying with the United States over control of the world, trying to extend its sway over the so-called Third World countries, and prompt them to choose the only true – i.e. Soviet style socialist – way of development, Soviet experts invented a peculiar version of 'the dictatorship of the proletariat'. In accordance with Marxist orthodoxy, for a society to reach in its evolution the stage of socialism, it was necessary first to pass through the stage of developed capitalism, which would generate not only material preconditions for a successful and sustainable socialist revolution, but would also create and strengthen the proletariat – the 'gravedigger of capitalism', which, later, through the exercise of its dictatorship, would lead society, via socialism, to communism. According to this orthodox Marxist theory, countries such as Mongolia, Vietnam or Cuba, which in their evolution had not yet gone through the capitalist stage,[35] could not become socialist. Obviously, such an interpretation of Marx would not have been in the interests of or liking to the Soviet leaders, since this would have meant, *inter alia*, that those countries would have fallen, at least for the time being, into Washington's and not Moscow's sphere of influence. To avoid such a theoretical obstacle with its negative consequences in the practical struggle over global domination, a theory was invented, which asserted that in the absence of a proletariat at home the world socialist system, i.e. Moscow, could play the role of 'proletariat's dictatorship'. Thus, the absence of internal conditions for socialism could have been compensated for by external assistance and support.

Today various theories for the promotion of democracy are using, *mutatis mutandi*, similar lines of reasoning. If there are no internal conditions for the emergence of liberal democracy, and especially for its sustainability in a specific country, the European Union, the Organisation on the Security and Cooperation in Europe (OSCE), NATO or Washington either alone or together with a 'coalition of willing' can serve the role of 'Big Brother', who would shore up and guide new regimes towards liberal democracy. I do not want to

[35] Of course, Russia herself in 1917 had only rather feeble shoots of capitalism which made, first, the Bolshevik coup possible, secondly its practice especially bloody, and thirdly its eventual failure inevitable. Lenin wrote in 1912: 'Russia is undoubtedly ... one of the most benighted, medieval and shamefully backward Asian countries' (Lenin, 'Democracy and Narodism in China', www.marxists.org/archive/lenin/works/1912/jul/15.htm).

equate, of course, Soviet attempts to spread its totalitarian ideology with all the efforts, even if sometimes misguided and hypocritical, to widen the circle of democracies. If a society indeed becomes prosperous and democratic due, *inter alia*, to external efforts, even if outsiders are not exclusively or primarily motivated by noble and altruistic concerns, so be it. Moreover, there are indeed governments, international organisations and other bodies that carry out rather painstaking and usually unappreciated work helping other societies gradually democratise and modernise. My point is about the limits of external efforts in the absence of internal factors that are necessary for democratisation. It is also about wishful thinking in the elaboration of theories that correspond to one's interests, be they altruistic or self-serving.

Thomas Friedman once put forward one of the most pertinent questions concerning the democratization of some societies, though he himself did not give any answers to it. He asked: '[W]as Iraq the way Iraq was because Saddam was the way Saddam was, or was Saddam the way Saddam was because Iraq was the way Iraq was?'[36] A general answer probably has to be that Iraq was ready for Saddam and a person like Saddam Hussein could not have come to power, and even less likely would have ruled there for decades, in a society that would have been very different from Iraq. Rulers deserve their societies and societies as a rule too deserve their rulers, though some dictators turn out to be too bloody, brutal and mad even for the societies that have created them; Idi Amin, Pol Pot, Saddam Hussein or Muammar Gaddafi excelled even in their own class. Similarly, it was nothing but the personality characteristics of the first president of independent Turkmenistan, Saparmurat Nijazov (the *Turkmenbashi* – the father of the Turkmen) that made Turkmenistan outstanding even amongst Central Asian authoritarianisms. Often chance plays a significant role in history of individual societies, and sometimes even in world history, more than any 'rule' of social development.[37] The fall of such leaders is therefore

[36] T.L. Friedman, 'The big question', *The International Herald Tribune*, 4–5 March 2006, p. 6.

[37] See, R. Müllerson, *Central Asia: A Chessboard and Player in the New Great Game*, London, Kegan Paul, Columbia University Press, 2007; the paperback edition of the same book was published by Routledge in 2012.

welcome on humanitarian grounds, though it may not signify that a society in liberating itself, sometimes with significant outside assistance, from such a tyrant will necessarily undergo genuine social revolution leading to freedom and prosperity. It would not even always be correct to call overthrows of bloody tyrants revolutions, since the new regime very often soon falls back on old habits. It is not atypical that new authorities, having come to power through external support, use, at least for a while, rhetoric that pleases the ears of their external supporters. However, when in power, they would often continue with policies that differ very little from those of their predecessors. And it is not that they all are necessarily hypocrites when promising to carry out democratic reforms. Very often liberal democratic minorities that genuinely promise reforms are as alienated from their own people as are the autocrats who rule.

One of the latest waves of regime changes, after the so-called 'colour revolutions' in some territories of the former Soviet Union, has been dubbed the 'Arab spring'. Like the 'colour revolutions', they too had internal causes as their main engines, though in some cases external factors played a significant role. One of the most important lessons of the 'Arab spring' should be, in my opinion, the reiteration of the strategic rule that external interference usually makes things worse, not better. This rule applies in two different scenarios: first, when for tactical purposes it is believed that incumbents deserve to be propped up; secondly, in cases when, on the contrary, outsiders for whatever reasons believe that it is necessary to support opposition forces. The rule of the thumb should be: don't support dictators but don't undermine them either. Often anti-Western, and especially anti-American, attitudes in some developing countries are counter-reactions to Western policies aimed at supporting pro-Western governments in power. The Castros' Cuba and the Ayatollahs' Iran are both reactions to Washington's support of the regimes of Fulgencio Batista in Cuba and of Shah Reza Pahlavi in Iran. Equally, one shouldn't be certain that the people of Iraq or Afghanistan would warmly remember those who liberated them from Saddam Hussein or the Taliban. The situation in both countries is far from optimistic. For example, according to a classified coalition report on Afghanistan obtained by *The New York Times*, 'American and other coalition forces here are being killed in increasing numbers by the very Afghan soldiers they fight alongside and train, in attacks motivated by deep-seated animosity between the supposedly allied forces'.[38] The same day when parts of that report were leaked, *The International Herald Tribune* reported that four French troops had been killed in northern Afghanistan and sixteen more were wounded when a soldier from the Afghan National Army whom the French were training, opened fire.[39] In August 2012 The New York Times once again noted the increase of attacks by Afghan solders on NATO troops as well as on their own colleagues.[40] The aggressive external involvement in the formation, evolution of and support for the Karzai Government in Afghanistan has done little good either for Afghanistan or for those who have been involved in the country. Not only are the Taliban and their Pakistani supporters, but also Afghan society as a whole, bracing themselves for the time when the Americans and its NATO allies leave the country. As the leaked February 2012 NATO report observes, 'Afghans frequently prefer Taliban governance over the Afghan [Karzai] government, usually as a result of government corruption'.[41] One of the most prominent British military commanders of the past, General Frederick Roberts, who for decades had served in Asia, and who intimately knew the region (he took part in the second British Afghan war of 1878–80) felt sure that 'the less the Afghans see us the less they will dislike us'.[42] This observation is no less true today than it was more than a century ago.

It may well be that in today's turmoil in the Arab world, as well as in certain disturbing developments in some other third world nations, we see a kind of return in these societies to their roots, so to say. For Islamists, whether so-called moderates or radicals, obtaining power in Muslim countries may be more natural than Arab socialists *à la* Gamal Abdel Nasser or Western oriented secular autocrats *à la* Anwar Sadat or Hosni Mubarak. In a way, and especially from the

---

[38] *The International Herald Tribune*, 20 January 2012.

[39] Ibid.

[40] R. Oppel, G. Bowley, 'Attacks on Afghan Troops by Colleagues Are Rising, Allies Say', *The New York Times*, 23 August 2012.

[41] Ben Farmer, 'Taliban intact and getting Pakistan backing, NATO report reveals', *The Telegraph*, 1 February, 2012.

[42] A. Forbes, *Afghan Wars, 1839–42 and 1879–80*, London, Seeley, 1892, p. 325.

Western perceptive (and also from the perspective of many people in those societies as well), this can be seen as a return to the dark ages since, for example, the status of women may quite predictably suffer even more, and so would some other limited freedoms and modest achievements. However, taking a few steps back, these societies may, hopefully, be able, starting from that set point, to build their own institutions, ones more adequate to the characteristics of their own societies, while also borrowing from other countries (not necessarily only from the West but also, say, from China) that which would help them become more prosperous and free.

The current Islamisation of some Middle Eastern countries, as a result of the 'Arab spring', is both inevitable and, in the long run, probably beneficial not only for the peoples of the region but for their neighbours as well. It is inevitable because these are traditional Muslim societies on whom alien models had been imposed for long periods, be it by Atatürk in Turkey or the secular autocrats of many Arab nations. It is beneficial in the long run because even if in some of these countries some categories of people may see their status, at least for the time being, worsening (e.g. women or religious minorities because of the introduction of the Sharia law), it is better to start the long and painful process of evolution towards a more free society earlier rather than later. The Soviet experience both in Soviet Central Asia and later in Soviet occupied Afghanistan shows that imposed personal freedoms (e.g., the improvement of the status of women), even if rather limited, are easily reversible realities.

Quite a few people in the West, and especially in Israel, are extremely worried about the prospect of the Islamisation of the Middle East. However, it may well be that when the West ceases to tell the East how to live, and also helps, through impartial mediation, resolve the Israeli-Palestinian conflict (which many in the region regard as a litmus test for the East-West relations in the Middle East), then Western and Muslim countries may indeed develop good-neighbourly relations as equals, even despite having different cultures and interests. Nikolas Gvosdev and Ray Takeyh, in writing about the US policy towards the 'Arab spring' and especially about NATO's intervention in Libya, observe that 'there has been a real shift in American attitudes, a willingness to take the risks of losing short-term security advantages in favour of encouraging long-term societal change'.[43] Such a shift would be indeed welcome, not in the sense of the military intervention in Libya, but because of the withdrawal of support from friendly autocrats, who had for far too long represented American interests, contrary to the interests and values of their own people, in the Middle East. After the first round of Egyptian parliamentary elections Bobby Ghosh made an interesting comment: 'The Islamists, it turned out, understand democracy much better than the liberal do.'[44] Indeed, in a country without liberal traditions democracy will never bring liberals to power. We see that Turkey can combine political Islam and democracy; why not Egypt or some other Muslim states? In the Middle East such a combination will certainly have better prospects than liberal democracy. Moreover, as Charles Kupchan writes, 'observers and policy makers should stop operating under the illusion that the spread of democracy in the Middle East also means the spread of Western values'.[45]

Amitai Etzioni in his book *Security First: For a Muscular, Moral Foreign Policy* maps some non-traditional fault-lines in the non-Western world. They are drawn not so much between different religions or cultures, as between what he calls 'Warriors' and 'Illiberal Moderates'.[46] The majority of people in non-Western, and specifically in the Muslim, world are not 'Warriors' ready to use violence for the promotion of their values; however, neither are they western-style liberal-democrats. They are, as Etzioni writes, 'Illiberal Moderates', i.e. 'those who disavow violence (in most circumstances) but who do not necessarily favor a liberal-democratic regime or the full program of human rights'.[47] As in many countries they constitute the absolute majority of the population, it is necessary to work with

---

[43] N.K. Gvosdev, R. Takeyh, 'Triumph of the New Wilsonianism', *The National Interest*, 4 January 2012 (http://nationalinterest.org/articledecline-western-realism-6274).

[44] B. Ghosh, 'Why the Islamists are Better Democrats', *The Time Magazine*, 19 December 2011 (http://www.time.com/time/magazine/article/0,9171,2101903,00.html).

[45] C. Kupchan, 'Diversity Wins', *Russia in Global Affairs*, 29 December 2011 (http://eng.globalaffairs.ru/number/Diversity-Wins-15426).

[46] Amitai Etzioni, *Security First: For a Muscular, Moral Foreign Policy*, Yale University Press, 2007.

[47] Ibid., p. 86.

them, and to rely mainly on them and not on a thin layer of liberals who usually lack domestic support and legitimacy. 'This [establishing good relations between Western and such non-Western countries] will work only as long as the West seeks a safe and peaceful world, not one in which all regime types are identical or in which the moral cultures are universally secular.'[48] Trying to convert 'Illiberal Moderates' into liberal-democrats would be not only futile; it would be also counter-productive. In that respect a remark is due. Etzioni writes that 'we should refrain from sending Special Forces or cruise missiles to transform others into supporters of the particular beliefs we champion'.[49] True. However, we would caution also against excessive preaching, missionarism and assertive democracy promotion, even without the help of Special Forces and missiles. Not only aren't all human rights equally important, but there are rights that aren't universal and some that may not (even in principle) be universalisable. Moreover, in some societies proselytizing may cause serious social unrests and conflicts; what is needed are conversations across cultural boundaries, and not the preaching of one's values as superior or the only true ones.

Nicholas Gvosdev, advocating *nation cultivation* instead of *nation building*, believes that '[N]ation building is an inherently revolutionary proposition that believes it is both possible and desirable to sweep away the past and install new institutions by fiat. Nation cultivation, in contrast, rests on the observations of Edmund Burke that sustainable, evolutionary change is possible only by working within the existing frameworks bequeathed by tradition and experience'.[50] He rightly observes that '[M]any nation-building failures of the last two decades—Somalia, Bosnia, Iraq and Afghanistan—resulted from the hasty and rapid importation of institutions that had no way to take root in the local society ... In retrospect, a nation cultivator might have supported the restoration of the monarchy in Afghanistan as a first step toward recreating a central authority capable of providing some degree of national unity and identity, rather than settling on elections as the source of sovereignty. After all, to have a

48 Ibid., p. 163.
49 Ibid., p. 92.
50 N. Gvosdev, 'The Era of Nation Cultivation', *The National Interest*, 25 May, 2012.

democracy, one must have a "demos"—a people'.[51] Of course, nation cultivation may be preferable to aggressive nation building, but it should also be demand-induced, not supply-stimulated.

3. PROBLEMS OF LIBERAL DEMOCRACY AND DEMOCRATIC CAPITALISM

The most important shortcoming of a proactive and voluntaristic promotion of liberal democracy stems from the simplistic and deterministic belief in the linear and unidirectional evolution of the world. Although it is true, as we have illustrated, that the more globalised the world becomes, the more homogeneous it turns out to be, this process is very slow, it is driven by fits and starts and never ends. Moreover, globalisation has its dangers as well as its limits. It may well be that at least in certain areas, in order to meet new challenges (e.g., run-away financial markets, uncontrolled migration flows, traffic in drugs and terrorism), societies would find it necessary to curb certain aspects and consequences of globalisation. As Dani Rodrik observes, 'we cannot have hyperglobalization, democracy, and national self-determination all at once. If we want hyperglobalization and democracy, we need to give up on the nation state. If we must keep the nation state and want hyperglobalization too, then we must forget about democracy. And if we want to combine democracy with the nation state, then it is bye-bye deep globalization'.[52] Although it has been the West that has been the engine of globalisation and homogenisation in the world, and at least until recently also its main beneficiary, it will not stay like that forever. In human history there has not been any political or economic system, empire or great power, whose dominance has not come to an end, whose ways of doing things, even if widely copied by others, have not at some point become out-dated. Taking into account that globalisation has accelerated changes and developments in many parts of the world, the rise and fall of great powers will also happen faster

---

[51] Ibid.

[52] D. Rodrik, *The Globalization Paradox: Why Global Markets, States and Democracy Can't Coexist*, Oxford University Press, 2011, p. 200.

than ever before in human history.[53] Even if it weren't for the current financial and economic crisis in the West, there is no doubt that the East, and first of all China, using *inter alia* Western scientific and even social achievements and combining them with its own traditions and inventions, will change the balance of power in the world. Trying to impose, even for benign ends, one's own model on other societies would put an end to social development, since it is not only through borrowing from others, but also through social experimentation and competition that humankind has progressively evolved.[54] Charles Kupchan writes that the 'crisis of governability within the Western world comes at a particularly inopportune moment. The international system is in the midst of tectonic change due to the diffusion of wealth and power to new quarters. Globalization was supposed to have played to the advantage of liberal societies, which were presumably best suited to capitalize on the fast and fluid nature of the global marketplace. But instead, mass publics in the advanced democracies of North America, Europe, and East Asia have been particularly hard hit – precisely because their countries' economies are both mature and open to the world'.[55] Moreover, it is not at all certain that existing and dominant social arrangements are well suited to facing new and unforeseen challenges.

---

53 Although Niall Ferguson's warning that imperial demise (and the US in his opinion is an empire and should openly recognize itself to be one) is not necessarily a centuries long process and can take place rather abruptly, may be overstated (N. Ferguson, 'Complexity and Collapse. Empires on the Edge of Chaos', *Foreign Affairs*, March-April, 2010), there is no doubt that the acceleration of social changes that is a result of and a part of globalisation means that changes in the balance of power in the world also happen much more quickly than centuries ago. Arvind Subramanian is less alarmist but he also observes that '[A]ccording to the projections, between 2010 and 2030 emerging markets and developing economies will increase their share of world GDP (at market-based exchange rates) by a whopping 19 percentage points and by 15 percentage points at PPP exchange rates. China's share of the world GDP (in PPP dollars) will increase from 17 percent in 2010 to 24 percent in 2030, and India's share will increase from 5 to 10 percent. China's economy (in PPP dollars) will be more than twice that of the United States by 2030' (A. Subramanian, *Eclipse: Living in the Shadow of China's Economic Dominance*, Peterson Institute, 2011 (Kindle editions), Loc., 2239).

54 See, e.g., D. Landes, *The Wealth and Poverty of Nations. Why Some Are So Rich and Some So Poor*, Little, Brown and Company, 1998, p. 38–39.

55 C. Kupchan, 'The Democratic Malaise. Globalization and the Threat to the West', *Foreign Affairs*, January-February, 2012.

In the opinion of Francis Fukuyama, '[L]iberal democracy is the default ideology around much of the world today in part because it responds to and is facilitated by certain socioeconomic structures. Changes in those structures may have ideological consequences, just as ideological consequences may have socioeconomic consequences'.[56] Globalisation and the development of technology have indeed had a serious impact on these socioeconomic structures; most importantly, they have eroded the relative strength of the middle class – the main pillar of liberal democracy – in the Western world. Societies are becoming more and more unequal and polarised. As Joseph Stiglitz wrote in 2011, '[T]he upper 1 percent of Americans are now taking in nearly a quarter of nation's income every year. In terms of wealth rather than income, the top 1 percent control 40 percent. Their lot of life has improved considerably. Twenty-five years ago, the corresponding figures were 12 percent and 33 percent'.[57] A similar trend, though not always as obvious, is taking place in most Western or Westernising societies. In Fukuyama's view, such a tendency undermines the very structure on which liberal democratic ideology and practices are based. It is difficult to disagree with him. If, say, Great Britain will continue losing its industrial and manufacturing base (which in the eighteenth and nineteenth centuries made possible its dominant global position) and contributed to the relatively even spread of wealth in society, and carries on relying on the financial services sector of the City of London as the main source of its revenue, it may indeed guarantee GDP growth for some time, but society will become ever more unequal, and the middle class smaller and weaker. Dan Hind has even written that 'on any conventional measure, the financial sector has been a disaster for the majority of the country [the UK]. The amounts devoted to saving the banks when the credit crisis began are so enormous that it is hard to grasp their significance – and we still don't know what the final reckoning will be'.[58]

---

[56] F. Fukuyama, 'The Future of History. Can Liberal Democracy Survive the Decline of the Middle Class?', *Foreign Affairs*, January/February, 2012.

[57] J. Stiglitz, 'Of the 1 %, by the 1%, for the 1%', *Vanity Fair*, May 2011.

[58] D. Hind, 'The Last Province of the Empire', Al Jazeera, 21 July 2012 (http://www.aljazeera.com/indepth/opinion/2012/07/201271972132896868.html).

It would be imprudent to remain content with Churchill's words, which for too many have become a mantra repeated *ad nauseam*, that 'democracy is the worst form of government except all those other forms that have been tried from time to time' (Winston Churchill is reported of having also said that 'the best argument against democracy is a five-minute conversation with the average voter'). Moreover, is it not necessary to seriously reflect on the first part of Churchill's statement ('democracy is the worst from of government') and not see it only as a defence (as such, it would be rather sharp but nevertheless superficial) of democracy but also as its critique? There are several shortcomings of liberal democracy that have become increasingly evident, as the world has become more and more globalised. First, modern democracy emerged in parallel with, evolved within, and its thriving was dependent on the nation-state, i.e., relatively homogenous, closed and self-sufficient entities. Today the trinity – democracy, the nation-state and hyperglobalization – are not possible all at the same time, as Dani Rodrik has shown. Today, even the nation-state in its traditional form, and democracy are not easily compatible. Historically, there has been a positive correlation between democracy and nationalism. Not anymore.

John Stuart Mill, one of the greatest liberal thinkers, argued that democracy could only flourish where 'the boundaries of government coincide in the main with those of nationality.'[59] His argument in support of this contention was based on an analysis of the necessary conditions for a flourishing democracy: 'Among a people without fellow-feeling, especially if they read and speak different languages, the united public opinion necessary to the workings of representative institutions cannot exist'.[60] Much later, in 1969, Leo Kuper wrote in the same vein asserting that: '[C]ultural diversity or pluralism automatically imposes the strictest necessity for domination by one of the cultural sections. It excludes the possibility of consensus, or of institutional integration, or structural balance between the different sections, and necessitates non-democratic regulation

59 J.S. Mill, *Utilitarianism. On Liberty, Considerations of Representative Government*, Basil and Blackwell, 1993, p. 394.

60 Ibid., p. 392.

of group relations'.[61] We see that historically the emergence and development of democracy was, if not conditioned, then at least facilitated by the homogenous nature of societies, and if they were not homogenous enough they had to be made such. As the Italian novelist and politician Massimo Taparellid'Azeglio famously put it in 1861: 'We have created Italy. Now all we have to do is to create Italians'.[62] To put it otherwise, without necessary homogeneity, d'Azeglio believed, the country would not even stay together, to say nothing about developing representative institutions. Today, however, most societies have become multicultural, and are increasingly becoming more and more multi-ethnic and multi-religious. In such a condition, nationalism has ceased to play any positive emancipatory role; its impact is increasingly becoming negative. Today, as we have already emphasised, it is the recognition and tolerance of diversity, the respect of the rights of minorities, be they ethnic, religious or sexual, which are essential in practically all societies. Of course, these values, which were alien for European societies at the age of the creation of the nation-states, are not at all opposite to the democracy of the twenty first century. But this democracy cannot aim, like the democracy of the eighteenth and nineteenth centuries, at constructing societies that are homogeneous in terms of languages read or spoken, religions professed or not professed; one of the important tasks of practically all societies, and not only the fledgling but also mature democracies, is the formation of fellow-feeling between diverse people and groups. However, in many societies, including some rich countries, nationalism is rearing its ugly head; yet, in the twenty first century the methods used to homogenise a country and create a nation within which representative institutions could flourish are unacceptable or even criminal (at least under international law), like ethnic or religious cleansing. Therefore, societies must find ways to create truly multicultural democracies, where different people and groups possess fellow-feeling based on common values and interests. This may be even more difficult than

[61] L. Kuper, 'Plural Societies: Perspectives and Problems' in L. Kuper, A. Smith (eds.) *Pluralism in Africa*, University of California Press, 1969, p. 14.

[62] S. Tharoor, '*E Pluribus*, India: Is Indian Modernity Working?' *Foreign Affairs*, 1998, vol. 77, No. 1, p. 128.

the parallel processes of democratisation and homogenisation of the nineteenth century, but there is no other way if human beings want to live in both democracy and in peace.

Equally damaging is the positive (or negative, depending on how one sees it) correlation, especially in the United States, between money and democracy. If in some so-called developing countries or emerging market economies one has to enjoy political power in order to become a billionaire, in the citadel of liberal democracy in order to be elected to a high political post one needs, if not himself to be a billionaire, then at least to be supported by and work for them. As Jeffrey Sachs writes, '[C]orporate wealth translates into political power through campaign financing, corporate lobbying, and the revolving door of jobs between government and industry',[63] and he claims that America is becoming a 'corporatocracy, a political system in which powerful corporate interest groups dominate the policy agenda'.[64] Another shortcoming of liberal democracy is an institution at the very core of democracy – periodic elections. They are causing short-termism in the policy-making of practically all Western liberal democracies. 'All these problems of short-termism are compounded by an antiplanning mentality',[65] observes Jeffrey Sachs. The inability to take necessary measures in the face of current financial and economic crises is only one of the signs of democratic short-termism. As Fukuyama observes, '[M]any people currently admire the Chinese system not just for its economic record but also because it can make large, complex decisions quickly, compared with the agonizing policy paralysis that has struck both the United States and Europe in the past few years'.[66]

Even more serious are the external problems of democracy in the globalised world. Institutions of modern democracy, having emerged within and adapted for the frame of the nation-state, and showing strains in the multicultural societies of today, are not appropriate and suitable for international relations, and do not work well at all

---

[63] J. Sachs, *The Price of Civilization. Economics and Ethics After the Fall*, The Bodley Head, 2011, p. 116.

[64] Ibid., p. 106.

[65] Ibid., p. 242.

[66] Fukuyama, 'The Future of History. Can Liberal Democracy Survive the Decline of the Middle Class', *Foreign Affairs*, January/February 2012.

when the earlier clear divisions between external and domestic affairs become blurred. Would democracy in international relations mean 'one state, one vote'? In that case a vote from Nauru and a vote from China would have the same weight, which from the point of view of a 'one man, one vote' system looks not only unfair but even ridiculous. Would it mean that democratic states should have stronger voices than non-democratic states, like a kind of weighted voting in international financial institutions where the weight of one's vote depends on the money one contributes to the organisation? In that case who would allocate such votes? Ideas of so-called cosmopolitan democracy[67] transcending state boundaries are able to address at best some of the concerns of a democracy deficit in the globalising world. Even within Europe most populations of the European Union member-states constantly grumble about the alienation of the EU institutions from the European voters, about a democracy deficit within the Union. And this is within a group of states whose histories, traditions and levels of development are relatively similar. There is even a positive (or negative, depending on how one looks at the problem) correlation between the power and effectiveness of international bodies on the one hand, and their 'democratic' credentials, on the other. The more 'democratic' an international body, the less power or authority it enjoys. Within the United Nations it is its Security Council, and especially its 5 permanent members, which is the most powerful and effective organ. Neither are more 'democratic' different informal groupings, such as G7, G8, G20 or G2. Or rather, one may justifiably conclude that this concept has very little room in the field of international relations. Today, if the concept of democracy has any relevance in an international society, which has been and remains in essence an interstate society, then it may be related to the development of a multipolar and diverse world consisting of several centres of power and thereby avoiding the emergence of one hegemonic centre. In that respect the relative decline of US power and strengthening of China, Brazil, Russia, Turkey and some other countries which are not following, in all matters, Washington's lead, may be seen as a step towards

[67] D. Archibugi, *The Global Common Wealth of Citizens: Toward Cosmopolitan Democracy*, Princeton, 2008.

the 'democratisation' of international relations. Of course, such a 'democratisation' of international relations raises as many questions as it solves. First, this means, and even more so than in domestic affairs (the natural embodiment of democracy), that democracy in international relations is messy. Secondly, these centres of power, forced to cooperate and compromise among themselves, exercise a dominant influence over smaller nations that may have little say on big issues. This may not be such a serious practical issue (though it is a serious problem of social psychology for smaller but proud nations) since an aggregate of compromises between the powers of such a 'concert' may be generally preferable for smaller actors than the dominance of one single power centre. Thirdly, there is a tendency of emerging or developing power centres turning into regional hegemonic powers. Although there will not be any global hegemonic power, there will be various regional hegemons with their zones of 'privileged interests', with their own 'Monroe' or analogous doctrines. To counter such a tendency, it would be necessary to also have regional 'concerts' that would balance the development of a single regional hegemon. Be that as it may, it seems that democracy in international relations would look more like a balance of powers than a 'one man one vote' system, though Hugh White, advocating the creation of a regional concert of great powers in Asia that would accommodate China's rise and balance it with the continuing American presence (though not the continuing domination) in the Asia-Pacific region, may be right that '[A] balance of power is that what emerges naturally if the great powers in a system fail to agree on a concert, and it is what happens if a concert collapses, as it happened in the years before 1914. By contrast, a concert is an agreement to minimise the risk of war that is inherent in the balance of power system'.[68]

Besides the crisis of liberal democracy there is also a crisis of capitalism. It seems that free market (capitalism) and liberal democracy, phenomena that on the one hand have presumed each other, are also increasingly in a state of constant rivalry or competition. The freer a market, the greater the economic inequality; the greater the

---

68 H. White, The China Choice: Why America should Share Power, Black Inc., 2012, (Kindle version), loc. 1785.

inequality, the less would there be democracy, and *vice versa*. Cambridge economist Ha-Joon Chang even writes that '[F]ree market and democracy are not natural partners',[69] though it has to be emphasised that Professor Chang is not speaking of 'market economy', but of 'free market' or rather 'unbridled markets', as advocated, for instance, by Milton Friedman and his followers. One of the most persistent market-friendly advocates of political freedoms, Karl Popper, already half a century ago incisively wrote that: 'Even if the state protects its citizens from being bullied by physical violence (as it does in principle, under the system of unrestrained capitalism), it may defeat our ends by its failure to protect them from the misuse of economic power. In such a state, the economically strong is still free to bully one who is economically weak, and to rob of his freedom. Under these circumstances, unlimited economic freedom can be just as self-defeating as unlimited physical freedom, and economic power may be nearly as dangerous as physical violence.'[70] As it was so more than half a century ago when Popper wrote these words, it is even more so today.

Economic inequality *de facto* and inevitably also increases political inequality, while political equality puts brakes on widening economic inequality. Strong democracy attained by curbing inequality almost inevitably also bridles market freedoms. Democracy tries to make a society more equal, while unbridled markets increase inequality. The result of such constant balancing is that in Western European liberal democracies (social democracies), these two spheres – political and economic – while supporting each other, have also constantly softened each other's negative impacts. The United States, in that respect too, differs considerably from Europe. Cambridge Professor John Dunn writes that 'America today remains a society uncomfortable with every surviving vestige of explicit privilege, but remarkably blithe in face of the most vertiginous of economic gulfs, and comprehensively reconciled to the most obtrusive privileges of wealth as such. Behind this outcome lies the continuing

[69] H.-J. Chang, *Bad Samaritans. Rich Nations, Poor Policies & the Threat to the Developing World*, Random House Business Books, 2007, p. 18.
[70] K. Popper, *The Open Society and Its Enemies*, Volume 2. Hegel & Marx, Routledge, 1996, p. 124.

vitality of its economy, the real source of the victory of the partisans of "distinction, or the English school of economists"'.[71] Or as Joseph Stiglitz has put it, 'instead of government tempering the excesses of the market, in America today the two have been working together to increase income and wealth disparities'.[72] There the market has prevailed over democracy while, say, in Sweden, governed for long periods by social democrats, there has been less room, as Dunn puts it, for 'distinctions and opulence',[73] i.e. democracy has exercised greater constraints on the market. Today, when there are serious doubts about 'the continuing vitality' of the American economy one may start questioning whether equality of opportunity without much effect on the equality of the outcome is not too narrow a concept. Moreover, as Stiglitz has well shown in his latest book,[74] 'the American dream', '*the land of equal opportunity*' has become a complete myth and social, both upward as well as downward, mobility has all but stopped working. Without equal opportunity, however, 'equal rights' also becomes an empty slogan instead of an enforceable right. This has had a nefarious effect also on the political sphere where the 'current system seems to operate on a "one dollar" one vote instead of "one person one vote" basis'.[75] Paul Krugman put it forcefully when he wrote: 'Extreme concentration of income is incompatible with real democracy. Can anyone seriously deny that our political system is being warped by the influence of big money, and that the warping is getting worse as the wealth of a few grows ever larger?'[76]

John Dunn also observes that within the liberal democratic movement 'the partisans of the order of egoism', i.e. capitalists, have defeated 'the partisans of equality',[77] i.e. democrats. One of the important causes of equality's defeat at the hands of economic

---

71 J. Dunn, *Setting the People Free. The Story of Democracy*, Atlantic Books, 2005, p. 127.

72 J. Stiglitz, *The Price of Inequality: How Today's Divided Society Endangers Our Future*, W.W. Norton & Company, 2012, p. 38.

73 J. Dunn, *Setting the People Free*, p. 130.

74 J. Stiglitz, *The Price of Inequality*, pp. 17–20.

75 Ibid., p. 119.

76 P. Krugman, 'Oligarchy, American Style', The *New York Times*, 4 November, 2011 (http://www.nytimes.com/2011/11/04/opinion/oligarchy-american-style.html).

77 J. Dunn, *Setting the People Free*, p. 134.

egoism has been that in the long run the uncompromising instruments for attempting to realize equality, and the rigidities inherent in its pursuit, have blunted equality's appeal as a goal.[78] Both the 1789 French and especially the 1917 Russian revolutions, where contrary to the American revolution of the eighteenth century, the aim was not so much, as Hannah Arendt had put it, 'freedom from oppression' as 'freedom from want', and one of the main requirements therefore was *égalité* (equality), have contributed to the existing balance (or imbalance) within today's understanding of the correlation between democracy and liberty. Arendt wrote that 'the inescapable fact was that liberation from tyranny spelled freedom only for the few and was hardly felt by the many who remained loaded down by their misery. These had to be liberated once more, and compared to this liberation from the yoke of necessity, the original liberation from tyranny must have looked like child's play'.[79]

The fact that radical attempts of liberation from 'the yoke of necessity' and the creation of more equal societies have so far led to tyranny, should in no way compromise the values of equality and freedom from want in the eyes of thoughtful individuals. It is possible to abuse all values and norms but this doesn't mean that we should therefore reject them. What is needed is a critical mind able to distinguish between a value and its abuse. Today, advanced liberal democracies have, in principle, got rid of the 'yoke of tyranny' and have alleviated the 'yoke of necessity' for most of their people, but one cannot be complacent since not only are there too many poor people even in rich European societies, but the 'war on terror' is attempting to bring back the 'yoke of tyranny'. For many other societies both tasks still constitute formidable challenges, and even mature democracies have to constantly find new balances between freedom and equality. Wolfgang Streeck, writing of 'the crises of democratic capitalism', whose heydays, in his opinion, were between the end of WWII and the end of the 1960s, observes that 'more than ever, economic power seems today to have become political power, while citizens appear to be almost entirely stripped of their democratic defences and their capacity to impress upon the political

---

[78] Ibid., p. 129.
[79] H. Arendt, *On Revolution*, Penguin Books, 1965, p. 74.

economy interests and demands that are incommensurable with those of capital owners'.[80] After the collapse of communism, the conflictual aspect of the correlation 'capitalism – democracy' is becoming more and more visible. Therefore one may be justified in asking whether the 'sell-by date' of at least some of the Western style political and economic institutions that the West is trying to export to other countries has not already passed.

Even if we answer this question in the positive – and there are serious grounds for such a conclusion – this would not yet mean that democracy has no future. However, Wang Hui, who believes that 'we need to rethink the parochial [i.e. Western] notion of democracy'[81] emphasises that:

> If constitutionally defined political rights cannot effectively pave the way for democratic participation by citizens; if these political rights cannot check the inequalities that exist with respect to race, gender and class; if these democratic rights cannot restrict monopolies, power and domination; if they cannot limit the increasingly market-like behaviour of political power or the growth in the authority of the market, then we must consider a broader and more complete concept of democracy.[82]

This conclusion of the Chinese scholar, who is critical of today's Chinese realities, carries considerable weight: China needs both political and economic reforms, but not the copying of the West, which itself is in dire need of political and economic reforms.

American philosopher Daniel Dennett, who writes that his sacred values are obvious and quite ecumenical, lists them in alphabetical order as 'democracy, justice, life, love, and truth'.[83] Is democracy really ecumenical and sacred? Does it have any intrinsic value at all or is its value wholly instrumental? David Held has written that '[W]ithin democratic thinking, a clear divide exists between those who value political participation for its own sake and understand it

---

80 W. Streeck, 'The Crises of Democratic Capitalism', *New Left Review*, 71, September-October, 2011.

81 Wang Hui, *The End of the Revolution: China and the Limits of Modernity*, Verso, 2011, p. 103.

82 Ibid.

83 D. Dennett, *Breaking the Spell: Religion as a natural phenomenon*, Penguin Books, 2007, p. 23.

as a fundamental mode of self-realisation, and those who take a more instrumental view and understand democratic politics as a means of protecting citizens from arbitrary rule and expressing (via mechanisms of aggregation) their preferences. ... According to this position, democracy is a means not an end'.[84] Therefore, if democracy does not deliver what people need (economic growth, stability, personal and societal security) its fate may be even more fragile than that of autocratic regimes. Amitai Etzoni observes that '[F]rom the extensive literature written on the question of what caused the fall of the Weimar Republic and the rise of the Third Reich, it is reasonable to conclude that liberal democracy lost legitimacy because it failed to address peoples' need to physical and economic security'.[85] However, notwithstanding that people cannot be satisfied with a democracy that does not deliver, the concept, in our opinion, has not only instrumental but also some intrinsic value (though we would not call it sacred, since often even those who most ardently strive for democracy do not know what to do with it once they have received it as a sudden 'gift'; sometimes they even start missing the certainties of a stable autocracy). The gist of democracy's intrinsic value is that humans (at least most of us and we believe, in principle, at least all adult and mentally non-handicapped persons), when their immediate needs for survival are met, are not content and happy if it is somebody else who decides what is good for them, what they are allowed to do and what they should not do.[86] There have always been those who have not been satisfied with only material well-being. However, Dennett himself observes that '[B]iology insists on delving beneath the surface of "intrinsic" values and asking why they exist, and any answer that is supported by the facts has the effect of showing that the value in question is – or

---

[84] D. Held, *Models of Democracy* (3d edition), Polity Press, 2006, p. 231.

[85] A. Etzioni, *Security First: For a Muscular, Moral Foreign Policy*, Yale University Press, 2007, p. 8.

[86] However, one should not underestimate the human desire for emotional comfort, which is provided often by relieving people from the need to constantly take difficult decisions and make their own choices. Some people often prefer that somebody else – the parents, a party, the government, God represented by the clergy – takes over the burden. Many feel comfortable only amongst their co-religionists or in the military (See, e.g., Jean-Francois Revel, *La Tentation Totalitaire*, Editions Robert Laffont, Paris, 1976).

once was – really instrumental, not intrinsic, even if we don't see it that way'.[87] Although democracy has this intrinsic value because only under democracy – as if by definition – human beings obtain their adulthood, become citizens instead of subjects, its primary value is instrumental – it has to contribute, and often indeed contributes, to the realisation of other values such as material prosperity, social stability, personal freedoms and security and scientific or artistic creativity. However, this is not what always happens, since even good intentions may pave the road to hell. Moreover, if we speak of those who are involved in democracy promotion in different parts of the world, we have to remember that according to the Bible, a Good Samaritan is the exception rather than the rule.

There are logical arguments favouring democracy over other forms of governance, such as 'a human being can be fully human only when he or she fully participates in the political life of his or her country', that democracy is 'a fundamental mode of self-realisation', or even that 'only democratic governance can put an end to famines'. These and other similar arguments are put forward by thinkers such as Jürgen Habermas and Amartya Sen.[88] However, such reasoning cannot persuade those who prefer pragmatic or emotional arguments to logical or rational reasoning, as many people do. One of such arguments in favour of democracy is best expressed by the Richard Rorty, the greatest pragmatist philosopher who passed away in 2007: '[F]ollowers of Dewey like myself would like to praise parliamentary democracy and the welfare state as very good things, but only on the basis of invidious comparison with suggested concrete alternatives, not on the basis of claims that these institutions are truer to human nature, or more rational, or in better accord with the universal moral law, than feudalism or totalitarianism'.[89]

---

87 D. Dennett, *op.cit*, p. 69.

88 Nobel economics prize winner Amartya Sen writes that 'famines are easy to prevent if there is a serious effort to do so, and a democratic government, facing elections and criticisms from opposition parties and independent newspapers, cannot help but make such an effort. Not surprisingly, while India continued to have famines under British rule right up to independence (the last famine, which I witnessed as a child, was in 1943, four years before independence), they disappeared suddenly with the establishment of a multiparty democracy and a free press' (A. Sen, 'Democracy as Universal Value', *Journal of Democracy*, 1999, No 3, p. 8).

89 R. Rorty, *Philosophical Papers*, Volume 1, Cambridge University Press, 2007, p. 211.

As Cambridge philosopher Simon Blackburn writes, Rorty 'opposes the tradition which descends from Locke or Kant to recent writers such as Jürgen Habermas and John Rawls, which seeks to prove that a democratic and liberal state is the only rational mode of social organisation. For such writers, someone who chose to live in an illiberal or undemocratic state would be trampling on his own reason. It is irrational to sell yourself into the mental servitude that a theocratic state demands. But for Rorty, this Enlightenment attitude with its talk of irrationality is useless. The right pragmatist observation is that theocratic states seem not to work very well, by comparison with liberal democracies – it is theocracies who lose refugees to us, and not vice versa. We can cope, and theocracies cannot'.[90] There are certainly some strong points in Rorty's arguments, though most of those millions who leave their war-torn and poverty-ridden countries behind do not at all seek democracy and liberalism in the West. Often they bring with them highly undemocratic and illiberal habits and traditions, and even try to spread them in countries that have given them refuge. Of course, it is possible to argue that Western societies are prosperous because they are democratic, though it may well be the other way round – it could be prosperity that leads to democracy. The truth is, probably, somewhere in-between, and where there is the chicken and where there is the egg depends on concrete circumstances.

I personally enjoy living in a liberal-democratic country and I believe that notwithstanding all its imperfections it is best for me and for my family. However, it would be a mistake to make from this personal observation the following extrapolations. The first such invalid extrapolation would be the belief that everybody is like me. I would call it the 'Bush fallacy' since it has been President George W. Bush the Junior, who has the most clearly and the most frequently expressed the belief that what truths are self-evident for the Americans are true for all and everywhere.[91] Such a worldview is deeply engraved in American consciousness. So, President Bush the

[90] S. Blackburn, 'Portrait: Richard Rorty', *Prospect Magazine*, Issue 85, April, 2003.

[91] President G.W. Bush, Commencement Address to the United States Coast Guard Academy (21 May 2003).

Senior, urging Deng Xiaoping to understand popular outrage in America as a reaction to the 1989 Tiananmen tragedy, wrote to China's paramount leader: 'It is not a reaction of arrogance or of a desire to force others to our beliefs but a simple faith in the enduring value of those principles and their universal applicability'.[92] If such a belief and acting upon it do not reflect some kind of arrogance (alloyed with a portion of naivety) then what is arrogance?

The second extrapolation is that even if democracy, especially liberal democracy, is in principle good for everybody (of which, having studied the issue in some depth, I am not so sure anymore) the problem is when and how to get there. One of the greatest contemporary philosophers Jürgen Habermas insightfully observes that it is necessary to 'relativize one's own views to the interpretive perspectives of equally situated and equally entitled others', and that the "reason" of modern rational law does not consist of universal "values" that one can own like goods, and distribute and export throughout the world. "Values" – including those that have a chance of winning global recognition – don't come from thin air. They gain their binding force only within normative orders and practices of particular forms of cultural life.'[93] Therefore, 'whenever an attempt has been made to impose a Western model of development on non-Western countries it has involved mass terror'.[94] Alastair Crooke, comparing Islamic and Western societies observes that

> [I]t is this clash of two views of human being: one view – the western one –privileges "individuality", and defines this "individuality" as the appropriate organising principle around which society should be shaped. The other view – the Islamist vision – see the human to be integral to wider existence; intractably linked, and not separated, as "an individual", from others and the world that surrounds him or her; which sees the human as a multi-dimensional creature – larger than the sum of his or her desires and appetites, whose ability to access innate moral values, as the basis of his or her responsibility to the

---

92 H. Kissinger, *On China*, The Penguin Books, 2011, p. 417.

93 J. Habermas, 'Interpreting the Fall of the Monument', in *Empire's Law. The American Imperial Project and the 'War to Remake the World'* (A. Bartholomew ed.), Pluto Press, 2006, p. 51.

94 J. Gray, *Black Mass. Apocalyptic Religion and the Death of Utopia*, Allen Lane, 2007, p. 147.

> community, becomes the organisational principle of economics, society and politics.[95]

Therefore, democracy in the Middle East, or in the Far East for that matter, cannot be like that in the West; though in the long run (and only in the long run and without forcible pushing from outside, as we constantly emphasise in this book), different societies may become, in certain important respects, more similar to each other. While Muslim and other non-Western societies may start paying more attention to individual liberties, at least some Western (especially Anglo-Saxon) societies will have to tame their excessive individualism and borrow some communitarian ideas and practices either from the East or from their own past. This means that, at least in some way, though not necessarily in different ways, the concept of truth is relative and contingent; so is the truth about the advantages and disadvantages of democracy.

4. LIMITS OF SOCIAL DEMOCRATIC CHOICE IN A GLOBALIZED WORLD

After WWII many Western European states found a remedy to the excesses of wild capitalism (as well as to the challenges of the communist ideas) in social-democratic policies and in the so-called welfare state, which seemed to be able to find a satisfactory balance between *liberté*, *egalité* and at that time even *fraternité*. However, today the nation-state and the national market economy – these cradles of human rights and democracy – are both in the process of radical change. The world market is not any more the sum-total of national markets; it is becoming more and more a real common market. The state has lost not only its ability to control world financial flows, but also its ability to protect its own population from the negative effects of fluctuations in global markets, especially the financial markets. The unfettered global market tends to drag down the protection of economic and social rights to the level of the lowest common denominator (e.g. cheap labour and longer working

[95] A. Crooke, *Resistance: The Essence of the Islamist Revolution,* Pluto Press, 2009, pp. 29–30.

hours in many Asian societies are certainly affecting employment and social protection in all OECD countries). Jack Donnelly has written that: '[T]he globalisation of production is weakening state-centric schemes for implementing economic, social and cultural rights, most dramatically in the wealthier countries of the Northern Hemisphere. It does not, however, seem to be creating viable alternative mechanisms'.[96] Donnelly correctly also emphasises that economic growth that had come about due to globalisation, and the new division of labour should not be confused with the growth of economic and social rights since 'human rights are about assuring minimum distributions of goods, services and opportunities to all, something that is by no means assured by economic growth'.[97] Sometimes rapid economic growth has been achieved in circumstances when economic and social rights, usually together with civil and political rights, like in Pinochet's Chile in the 1970s and 80s, have been severely curbed.

The process of globalisation negatively affects not only economic and social rights, but also civil and political rights. The inability of democratically elected governments to protect their constituencies from the negative global effects (e.g. the crash of financial markets or the effect of cheap child labour from some Asian countries) means that democracy has become less effective, and political rights less important. The dilemma which globalisation has posed for social democrats has been well summarized by Dominique Strauss-Kahn, a leading French socialist, a former minister in the Mitterrand and Jospin governments and the former chief of the IMF: '[T]he success of post-war democracy rests on the equilibrium between production and redistribution, regulated by the state. With globalization, this equilibrium is broken. Capital has become mobile: production has moved beyond national borders, and thus outside the remit of state redistribution .... Growth would oppose redistribution; the virtuous circle would become the vicious circle.[98]

---

[96] J. Donnelly, 'Social Construction of International Human Rights', in T. Dunne, N.J. Wheeler (eds.), *Human Rights in Global Politics,* Cambridge University Press, 1999, p. 94.

[97] Ibid. p. 95.

[98] D. Strauss-Kahn, 'What is a Just Society?' in *Where now for European Social Democracy*?, Policy Network, 2004, p. 14.

The creation in the aftermath of WWI of the International Labour Organisation (ILO) was the world's (this was when only the Western world mattered) response to two problems: the workers movements for their rights, in which many saw 'the spectre of communism' haunting the Western world, and the need to level the playing field for competing national capitals. The ILO is the only specialised agency of the UN that was created before WWII, i.e. before the creation of the United Nations Organisation, and before human rights would become an international issue (this happened together with the creation of the UN in 1945). Moreover, the mandate of the ILO has been the promotion of social and economic rights, which are considered to be the second-generation rights (if human rights at all) *vis-à-vis* the first generation (civil and political) rights. This is all very interesting and significant because it indicates that it was not so much human rights, but other interests that guided the founders of the ILO. International concern for workers' rights was not so much due to the unease about the welfare of the workers, though they naturally benefited from it. The ILO was established primarily for the sake of the survival of capitalism, and in order to mitigate rivalry between employers from different Western capitalist countries by creating for them more or less equal labour costs (approximately the same working hours and conditions, minimal paid holidays, etc.). Such an arrangement, however, was realistically possible and worked relatively well between a limited number of countries that were approximately at the same level of economic and social development. Can this experience be repeated worldwide today?

Of course, the ILO is an organisation with universal membership, but it is no secret that working conditions, worker pay and other labour factors between countries and regions differ hugely, and therefore the effectiveness of ILO's efforts is rather limited. Today, it is not only European societies or societies of European extraction that are competing with each other, as it was after WWI. Today, it is societies at very different levels of economic, social and political development. It would be impossible to demand that their labour costs and conditions were even approximately the same. In a global world, capital benefits from a 'race to the bottom', i.e. it moves to places where the costs of labour are lower, thereby dragging down the social safety nets of richer countries. The same effect is seen from increased migration from the poorer regions to the richer ones. Therefore, when social democratic or socialist parties come to power in some European countries, they are unable to continue with the traditional policies of the welfare state. As the right and right-of-centre policies, which until recently were trumpeted as the panacea for all the socioeconomic ills ('no more bust and boom, only boom' was the slogan constantly repeated by Gordon Brown, the former Chancellor of the Exchequer and later Prime Minister of the United Kingdom), have bankrupted the Western world, the left and left-of-centre parties have not offered any plausible answers to today's challenges.

The capitalist system, in competing with the economically ineffective, politically oppressive and ideologically utopian communist system, turned out to be much more effective, freer, as well as more pragmatic than its nemesis; however, it was in comparison with the communist system of the Cold War era. The triumph of capitalism over a failed social experiment should not make us complacent and closed to the search for remedies, reforms, and if need be, revolutionary alternatives to an existing dominant system that is clearly in crisis. Jeffrey Sachs writes that today 'America's weaknesses are warning signs for the rest of the world' and that 'the society that led the world in financial liberalization, round-the-clock media saturation, television based election campaigns, *is now revealing the downside of a society that has let market institutions run wild over politics and public values*'[99] (emphasis added, RM).

5. *ANY VIABLE ALTERNATIVES?*

It would be wrong, in our opinion, to even ask: where is the world going to? The very fact of posing such a general question would imply that we might be all moving in the same direction, that we accept a unidirectional, linear evolution of the world towards some singular end. This would also imply a teleological approach to history. The world, though interconnected, is going in different

---

[99] J. Sachs, *The Price of Civilization: Economics and Ethics after the Fall*, The Bodley Head, 2011, p. xi.

directions and one should not become too despondent about that. What is required is to learn to live with it and collectively manage it.

Not many would disagree with the statement that '[T]he shift in power and wealth from West to East in the twenty-first century is probably as inevitable as the shift from East to West that happened in the nineteenth century'.[100] The rapid rise of China, and also the increasing potential of Brazil, India, Russia, Turkey, Vietnam and the earlier economic miracles of authoritarian Asian tigers (South Korea, Taiwan), have led some authors to write, often with apprehension, about authoritarian capitalism as one of the potential models for the future. For example, Russian analyst Sergei Karaganov, observes that there is another aspect of the emerging *New Epoch of Confrontation* (NEC), 'namely, the emerging struggle between two models of development – liberal-democratic capitalism of the traditional West, and "authoritarian capitalism" led by the Asian "tigers" and "dragons"'.[101] Israeli strategist Azar Gat, similarly, observes that 'authoritarian capitalist states, today exemplified by China and Russia, may present a viable alternative path to modernity, which in turn suggests that there is nothing inevitable about liberal democracy's ultimate victory – or future dominance'.[102] One of the most eloquent critics of all forms of capitalism Slavoj Žižek warns that 'the virus of this authoritarian [Lee Kuan Yew's and Deng Xiaoping's] capitalism is slowly but surely spreading around the globe'.[103]

Whether it is China and Russia that are showing or will show us a possible future model, we really do not know, but there is indeed 'nothing inevitable about liberal democracy's ultimate victory – or future dominance'. That much has to be made absolutely clear. Joshua Cooper Ramos even writes that believing, for instance, that 'the triumph of democracy and capitalism is inevitable should disqualify you immediately from a serious position in foreign policy.'[104]

---

100 I. Morris, op. cit., p. 615.

101 S. Karaganov, 'A New Epoch of Confrontation', *Russia in Global Affairs*, No 4, 2007.

102 A. Gat, 'A Return of Authoritarian Great Powers', *Foreign Affairs*, July/August, 2007, p. 60.

103 S. Žižek, op. cit, p. 130.

104 J. Cooper Ramos, *The Age of the Unthinkable: Why the New World Disorder Constantly Surprises Us and What We can Do About It*, Little, Brown and Company, 2009, p. 37.

One may also add that the belief in the eventual triumph of any particular economic, social or political arrangement should have the same disqualifying effect. However, unfortunately this is not the case. On the contrary, in the West only a faithful following of the idea of supremacy and inevitable triumph of liberal democracy seems to guarantee a high position in foreign as well as domestic policy (it goes without saying that in autocracies this is an iron rule of social, political and even economic advancement). Such a mindset supports the status quo. If in the halcyon days of liberal democratic capitalism such an attitude could have indeed strengthened the domestic and international arrangements that worked relatively well, in the troubled days of radical transformations, such a mindset becomes counterproductive and dangerous. It is reminiscent of the Soviet Union in the final years before its demise, when continuing as usual paved the road to its collapse (though the reform attempts only precipitated the inevitable). Therefore our advice to the Western political elites would be: love your own nonconformists instead of concentrating your love on Russian or Chinese dissidents or Syrian 'activists'. Most of Western non-conformists wish good for their country, and some of them may well have ideas whose realisation could show a way out of the current economic, political and social crises in the Western world.

For some societies, like China, Vietnam or even Russia, it may indeed be that some form of authoritarian capitalism will be, at least for some time, their model of development, while, say, European nations may continue experimenting with various forms of liberal-democratic market economy. The choice of different models will depend on various factors among which history, religion, size, geography and demography may all be significant contributing factors. Sometimes chance may play a crucial role. However, it is important to note that the relatively small Asian authoritarian tigers gradually became less authoritarian and more democratic, and big ones are not so averse to the pull of democratic ideals either. As Kishore Mahbubani observes, though China remains a 'politically closed society', it is 'in social and intellectual terms an increasingly open society'.[105] Moreover, China is also experimenting with political

[105] K. Mahbubani, *The New Asian Hemisphere. The Irresistible Shift of Global Power to the East*, Public Affairs, 2008, p. 139.

reforms, though slowly and cautiously, and rightly so. Azar Gat, who with apprehension writes of the possibility of authoritarian capitalism as an alternative to liberal democratic capitalism, observes at the same time that 'institutionally, the regime in China is continuously broadening its base, co-opting the business elites into the party, democratizing the party itself, and experimenting with various forms of popular participation, including village and some town elections, public opinion surveys, and focus group polling – all of which are intended to ensure that the government does not lose the public's pulse'.[106] Naturally, as we have already said, such a potentially positive correlation between economic development and democracy does not get realised automatically; economic development is only one of the important facilitators of the evolution of democratic institutions. This means that China is shedding some of its authoritarian traits while acquiring some democratic ones. This is an important and positive trend, from which first of all China would benefit. It may, in various ways, be beneficial also for the West, though the latter may also find that some of the policies of a more democratic China may be contrary to what the West would expect. Democracy in China is for the Chinese people. What is important is that this process goes at its own pace without being hastened from the outside. A more democratic China will not necessarily be more amenable to Western or American interests (a more democratic China may well be more nationalistic too). Equally, Chinese democracy will certainly be one with 'Chinese characteristics'.

Turkey's evolution under the government of Recep Tayyip Erdogan's *Justice and Development Party* may well show the way for some other Muslim countries. There, market economy, i.e. capitalism, is pooled with Islam and democracy. This combination may be quite different from Western liberal democracies, which Turkey has tried to emulate (at least until recently) in its aspiration to join the European Union. However, already some years ago Samuel Huntington insightfully predicted that 'at some point Turkey could be ready to give up its frustrating and humiliating role as a beggar pleading for membership in the West and to resume its much more

---

[106] Gat, op. cit., p. 74.

impressive and elevated historical role as the principal Islamic interlocutor and antagonist of the West'.[107] It seems that this time may have arrived. Although Walter Russell Mead's comment in a newspaper article that '[E]urope looks less and less to the Turks like a model to imitate and more and more like a fate to avoid',[108] seems to be slightly exaggerated, or at least premature, there is certainly some truth in it. Turkey has become not only economically more successful and politically more assertive, but also more authentic. Ted Galen Carpenter writes of Turkey: 'Turkish leaders chafe at being expected to follow Washington's lead on every issue. Deferring to the United States may have made sense in the bipolar strategic environment of the Cold War, when Soviet power and intentions appeared to pose a serious threat to Turkey's security and the United States was the only country that could provide effective protection. But the situation in the twenty-first century is much different. The possible threats are both less serious and more diffuse. Therefore, blindly following Washington's policy lead is not only unnecessary; it could be counterproductive to Turkey's interests'.[109] And Washington should not be frustrated with an ally that, instead of always replying 'Yes, Sir', sometimes dares to express its own opinion. The world cannot be ruled from one centre, be it Washington, Brussels, Beijing or Moscow.

Of course, it should be welcome when individuals or societies strive to become better and more successful, if necessary through borrowing, *inter alia*, from the experiences of others. However, if in their strivings they have to give up their identity, many of them become torn, whether they are individuals or societies. Therefore Turkey, in following an authentic path that may differ from those pursued by other, and primarily Western, countries, should not be deplored. Each society has to find its own combination of characteristics specific to its own history, traditions, interests, as well as principles and patterns of behaviour that are common to all successful societies. There are more and more of those, both among Muslim

---

107 S. Huntington, *The Clash of Civilizations and the Remaking of world Order*, Simon & Schuster, 1996, p. 178.

108 W.R. Mead, 'The Euro's Global Security Fallout', *The Wall Street Journal*, 18 June 2012.

109 T. Galen Carpenter, 'The End of the U.S-Turkey Alliance?', *The National Interest*, 20 January 2012.

and Western authors, who see Atatürk's reforms and secularization (Westernization) of Turkish society not so much as an example of the progressive march of history, but as a continuation of Western colonialism by other means and through indigenous autocrats.[110] Tariq Ramadan, for example, writes: 'But except for an elite, a tiny minority of intellectuals frequenting the corridors of power, most people in Muslim-majority societies, particularly Turkey and the Arab countries, generally understand "secularization" as models of dictatorial, anti-Islamic regimes than have been imported from the West, a fact that any debate over the place of religion and the state must take into account, instead of falling into sterile and counter-productive terminological dispute'.[111] This is an appropriate warning to be taken heed of by all those who promote democracy, secularization and modernity in that part of the world.

Why cannot the world consist, for instance, of a social-democratic Europe, a libertarian capitalist America (probably joined by some other Anglo-Saxon societies), state-capitalist China and even Russia? A serious problem with such a scenario for the future is that all these forms have already revealed their deficiencies and limits. We have already discussed the serious problems facing liberal democratic capitalism and social democracy. Authoritarian or state capitalism may indeed be more efficient in responding to some new challenges, but its main problem, especially in the longer term, is that every authoritarianism limits human freedom, and the latter is not only an important value in and of itself and one that starts to be increasingly demanded when bread and butter problems become less acute,[112]

---

110 See, e.g., T. Ramadan, *The Arab Awakening: Islam and the New Middle East*, Allen Lane, 2012, pp. 81–86; A. Crooke, *Resistance: The Essence of the Islamist Revolution*, Pluto Press, 2009, pp. 53–4, 56, 59.

111 T. Ramadan, *The Arab Awakening*, pp. 85–6.

112 Richard Rorty writes that in order to extend equal respect for all the people we do not need to become more rational or reasonable. Rational or reasonable people can well be racists, rapists or thieves. We need, as Rorty writes, security and sympathy. He writes: 'By "security" I mean conditions of life sufficiently risk-free .... By "sympathy" I mean the sort of reaction ... that white Americans had more of after reading Uncle Tom's Cabin than before, the sort that we have more of after watching TV programs about the genocide in Bosnia. Security and sympathy go together, for the same reason as peace and economic productivity go together. The tougher things are, the more you have to afraid of, the more dangerous your situation, the less you can afford the time or effort to think about what things might be like for

but also a vehicle for economic development.[113] At the same time, it is impossible to deny that at least in China, as well as in some other Asian countries, state capitalism has achieved impressive results in terms of economic growth as well as poverty reduction. Therefore, quite a few people in the West, both politicians and experts, perceive, in the existence and success of state capitalism, a threat to Western values and ways of life. However, in reality they fear that the success of state capitalism may undermine Western dominance. Ian Bremmer, for example, writes of state capitalism as 'a form of bureaucratically engineered capitalism particular to each government that practices it. It's a system in which the state dominates markets primarily for political gain'[114] and that the world may be 'on the verge of a new global struggle – one that pits free-market capitalists and state capitalists in a battle to win over countries that might still tip either way'.[115] Although it may be true that governments in state capitalist countries use the economic system for political gain (as if the use of the political system for economic dominance would be preferable), this is not inevitably the case. Even if the main political aim of the government is to stay in power (this applies equally to both democratic and authoritarian governments, though the methods of securing that aim differ), this aim can be sustainably secured only if the economic system delivers, i.e. if from it benefits not only a narrow elite but also the majority. In a case where the economic system fails, the political power would also be in danger. Furthermore, if in a peaceful rivalry state capitalism prevails over free market capitalism, so be it. This would mean that the more adequate, in concrete circumstances of time and space, system prevails. That the real worry of Bremmer is not at all the fate of the world but only of the American

---

people with whom you do not immediately identify. Sentimental education only works on people who can relax long enough to listen' (R. Rorty, 'Human Rights, Rationality, and Sentimentality', in *On Human Rights. The Oxford Amnesty Lectures 1993* (S. Shute, S. Hurley eds.), Basic Books, 1993, p. 128). Similarly, economic development and security are, if not sufficient then at least necessary, preconditions and facilitators of the development of democracy.

113 A. Sen, *Development as Freedom*, Oxford University Press, 1999. In my opinion, the title of the book may have also been 'Freedom as Development'.

114 I. Bremmer, *The End of the Free Market: Who Wins the War between States and Corporations?* Portfolio, 2010, (Kindle version), Loc. 365.

115 Ibid., Loc. 377.

dominance of it, can be seen from the following excerpt from his book:

> As the world recovers from the global recession and investors regain their appetite for risk, what if we discover that state-capitalist governments mean what they say about diversifying away from the dollar to diminish its status as the world's reserve currency? In other word, what if they slowly reduce their willingness to finance America's debt by buying U.S. Treasury bills?[116]

This statement hardly needs comments except one: the main threat for the United States of state capitalism becoming a dominant arrangement is that it may end almost an absurd situation where those who are dominated are forced to finance those who dominate them.

Ian Bremmer writes that 'state capitalists see markets primarily as a tool that serves national interests, or at least those of ruling elites, rather than as an engine of opportunity for the individual'.[117] This observation seems to be true, but does its truth not express, at least partially, the underlining characteristics of differing societies? While Anglo-Saxon societies are at the individualistic end of the spectrum, societies like China and Russia are closer to the collectivistic or communitarian end. Therefore, while state capitalism may be quite alien, even unacceptable, in the United States, it may be much more natural for China or even Russia.[118] Thus, free market capitalism and state capitalism are not simply two different economic models for an abstract society; rather, they correspond to two (and probably more) different historically evolved types of society. The problem, if this can be considered at all a problem, with state or authoritarian capitalism and with its possible domination, especially in the long run, is different. As we have seen, successful authoritarianisms tend

---

[116] Ibid., Loc. 2482.

[117] Ibid., Loc., 783.

[118] This observation to an extent may explain also the relative ease with which utopian communist ideology was accepted and became practiced in countries like Russia and China and not in societies where they originated, i.e. in Western societies. In Eastern societies Western collectivistic ideas superimposed on Eastern communitarian traditions and practices that explains equally the initial 'success' of these ideas and also the eventual failure of these experiments. Obviously, Eastern societies need more individualism, not more Western communitarian ideas, while Western societies need more collectivism.

in their evolution to become more liberal and more democratic. One should, of course, welcome this trend. Naturally, there are many pitfalls on the road to a realisation of this trend, and even if the trend succeeds and, say, China and Russia become considerably more democratic, they will not be Western style liberal democracies; and even if they would, this would not mean that they would accept guidance from Washington.

Today we see at least three competing and struggling forms of capitalism: the liberal-democratic capitalism of the Anglo-Saxon variety; the social-democratic capitalism of Scandinavia (practiced also in Germany and some other Western European countries); and state capitalism as exemplified primarily by China and Russia. The most plausible and positive outcome could be a kind of peaceful competition between them, in the process of which all models would be ready to borrow from each other that which works best. One thing is certain, that the West does not have, and should not even pretend to have, a monopoly on truth. As Charles Kupchan writes,

> [C]learing the way for a more inclusive global order entails recognizing that there is no single form of responsible government; the West does not have a monopoly on the political institutions and practices that enable countries to promote the welfare of their citizens. As long as other countries adhere to reasonable standards of responsible governance, the West should respect the political choices as a matter of national discretion and as a reflection of the intrinsic diversity of political life.[119]

It may well be that while the East could gradually become more democratic and liberal (while not becoming a Western style liberal democracy), the West, in order to regain some governance lost to market forces (especially those of the financial markets), would have to increase the role of the state both domestically as well as internationally. Sergei Karaganov may be at least partially right when he writes that '[T]he existing model of Western capitalism based on a society of almost universal affluence and advanced democracy cannot withstand a new competition. Not only will the authoritarian

---

[119] C. Kupchan, *No One's World: The West, the Rising Rest, and the Coming Global Turn*, Oxford University Press (Kindle version) Loc. 3322.

regimes have to drift towards greater democracy in the medium term. Western democracies, too, will have to drift towards more authoritarianism. This will be a retreat, a post-modern theory of convergence'.[120] *Cum grano salis*, there seems to be some truth to such a statement. However, if the Eastern drift towards greater liberty and democracy is well within the overall long-term tendency of the evolution of humankind, a widespread and sustainable drift towards more authoritarianism goes against the general long-term trend of transformations that have taken place in the world. Therefore, the term 'more authoritarianism' may not accurately reflect what the West needs in order to compete with the rising East. Rather, one may think of more collectivism in the West instead of glorifying rampant individualism *à la* Ayn Rand; individual liberties balanced with social responsibilities; a greater role for the state, though not so much as a redistributor of wealth as the main protector of people from the negative effects of markets; and the acceptance of the truth that that there is no single true socioeconomic and political arrangement suitable for all. Charles Kupchan's prediction that 'it is more likely that emerging powers will follow their own unique paths to modernity as they rise, ensuring that the next world will not just be multipolar, but also politically diverse' and that therefore 'the emerging world is poised to consist of a multiplicity of different kinds of regimes; considerable political diversity, not political homogeneity among Western lines, lies ahead',[121] seems to characterise current trends better than simplistic 'end of history' or 'history is on our side' blueprints. Even such a free-market enthusiast as Niall Ferguson has recently published an article entitled *We're All State Capitalists Now* where he writes that '... the question today is not whether the state or the market should be in charge. The real question is which countries' laws and institutions are best, not only at achieving rapid economic growth but also, equally importantly, at distributing the fruits of growth in a way that citizens deem to be just'.[122] Who could argue with that?

---

[120] S. Karaganov, 'A Revolutionary Chaos of the New World', *Russia in Global Affairs*, 28 December, 2011.

[121] C. Kupchan, 'Diversity Wins', *Russia in Global Affairs*, 29 December 2011, http://eng.globalaffairs.ru/number/Diversity-Wins-15426.

[122] N. Ferguson, 'We're All State Capitalists Now', *Foreign Policy*, 9 February, 2012.

Chapter Three

ON THE FUTILITY AND DANGER OF EXTERNAL ATTEMPTS TO 'DEMOCRATISE' CHINA

Although active and forceful policies of regime change are usually practiced *vis-à-vis* smaller countries in the periphery of the non-liberal-democratic world, the idea of changing the political regime in the world's most populous country is not a rare one. Political scientist Aaron Friedberg, for example, writes that 'a liberal democratic China will have little cause to fear its democratic counterparts, still less to use force against them'. Therefore, he opines: 'Stripped of diplomatic niceties, the ultimate aim of the American strategy [should be] to hasten a revolution, albeit a peaceful one, that will sweep away China's one-party authoritarian state and leave a liberal democracy in its place.'[1] However, in Henry Kissinger's much more realistic view, such policies would almost inevitably lead to a confrontation between the two most powerful states in today's world – the United States of America and the People's Republic of China. He warns American elites of the dangers of such a strategy *vis-à-vis* of the Asian giant: 'U.S. strategic concerns are magnified by ideological predispositions to battle with the entire nondemocratic world. Authoritarian regimes, some argue, are inherently brittle, impelled to rally domestic support by nationalist and expansionist rhetoric and practice. In these theories – versions of which are embraced in segments of both the American left and the American right – tension and conflict with China grow out of China's domestic structure. Universal peace will come, it is asserted, from the global triumph of democracy rather than from appeals for cooperation'.[2] So, the American (Western) dilemma seems to be: to deal with China as it is, or to try to change its fundamental characteristics.

In this chapter we would analyse China's democratic potential, what would be the role of external factors in democratising China,

---

[1] H. Kissinger, 'The Future 7/of U.S.-Chinese Relations: Conflict Is a Choice, Not a Necessity', *Foreign Affairs*, March-April 2012.

[2] Ibid.

and what a more democratic China would mean for its own people as well as for the wider world.

1. CHINA'S RISE AND THE CHANGING BALANCE OF POWER

It was pragmatic Deng Xiaoping who, after the Tiananmen tragedy of 1989, where hundreds of people died and when China was ostracized by the West, called his countrymen to 'observe developments soberly, maintain our position, meet challenges calmly, hide our capacities and bide our time, remain free of ambition, never claim leadership'.[3] Although only slightly more than two decades have passed since 1989, the world of 2012, when this book was mainly written, belongs not only to a new century and millennium; today we also live in a different political epoch in comparison with 1989. The balance of power in the world has since then radically changed at least twice – from the Cold War bi-polar system, through a unipolar moment, to a new balance of power where China is already/still second, but rising fast. Is Deng Xiaoping's advice still valid? Is this a moment for the crouching tiger or will the dragon continue to remain hidden?

Goldman Sachs has predicted that China's economy will become the world's largest by approximately 2027, and by 2050 the three largest economies in the world will be China, followed by a closely matched United States and India, and trailed by Brazil, Mexico, Russia and Indonesia.[4] The following graphs show Goldman Sachs' predictions of world economic power in both fifteen and forty years.

Due to such analysis it is not surprising that the US National Intelligence Council Report of November 2008 foresaw the emergence by 2025 of a 'multipolar world without multilateralism'[5] where 'the wealth is moving not just from West to East but is concentrating more under state control',[6] where 'we are unlikely to see an overarching, comprehensive, unitary approach to global governance', where

[3] W. Hutton, *The Writing on the Wall: China in the 21st Century*, Little, Brown, 2006, p. 220.
[4] D. Wilson, A. Stupnytska, 'The N-11: More than an Acronym', *Goldman Sachs Global Economic P*apers, 153, 28 March 2007, pp. 8–9.
[5] *Global Trends 2025: A Transformed World*, NIC Report, November 2008, pp. 81.
[6] Ibid., 8.

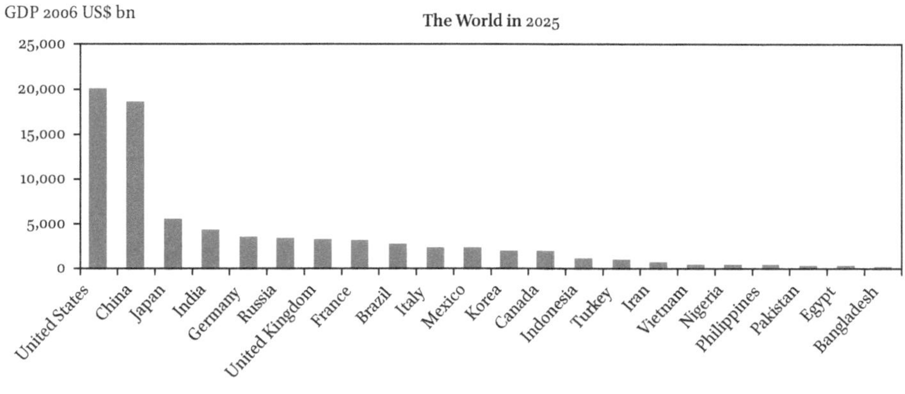

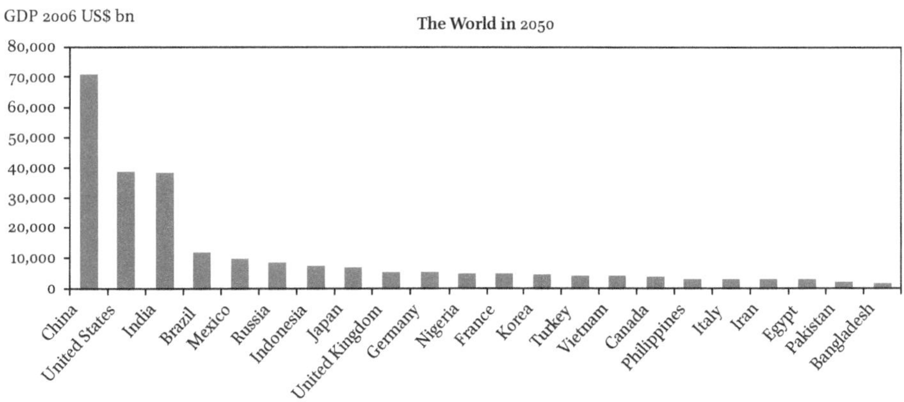

The graphs show Goldman Sachs' predictions of world economic power in both fifteen and forty years. (Reproduced from D. Wilson, A. Stupnytska, 'The N-11: More than an Acronym', Goldman Sachs Global Economic Papers, 153, 28 March 2007, pp. 8–9.)

'strategic rivalries are likely to revolve around trade, investment, technology innovation, and acquisition', where 'increasing worries about resources – such as energy and water – could easily put the focus back on territorial disputes or unresolved border issues'.[7] This Report was written just before the current world economic and

[7] Ibid., pp. 81–2.

financial crisis began to bite. The crisis has only accelerated some of these trends.

This new world would be quite different from the bi-polar and powder keg like stability of the Cold War (i.e. stability until the explosion, which thankfully did not occur); it would also considerably differ from the short post-Cold War period of unilateral American dominance. Due to the number and variety of actors in the world, the emergence of new centres of power, and the exacerbation of existing problems (terrorism, poverty, environment, food and energy shortages), and the surfacing of new still unknown challenges, this would certainly be one of the most complex international systems that has ever existed. Besides formal institutions such as the United Nations, EU, AU, NATO, OSCE and many others, there are informal but potentially more influential bodies like the G20, BRICS or even the G2 emerging. However, Ian Bremmer may well be right that the future world belongs to the G-0, i.e. to a world where no state or even group of states governs the world.[8] Be this as it may, in all the predictable scenarios of the future world China's role is indispensable and prominent. What may such transformation mean for China and for the world?

2. MODERNIZING CHINA – A DEMOCRATIC CHINA?

As China is becoming economically stronger and stronger, experts argue whether the world's most populous country will (or even have to) become also more democratic and liberal, more like contemporary developed Western societies, or whether it will modernize by borrowing from the West only those features that suit Beijing while retaining and developing its specific Asian or Chinese characteristics. The first scenario was some years ago bluntly expressed by Will Hutton: 'The general argument ... is that if the next century is going to be Chinese, it will be only because China embraces the economic and political pluralism of the West in general, and our Enlightenment institutions in particular modified, of course, for the

[8] I. Bremmer, *Every Nation for Itself. Winners and Losers in a G-Zero World*, Portfolio Penguin (Kindle version), 2012.

Chinese experience'[9] and that 'eventually the Communist leadership will have to accept that China must become a pluralist representative democracy'.[10] Kishore Mahbubani, on the contrary, writes that 'the West had actually triumphed [in the Cold War with the Soviet Union] because of the strength of its economic system – free market economics – and not because of its political system ... In contrast to Gorbachev, Deng Xiaoping well understood the real sources of Western strength and power. He had no illusion that Western values were responsible for Western successes'.[11] Israeli strategist Azar Gat is of the opinion that 'a possible ideology for China would emphasize Chinese ways, incorporate Confucian values of meritocratic-technocratic hierarchy, public service, social harmony, and be presented as a contrast to liberal divisiveness and individual irresponsibility'.[12]

Then, as some experts correctly note,[13] to discuss democracy's achievements and perspectives in China, it is necessary to compare today's China not with today's Sweden or Finland, but with yesterday's China. Mahbubani rightly observes many Western commentators 'cannot see beyond the lack of a democratic political system. They miss the massive democratization of the human spirit that is taking place in China'.[14] My own experience of communicating with Chinese students, professors as well as state or even communist party officials in China testifies to the effect that today's China is hugely different, say, from the former Soviet Union (I don't have a personal experience of Mao's China) in terms of not only its

---

9 W. Hutton, *The Writing on the Wall: China in the 21st Century*, Little, Brown, 2006, p. X.

10 Ibid., p. 34.

11 K. Mahbubani, *The New Asian Hemisphere. The Irresistible Shift of Global Power to the East*, Public Affairs, 2008, p.44.

12 A. Gat, *Victorious and Vulnerable: Why Democracy Won in the 20th Century and How it is Still Imperiled*, Rowman& Littlefield Publishers, 2010, p. 73.

13 E.g. Daniel Deudney and John Ikenburry, though from my point of view somewhat too optimistically, or rather seeing the world in too deterministic terms as moving towards an inevitable goal, argue that though 'China and Russia are not liberal democracies, they are much more liberal and democratic than they have ever been – and many of the crucial foundations for sustainable liberal democracy are emerging' (D. Deudney, G.J. Ikenburry, 'The Myth of Autocratic Revival', *Foreign Affairs*, January-February, 2009).

14 Mahbubani, op. cit., p. 18.

economic effectiveness, but also of its intellectual openness and critical analysis of existing challenges. These debates may not (yet) be at the level of the intellectual diversity and sophistication of views expressed at academic gatherings, say, at the London School of Economics (LSE) or King's College, London (chosen because of my long personal experience), but they certify that China is not a closed society anymore.

The truth about China's evolution is probably (as it often, though not always, is) somewhere in between Hutton's and Mahbubani's predictions. Yang Yao observes that 'ultimately, there is no alternative to greater democratization if the CCP [the Chinese Communist Party] wishes to encourage economic growth and maintain social stability'.[15] But it may be indeed so only ultimately, and it should be a gradual progression ('crossing the river by touching the stones', in Deng Xiaoping words) rather than in one go through some variation of 'shock therapy'. First of all, liberal democracy, or rather its absence in China, is not what worries the majority of the Chinese people day to day, and secondly, the danger of possible (or even probable) instability and chaos as would be consequenced by such a shock experiment is too great a risk. Randall Peerenboom is not wrong when he writes that 'not everyone assigns the same value to civil and political freedoms relative to social order. Social order ranks much higher in the normative hierarchy of most Chinese than it does in the normative hierarchy of many Westerners, in part because stability is precarious in China. The consequences of instability for China, the region, and the world would be severe. Adopting this measure virtually assures a wide margin of deference to restrictions in the name of public order.'[16] There is no doubt that China's democracy, if and when it eventually unfolds, will be quite different from Western style liberal democracy, though obviously there have to be some general common principles and features that would allow us to call it democracy, whether it be with American, European or Chinese characteristics.

---

[15] Yang Yao, 'The End of the Beijing Consensus', *Foreign Affairs*, 2 February, 2010.

[16] R. Peerenboom, *China Modernises. Threat to the West or Model for the Rest*, OUP, 2007, pp. 124–25.

We believe that China will gradually become more open not only economically but also politically. Firstly, there is indeed a correlation, mostly positive though quite controversial,[17] and in some circumstances even negative, between economic development and market freedoms on the one hand, and personal and political liberties on the other. However, in this correlation it is more prosperity that contributes to the evolution towards democracy than democracy contributing to prosperity. Yet, such a positive correlation is a long-term tendency, and it would be wrong and dangerous to hasten this process. In the shorter term, it may even be that for the sake of economic development and social stability some restrictions of personal and political liberties would be, if not necessary then at least, unavoidable. American human rights expert Jack Donnelly, in analysing the experience of Brazil and South Korea, finds that 'some repression is likely to be "required" (or at least extraordinarily difficult to avoid) in pursuit of what can be called the structural task of removing institutional and sociocultural barriers to the development and the political task of assuring conformity with development plans'.[18] The former mayor (1995–2001) of Shanghai Xu Kuangdi has been reported arguing that this is all part of the plan: 'Let's look at our neighbouring Asian countries,' he said. 'South Korea: its peak developing speed was reached using military rule.... Indonesia was successful during the reign of Suharto but recently it has faced stalemate and difficulties'. The reason that democracy is an obstacle to economic progress, Mr Xu continued, is that 'the poor people want to divide the property of the rich people.... If we Chinese copied the directly elected situation today, people will say, "I want everyone to have a good job." Someone will say, "I will divide the property of the rich people to poor people", and he will be elected. It is useless: parity will not solve the problem of economic development. That is why we are taking a gradual and step-by-step approach in reform. As Mr Deng said, we will cross the river by touching the stones. We will

---

[17] On dialectical relationship between market economy and democracy see more in R. Müllerson, *Democracy – A Destiny of Humankind? A Qualified, Contingent and Contextual Case for Democracy Promotion*, NovaPublishers, 2009.

[18] J. Donnelly, *Universal Human Rights in Theory and Practice*, Cornell University Press, 1989, p. 187.

not get ourselves drowned, and we will cross the river.'[19] Of course, this was said by a former high official in the Chinese Communist Party hierarchy and it all sounds, and to an extent it certainly is, self-serving. However, this does not necessarily mean that it is all wrong, or that the man and those of his ilk are all hypocrites. Moreover, perceptions matter, and the perceptions of Chinese officials matter more on matters Chinese than those of outsiders.

In this respect it is important to note that it was not so much the shoots of Chinese democracy, though they certainly were too, that were suppressed in Tiananmen Square in 1989. One of the most prominent current Chinese intellectuals, Wang Hui, observes that 'as a movement for social self-preservation, the 1989 social movement was inherently a spontaneous protest against the proliferating inequalities spawned by market expansion, and a critique of the state's handling of the process of reform; as a movement of social protest, however, it also pursued a critique of authoritarianism and the methods of authoritarian rule'[20] and that '... the state-led neoliberal economic policies led to the social upheaval, while the post-upheaval stabilization became the proof of the social expansion of the legitimacy of state power'.[21] There seems to have indeed been a crucial choice between a political 'shock therapy' had the authorities attempted to meet various demands of protesters, which could have ended with the country in turmoil and freefall on the one hand, and the continuation of market oriented economic reforms that were quite painful for many Chinese on the other. It would have been impossible to carry out such radical reforms using democratic means. Therefore, we may say that in 1989, in Tiananmen Square, it was capitalism that prevailed over democracy. Mr Xu Kuangdi is right that the people would not have voted for those reforms that have made China the number two economy in the world. Some of the incidents and developments of 2012, though much less dramatic than those of 1989, have similarities with the events that took place

---

19 C. Hayes, 'The Great Leap', *The Nation*, 11 January, 2010.
20 Wang Hui, *The End of the Revolution: China and the Limits of Modernity*, Verso, 2011, p. 30.
21 Ibid., p. 34.

twenty-three years earlier. Wang Hui, in writing about the dismissal in spring 2012 of Chongqing party boss Bo Xilai, for example, observes that

> The aim of the current manoeuvres is to clamp down on political freedoms in order to make it easier to drive through deeply unpopular neoliberal measures. In the late 1980s, after some failed attempts to push through "price reforms" on many basic commodities, the death of the former party leader Hu Yaobang – deposed several years before partly because of his leniency over student demonstrations – inspired the discontent that manifested itself in Tiananmen Square and elsewhere. After the students had been repressed, the price reforms were pushed through without further protest. It is a pity that during the current celebrations of the 20th anniversary of Deng Xiaoping's "southern tour" and his call for the speeding up of reforms, nobody is mentioning that the precondition for the accelerating marketisation of 1992 was the crackdown of 1989.[22]

In a way, the situation in 1989 may have been comparable to what General Pinochet embarked on in Chile in the 1970s with the encouragement and help of Washington. A simultaneous introduction of political (democracy) and economic (market) reforms may work only in small countries, and even there, favourable internal and external conditions and facilitators are needed. How things can go terribly wrong, when in a weak, unstable and ethnically divided country market oriented economic and democracy-oriented political reforms are introduced simultaneously, can be seen in the case of certain developments in a small Central Asian country – Kyrgyzstan.

3. *A SMALL DIVERSION TO ILLUSTRATE THE POINT – THE KYRGYZ TRAGEDY OF 2010*

To illustrate this point, let us make a small diversion and look into the attempts of a simultaneous introduction of democratic and market reforms in a small neighbour of China – Kyrgyzstan. In the summer of 2010, a simmering interethnic conflict in Southern Kyrgyzstan – a former Soviet republic in Central Asia which

---

[22] Wang Hui, 'The Rumour Machine: The Dismissal of Bo Xilai', *London Review of Books*, 10 May 2012.

had recently undergone one of those 'colour' revolutions, a Tulip one –exploded in violence. The author of this book was a member of *The Independent International Inquiry Commission* (Kyrgyz Inquiry Commission or KIC), which looked into the causes of the conflict, how it played out in June 2010, who may have been responsible and also recommended measures aimed at healing the wounds and preventing such bloody conflicts occurring in future.[23]

In some ethnically mixed societies, and Kyrgyzstan is a fine example of such a society, the parallel introduction of market reforms and democratization may contribute to the potential for inter-ethnic conflicts. Unfortunately, there is no irony in an assertion that the simultaneous introduction of two generally necessary and positive reforms may not only cancel each other out, but may have disastrous outcomes; or, to put it otherwise, in social life, in contrast to arithmetic, one plus one may result in minus two. Amy Chua has mapped the negative effects of processes of globalisation in societies characterized by the presence of so-called *market-dominant minorities* (e.g. Indians in east Africa, Lebanese in West Africa, Ibo in Nigeria, Tutsi in Rwanda, Chinese in several Southeast Asian countries and Jews in many societies). She even argues that, 'the global spread of free market democracy has [...] been a principal, aggravating cause of ethnic instability and violence throughout the non-western world'.[24] This pessimistic conclusion is grounded in the reality that in some developing and post-communist countries there are minorities—perhaps better educated and more entrepreneurial than the majority population—who may also own more land or may otherwise be in a better position to benefit than the rest of the population, i.e. more than the majority, from the liberalisation of markets. The simultaneous introduction of democracy, which almost inevitably gives political power to the economically non-dominant majority (i.e. the poorer part of the population), can release suppressed discontent that creates a combustible mixture ready to explode in xenophobia,

---

23 *Report of the Independent International Commission of Inquiry into the Events in Southern Kyrgyzstan in June 2010.* Helsinki, May 2011 (http://www.cmi.fi/black-sea-and-central-asia/kyrgyzstan-inquiry-commission.html).

24 A. Chua, World of Fire, Arrow, 2004, p. 187.

ethnic cleansing or even in acts of genocide. In such cases, of course, there is neither market nor democracy. Amy Chua concludes that 'the United States should not be exporting markets in the unrestrained, *laissez-faire* form that the west itself has repudiated, just as it should not be promoting unrestrained, overnight majority rule—a form of democracy that the west has repudiated.'[25] Although in the West majority rule came not overnight, but only through sometimes centuries-long processes of trial and error, Amy Chua's warning must be taken seriously.

In southern Kyrgyzstan, the differences in lifestyles between the historically sedentary Uzbeks and nomadic Kyrgyz, which had existed for centuries, resulted in a situation where the Uzbeks were generally economically better off than the Kyrgyz. Centuries, or even as recently as decades, ago this did not matter much because these two communities did not mix a great deal (the Kyrgyz primarily lived in the countryside, while the Uzbeks were mainly city dwellers, and hence their ways of making a living were also different), and in addition, Soviet (before Russian) dominance did not allow for any discontent to explode. However, the migration wave of Kyrgyz to the newly industrialized southern cities, which had commenced as recently as the 1960s, increased rapidly when Gorbachev initiated his glasnost and perestroika reforms, and was further boosted at the end of 1991 by the establishment of an independent Kyrgyzstan. To simplify a bit, while the Uzbeks benefited more from the perestroika (economic liberalization), the Kyrgyz benefited more from glasnost (political opening). Therefore, by the 1990s, inter-ethnic clashes in southern Kyrgyzstan had, as a contributing factor, the combined effect of a simultaneous introduction of elements of market economy and democracy under Gorbachev. Uzbeks were better positioned to benefit from economic reforms; they had better entrepreneurial skills and, having some starting capital (albeit rather meagre by Western standards), they had a head start in regards to economic benefits as well. On the contrary, at the political level, the majority Kyrgyz had the upper hand. Through

---

25 Ibid., p. 17.

more or less democratic processes, they secured for themselves an overwhelming majority in legislative bodies at all levels, as well as in all important executive posts, and started to dominate the judiciary, law enforcement and military. Using their political, administrative as well as simply numerical power, they not only denied the Uzbeks effective access to higher administrative posts, law enforcement and the judiciary, but they also used these posts as leverage to force Uzbek businessmen to pay up. What is the point in having political power, they argued, if one cannot convert it into an economic benefit and wellbeing? The practice of using (abusing) political power for economic ends became especially widespread under Bakiyev's presidency (Kurmanbek Bakiyev became the President of Kyrgyzstan in 2005 as a result of the so-called 'Tulip revolution' that overthrew the first President of the independent Kyrgyzstan – Askar Akayev), and unfortunately it continues even today. The KIC Report emphasizes: '[R]acketeering had an ethnic dimension, as the membership of criminal networks was primarily Kyrgyz whereas southern businessmen were mainly Uzbek. Small and medium entrepreneurs in particular were in a vulnerable position. Café owners and car repair shopkeepers suffered the most. The money they were required to pay to criminal groups rose constantly and threatened to make the businesses unviable. "Raiding", the forced sale of a profitable business for a token sum, was also widespread' (paragraph 116 of the Report). If during Akayev's reign there were certain limits to such extortion, under Bakiyev, this all took the form of almost official racketeering. Such a situation could not last indefinitely, and when all the other components for the explosion came together, it was a relatively minor incident and rumours (by the way, exaggerated, distorted and spread over social media, which seems to be widespread practice in various conflictual situations) that triggered a bloody inter-ethnic clash. As a result, during three days of clashes more than 400 people, mostly ethnic Uzbeks, were killed and thousands of houses burnt, other property destroyed or looted. Having studied all the evidence and the Kyrgyz Inquiry Commission considered that 'if the evidence of the acts identified above committed during of the attacks on the *mahallas* [a traditional Uzbek neighbourhood] were proven beyond reasonable doubt in front of a competent court of law that court would conclude that they constituted crimes against humanity. Therefore the KIC is of the opinion that these acts would qualify as crimes against humanity'.[26]

This sad example is especially important as a warning since Kyrgyzstan has been often touted as an example to be followed by other Central Asian countries in terms of democratisation and individual liberties. It had also undergone one of those 'pro-democracy' 'colour revolutions' welcomed and supported by the West. However, like in many other situations, it was not shoots of democracy, but that of anarchy and chaos, that prevailed. Notwithstanding post-crisis constitutional referendum, the end of 2010 Parliamentary and 2011 Presidential elections, the situation in Kyrgyzstan remains potentially explosive since none of the underlying factors that led to the June 2010 bloody tragedy have been seriously addressed.[27] An International Crisis Group (ICG) report of March 2012 that speaks of widening ethnic divisions in Kyrgyzstan's South found that 'while a superficial quiet has settled on the city [Osh], neither the Kyrgyz nor Uzbek community feels it can hold.'[28]

4. BACK TO CHINA: REFORMS NOT REVOLUTION

Daron Acemoglu and James Robinson write: 'There was a real sense in 1989 that the Tiananmen Square demonstrations would lead to greater opening and perhaps even the collapse of the communist regime'.[29] However, they do not even reflect on what would have replaced the communist regime in China. What would have been the chance that the collapse 'the communist regime' would have resulted in, or at least would have been followed by, some kind of movement towards liberal democracy, which would have continued market reforms? Anybody who has some knowledge of Chinese

---

26 *Report of the Independent International Commission of Inquiry into the Events in Southern Kyrgyzstan in June 2010.* Helsinki, May 2011, para. 266 (http://www.cmi.fi/black-sea-and-central-asia/kyrgyzstan-inquiry-commission.html).

27 See, e.g., I. Greenberg, 'Cenral Asia's simmering instability', *The National Interest*, 9 August, 2012.

28 ICG Asia Report No. 222, *Kyrgyzstan: Widening Ethnic Divisions in the South*, 29 March 2012.

29 D. Acemoglu, J. Robinson, Why Nations Fails: The Origins of Power, Prosperity and Poverty, p. 440.

history and today's problems and challenges, should be shivering, when soberly reflecting on the state of today's world, and not only of China, had the Chinese leaders allowed American advisors, as President Yeltsin of Russia did, to experiment on their country. Not only the United States, but the world community as whole, even without the current financial and economic crisis, would not have been able to cope with the turmoil that could have realistically engulfed China if the authorities were to have suddenly lost control. As we will discuss below, external assistance in carrying out political and economic reforms, even in relatively small countries that have had their regime changes, has its limits. If reforms go astray in a country like China, the whole world community would be helpless. In today's world, instability in even a small African country may have effects that are not limited only to that country or region. That is why in the 1990s, not only the ECOWAS (the Economic Community of Western African States) but the West too chose to intervene in the civil wars in Liberia and Sierra Leone. Instability in China would shock the world and no outside intervention could prevent an instability that would negatively affect not only China and its neighbours, but the whole world.

Acemoglu and Robinson, correctly emphasising the character and role of political and economic institutions in making a society either prosperous or poor, differentiate between extractive and inclusive institutions.[30] If the former cater for the governing minority and reflect their interests, the latter represent the population as whole, and it is they that take account of the interests of various groups in society. Such institutions are usually paired: extractive economic institutions correspond to extractive political institutions, and *vice versa*, inclusive economic and political institutions also as a rule go hand in hand, though there may be, usually only temporary, discord between them. For example, today's China, as Acemoglu and Robinson explain, has relatively inclusive economic institutions that coexist with wholly extractive political institutions. While extractive institutions make societies poor, inclusive ones form the basis of success. However, as with practically all even profound and eloquent

---

[30] Acemoglu, Robinson, op. cit, p. 439.

(sometimes especially with the profound and eloquent, as we discussed above) studies that try to single out one factor or a single phenomenon that, at the end of the day, makes all the difference between success and failure, they too seem to considerably simplify reality in order to keep their theory profound and eloquent. For example, they recognise that while Chinese economic institutions have become relatively inclusive, extractive political institutions severely limit the role of economic institutions and put brakes on Chinese economic development. Theoretically, or abstractly if you like, this is correct. But the devil is not only, as it is usually said, in the details, but also in the concrete circumstances of time and place. Not all political institutions that are neither democratic nor inclusive, in terms of Acemoglu's and Robinson's definition, are entirely extractive either (i.e. the authorities do not necessarily exploit the people for the purpose of grabbing for themselves and their retainers as much as possible). Although as a general principle, the idea of extractive and inclusive institutions and the correspondence between them is interesting and even useful, it is only if it is not absolutised and relied upon as the ultimate explanation for the success and failure of all societies - there a quite a few examples showing that what the authors call extractive political institutions, but what would be more accurately defined as authoritarian or semi-authoritarian, may co-exist with and even be beneficial for inclusive economic institutions, at least for a while. Moreover, let us take some liberal democracies (say, the United States), whose institutions – both political and economic – should all be, as if by definition, inclusive, i.e. not extractive. But can we indeed honestly say that they are all entirely inclusive? A careful reading of the latest works of some serious American economists[31] testifies that at least some American economic institutions are rather extractive, i.e. they benefit more the upper 1% of the population than the rest. As Joseph Stiglitz writes (not about China, but about the United States), '[W]hen the wealthiest use their political power to benefit

---

[31] See, e.g., J. Stiglitz, *The Price of Inequality: How Today's Divided Society Endangers Our Future*, W.W. Norton & Company, 2012; J. Sachs, The Price of Civilization. Economics and Ethics after the Fall, The Bodley Head, 2011.

excessively the corporations they control, much needed revenues are diverted into the pockets of a few instead of benefiting society at large'.[32] And this is a comment that also applies to political institutions, not only economic ones. It is the former that allow the latter to be used in an extractive manner.

An article by B. Bueno de Mesquita, G.W. Downs, probably inadvertently, reveals the sensitivity and delicacy of Western human rights diplomacy and the promotion of democracy in non-Western countries. These American authors are right in observing that today there are some autocrats who open up the economies of their countries, carry out successful market-oriented reforms, but suppress civil and political rights.[33] Indeed, there are. However, there is nothing new in this. Chile under General Pinochet, South Korea under military rule and Taiwan until relatively recently have all had such autocrats in power. The authors of the article, however, lament that today's autocrats, while granting their populations so-called 'standard public goods', such as public transportation, primary and secondary education and public health, all which contribute to economic growth, restrict so-called 'coordination goods', such as civil and political rights. The reason for such policies is quite obvious. As the authors themselves state, '... the suppression of coordination goods keeps autocrats in power. An autocrat who permits both freedom of the press and civil liberties reduces the chances that he will survive for another year by about 15 to 20 percent'. Asking what the West or international bodies have to do about it, the authors answer: '...the United States, the European Union, aid agencies and other donors must keep exerting pressure to change'.[34] To put it otherwise, they call on such regimes to voluntarily opt for regime change, since by opening up their societies to civil and political rights autocrats shorten their life expectancy (at least in political terms, though in some countries in physiological as well), as the authors rather convincingly prove. If the regimes do not voluntarily

32 Stiglitz, *The Price of Inequality*, p. 83.

33 B. Bueno de Mesquita, G.W. Downs, 'An open economy, a closed society', *International Herald Tribune*, 17 August, 2005.

34 Ibid.

shorten their rule, the West must keep exercising pressure until they go.

Does this mean that the West should have pressured, for example, Mohamad Mahathir of Malaysia or Lee Kuan Yew of Singapore out of office because they secured to their people only 'standard public goods'? We do not think so. Limitation on some civil and political rights, such as the freedoms of expression or association, though deplorable, should not be cause for exercising pressure on the leadership with the aim of getting them out of office, especially if the population itself does not actively demand such change and the leadership indeed secures 'standard public goods'. The problem is that only very few authoritarian rulers secure 'standard public goods', while some dictators (such as General Pinochet of Chile or the military rulers of Argentina, supported by Washington) become too bloody and start using repression to quell popular discontent. Then even successful market reforms should not save autocrats from pressure that may indeed get them out of office. But until autocrats deliver, and do not turn bloody (like General Pinochet), there is no reason for undermining them, since one may instead have non-delivering autocrats in power.

Acemoglu and Robinson write that 'first, growth under authoritarian, extractive political institutions in China, though likely to continue for a while, yet will not translate into sustained growth, supported by truly inclusive economic institutions and creative destruction. Second, contrary to the claims of modernization theory, we should not count on authoritarian growth leading to democracy or inclusive political institutions'.[35] Both of these thoughts also ring true, and the authors illustrate their point by showing how in various countries the attempts of economic reforms under autocratic regimes have failed.[36] However, are we not here in a kind of catch-22 situation? Under extractive political institutions inclusive economic institutions either do not materialize or even if they do emerge, they would not be sustainable; and in any case, relatively inclusive economic institutions, like those in today's China, do not necessarily

35 Acemoglu, Robinson, op. cit., p. 445.
36 Ibid., pp. 446–448.

lead to inclusive political institutions or democracy. It is true that inclusive economic institutions do not automatically lead to democracy or inclusive political institutions, but they certainly support and facilitate the emergence and development of the latter. But for this tendency to materialise those, whose interests would be realised by inclusive political institutions (usually the majority of the people), should work and sometimes even fight hard. As the experience of several countries (e.g., South Korea, Taiwan) testifies, relatively inclusive economic institutions form a basis for sustainable political reforms and democratisation. If we compare the two biggest end-of-the-twentieth-century social, political and economic reforms in China under Deng Xiaoping and in the Soviet Union under Gorbachev – I would put my money on the Chinese experiment, where changes were started by gradual, localised and calibrated economic reforms. At the same time, we don't believe that, due to various reasons, such a blueprint of reforms would have been possible in the Soviet Union, but this is a different matter and there is more about that in the chapter on regime changes in Russia. For the USSR under Gorbachev, the Chinese model of reforms would have been all but impossible.

One of the differences between Deng Xiaoping's and Gorbachev's reforms, as correctly observed by some experts,[37] was that while Deng started with reforming the economy (first rural, and only later urban) leaving the political regime intact, Gorbachev pursued political and economic reforms simultaneously. However, Gorbachev could not start any serious economic reforms without first getting rid of his Politburo colleagues, for whom the colour of the cat was more important than its mice-catching abilities. This, combined with the multi-ethnic character of the USSR, which in itself was a legacy of the Czarist Empire, inevitably led to the collapse of this multi-ethnic Leviathan.

By now it should be clear that China's model of modernization has been successful while Russia's way of introducing simultaneous political and economic 'shock therapies' was quite disastrous. Dmitri

[37] See, e.g., A.C. Lynch, 'Deng's and Gorbachev's Reform Strategies Compared', *Russia in Global Affairs*, 24 June 2012.

Trenin writes: 'In 1990, Russia's GDP had been roughly the size of China's. Two decades later, China's was four times as large as Russia's'.[38] Since 1990 the number of people in poverty in China has fallen by more than 300 million, which is a great contribution to global progress toward the implementation of the UN Millennium Development Goals (MDGs).[39] In fact, it should be clear by now that without China's reduction of poverty (plus India's smaller but still significant contribution), it would be impossible for humankind to achieve the MDG target of halving the share of the population living in poverty by 2015. Since 1978 more than 600 million Chinese people have been lifted out of poverty, an achievement of staggering proportions. And the significant role of the Chinese state in these transformations has to be emphasised. Wang Hui, who is often critical of the Chinese state (and of other states as well), in underlining the important, and even increasing role of the state in the world, writes on the reasons for the successful transformations in China:

> Next, the role of the state is undergoing transformation not only within the realm of global relations but in domestic relations as well. Simple descriptions of the role of the Chinese state as "totalitarian" often confuse the positive with the negative aspects of the role of the state. China did not undergo "shock therapy" in its period of reform, as did Russia but was significantly more skilled at economic regulation than the latter country. That the Chinese financial system has shown itself to be relatively stable is due to the fact China has not entirely pursued the neoliberal path, and this is the product of conscious policy planning rather than the limitations imposed by social movements, social contradictions and the socialist tradition.[40]

Fantasising for a moment and assuming that eventually most of the countries in the world, including the major powers such as China and Russia, will all be democracies, let us ask: will such a world be free of major tensions and conflicts? We do not think so, and the

---

[38] D. Trenin, *Post-Imperium: The Dynamics of Former Soviet Eurasia*, Carnegie Endowment for International Peace, 2011 (Kindle version), loc. 1903.

[39] *China's Progress Towards the Millennium Development Goals 2008*. Report: Ministry of Foreign Affairs of the People's Republic of China – the United Nations System in China, p. 4.

[40] Wang Hui, *The End of the Revolution: China and the Limits of Modernity*, Verso, 2011, p. xxvii.

reason is not only that the rivalry over energy resources, food and water and many other scarcities will remain; there would also remains the question: who will lay down the law in such a 'democratic paradise'. Is the United States ready to follow the lead of a democratic People's Republic of China, accept Chinese recipes for the solution of Middle Eastern conflicts and put its military under Chinese command in certain world troublespots? Hardly. As Trenin writes, '[T]he question is over the direction of China's foreign policy, should more nationalistic trends prevail in Beijing, either as a result of hardening of the stance of the subsequent Communist Party leadership or *as a result of the fall of the communist dynasty and the emergence of a more democratic, nationalistic, and warlike China*. This may be the horizon of 2025–2030'.[41] Like in the case of the current changes in the Arab world, more democratic does not at all equal more Western oriented. Therefore the future of the world will depend on, among many other factors, (1) what would be the reaction of the rest of the world, especially that of Washington and its allies, to China's rise and (2) how will Beijing use its increasing strength?

5. THE WORLD'S REACTION TO CHINA'S RISE

Since the late 1970s, when Deng Xiaoping's economic reforms started China has witnessed accelerating economic development, and even the world financial and economic crisis of 2007–2009 only slowed down GDP growth to a level that for most world economies would have been a blessing. China's military expenditure, though in absolute terms well below that of the United States, in percentage to GDP, is one of the world's highest. Never, since the fifteenth century Ming dynasty's admiral Zheng He's navigations to far-away places, has Beijing been so active, not only in Asia but also on other continents.[42] And although China has mainly been interested in the

[41] Trenin, op. cit., loc. 1935.

[42] See, e.g., C. Aleden, Zhang Chun, B. Mariani, S. Large, 'China's Growing Role in African Post-Conflict Reconstruction', Global Review (SIIS), 2012, No. 1; R.Baker, Zhixing Zhang, 'The Paradox of China's Naval Strategy', Stratfor, 17 July 2012.

mineral and energy resources of those far-away places, Beijing is also participating in post-conflict reconstruction in African countries, helping them build infrastructure objects as well as special trade and economic cooperation zones, and China's terms of loans tend to be better than those from Western companies.[43] As Deborah Brautigam concludes, while 'Westerners support government and democracy, the Chinese build roads and dams'.[44] Zambian economist and writer Dambisa Moyo observes that '[I]n 2009, China became Africa's largest trading partner. Chinese foreign direct investment (FDI) is also steadily increasing. In 2010, China's FDI in Zambia topped $1bn, creating 15,000 jobs, and estimates for 2011 have the figure above $2,4bn. In exchange for copper and other resources, China is providing Zambia with much needed capital investment, jobs, and infrastructure'.[45] Dr Moyo emphasises her first-hand experience of the positive impact that Chinese investment has had on her country, and she is astonished that Chinese investments in Africa have garnered so much criticism in Western media. As she points out, Chinese investments in Africa stand favourably against the Washington led invasions of other resource rich countries, such as Afghanistan and Iraq, in a bid to gain dominion over scarce resources.[46] In his speech to the gathering of African leaders on 19th July 2012 in Beijing, President Hu Jintao pledged to lend $20 billion to African governments for infrastructure and agriculture in the next three years.[47] Nevertheless, an article in the New York Times that informed the readership about this fact did not, however, fail to make the traditional Western comments about China's relations with African countries: Beijing is offering its aid 'without conditioning it on human rights performance or governance' (i.e. without interfering in the internal affairs of African states), its projects — roads, pipelines and ports — have

---

[43] D. Brautigam, 'Africa's Eastern Promise', *Foreign Affairs online*, 5 January, 2010.
[44] Ibid.
[45] D. Moyo, 'If I Ruled the World: We need a global framework that follows China's lead', *Prospect*, 12 July 2012, p. 6.
[46] Ibid.
[47] J. Perlez, 'With $20 Billion Loan Pledge, China Strengthens Its Ties to African Nations', *New York Times*, 19 July 2012.

focused on benefiting China's extractive industries, not the African people, and China uses its own workers to carry out most of these projects.

Beijing has also activated, as Joshua Kurlantzick calls it, its 'charm-offensive'. He observes that 'polls show that people in Africa and Latin America have more positive feelings toward China than toward the United States'[48] and a 2005 BBC poll carried out in twenty two countries across several continents found that a majority believed China plays a more positive role in the world than the United States.[49] This has set alarm-bells ringing in Western capitals, and raised concerns among some of China's neighbours, such as Russia, Kazakhstan, Japan, Vietnam and the Philippines. American historian Arthur Herman, though pouring vitriol more on the American Democratic Administration in the United States than China, sounds quite hysterical: 'By their carelessness Congress and the Obama administration are steadily handing over control of America's economic and financial future to a handful of Chinese officials and generals in Beijing'.[50] Another Asian rising star – India, which has had strained relations with its North-Eastern neighbour, is also worried since 'as China's and India's economies continue to grow, the two countries will vie for greater influence, competing for both markets and resources'.[51] China's rise is met with as much enthusiasm as fear. Neighbours may be alarmed by its growing might, but there is greater support from other continents. However, even those who dislike China, or are afraid or envious of the rising Middle Kingdom should wish it well, since without China the current crisis would have been much more serious, and longer term economic perspectives would be rather bleak.

How will Washington and Beijing behave in the process of a change in their relative powers? One positive factor may be that China and America are economically and financially so interlocked and interdependent that one cannot seriously hurt the other

---

[48] J. Kurlantzick, Charm Offensive. How China's Soft Power is Transforming the World, Yale University Press, 2007, p. 9.

[49] Ibid.

[50] A. Herman, 'China's Debt Bomb', *The Washington Post*, 8 February, 2010.

[51] B. Peer, 'Clash of the Tigers', *Foreign Affairs* online, 6 January, 2010.

without suffering itself; they are locked in a so-called 'mutually assured economic destruction' (MAED instead of the Cold War period MAD between the US and the USSR). However, Arthur Herman, in his desire to attack both President Obama and China, is more alarmist and not as certain of such a linkage working: 'Today, some experts argue that rational self-interest will prevent China from waging this kind of economic warfare, because crippling the U.S. would also severely wound its own economy. However, on an issue like Taiwan or Japan, rational judgment can take a backseat to national pride, and the desire to reverse old humiliations'.[52] Once again, there is almost a visceral assumption that it is only Beijing, not Washington, which may act irrationally, even contrary to its own rational self-interest (still, as defined in Washington). It is not clear why Herman refers to Japan, but it seems pretty certain that a stronger China will react even more forcefully to any attempts to test Beijing's position on issues that the country's leadership, and also importantly the Chinese people, consider as 'non-negotiables': Taiwan, Tibet and Xingjian as integral parts of China. On these issues any serious challenge will indeed result in a strong reaction from Beijing. Moreover, as American experts Graham Fuller and Frederick Starr write, 'it would be unrealistic to rule out categorically American willingness to play the "Uighur card" as a means of exerting pressure on China in the event of some future crisis or confrontation'.[53] Charles Horner also believes that 'China's problems in Xingjian cannot but become a temptation for the United States if a future deterioration in Sino-American relations focuses attention on China's most deeply-seated structural weaknesses'.[54] The same considerations apply to Tibet as well. This must indeed be on Chinese minds, and who could blame them for that. Then, there are of course the maritime delimitation disputes in the South China Sea between China, Brunei, Malaysia, Philippines and Vietnam, in which the

---

52 A. Herman, op.cit.

53 Graham E. Fuller and S. Frederick Starr, *The Xingjian Problem, Central Asia-Caucasus Institute*, Paul H. Nitze School of Advanced International Studies, The Johns Hopkins University, 2006, p. 46.

54 C. Horner, 'The Other Orientalisms: China's Islamist Problem', *The National Interest*, No. 67, Spring, 2002, p. 45.

United States takes a keen interest,[55] and which may trigger conflicts if not handled cautiously.[56]

Many in Washington see America's trade deficit and dependence on Chinese credit as a national security problem, rather than merely an economic predicament. China, which emerged fairly unscathed from the global recession, clearly considers itself to be on a roll. One (unnamed) Chinese official was reported to have told the *Financial Times*: "We used to see the U.S. as our teacher but now we realize that our teacher keeps making mistakes and we've decided to quit the class. Market capitalism is so yesterday, state capitalism so now. A new role model for the developing world: state, authoritarian capitalism.'[57] Even before the world financial and economic crisis of 2007–2009 (and still continuing at the time of writing) some experts had argued that so-called authoritarian capitalism might be a workable substitute model of the development for liberal-democracy. The current crisis, which started in the liberal-democratic West and spread all over the world (affecting China less than most countries) gives additional weight to the understanding that not only are there other models of modernisation and development besides liberal democracy and liberal markets, but also that liberal democracies, in order to continue prospering may have to learn several things from China. So, British journalist and economist Anatole Kaletsky in an article with the intriguing title of '*We need new capitalism to take on China*' writes: 'As a leading US diplomat told me: "Since the crisis, developing countries have lost interest in the old Washington consensus that promoted democracy and liberal economics. Wherever I go in the world, governments and business leaders talk about the new Beijing consensus—the Chinese route to prosperity and power. The West must come up with a new model of capitalism that's consistent with our political values. Either we reinvent ourselves or we

---

[55] See, e.g., *Cooperation from Strength: The United States, China and the South China Sea*, Center for a New American Security, January, 2012.

[56] See, e.g., a special issue of the Italian journal of international relations *The International Spectator*, No 2 of June 2012 'A Rising China and Its Strategic Impact' and especially Michael Yahuda's 'China's Recent Relations with Maritime Neighbours' in the same issue (pp. 30–44).

[57] I. Stelzer, 'China v. world as a trade war comes closer', *The Sunday Times*, February 14, 2010.

will lose."[58] And Kaletsky concludes that 'if the West isn't to slide into irrelevance, governments must be much more active in taking control of the economy'.

The end of the Cold War and the collapse of the Soviet Union were followed by the emergence of dozens of small or medium sized new states, many of which almost by default chose Western style liberal democracy and free markets. Politically they exercised bandwagonning, i.e. joining the stronger and victorious side. Their choice was dictated not only by strategic calculations, but also for ideological reasons; having shed off Moscow's domination, which emphasised collective values, they naturally opted for Western institutions and values. This may have given additional grounds to the belief that eventually the whole world would become westernized, i.e. the liberal-democratic free market model was seen as triumphant. However, this was not to be the case. Countries such as China, Russia as well as many others could not, and in the case of China even did not attempt, to join this victorious club. If Yeltsin's Russia attempted to follow the Western lead and failed miserably, China never tried to do it at all. Moreover, Beijing, having seen what had happened to the Soviet Union and Russia, has become even firmer in its resolve not to repeat the Soviet or Russian experience.

John Ikenberry takes a relatively optimistic view on China's rise. However, his vision is to a great extent premised on the assumption that differently from all earlier international systems, which were dominated by a leading power that had always been eventually forced to give up its leadership to a new power, the United States, as a leading state, has purposefully worked on the creation of an international system of liberal-democratic capitalist states of universal appeal that is 'hard to overturn and easy to join'.[59] This is a Hegelian, Marxist or Fukuyamean 'the-end-of-history-and-the-last-man' type vision of the evolution of the world towards a final universal model. All such projects, envision they a worldwide Christendom, Islamic Caliphate, communist paradise or liberal-democratic free-market

---

58 *The Times*, February 4, 2010.

59 G.J. Ikenberry, 'The rise of China and the future of the West: Can the Liberal System Survive?', *Foreign Affairs*, 2008, vol. 87, No. 1, p. 28.

capitalism are doomed. The world is simply too big, too complicated and too diverse to be governed or led from one centre, to evolve in the same direction and to the same final destination. Although at the end of the process of our journey from an African village to a global megalopolis, Homo sapiens, although competing, cooperating and borrowing from each other, will in some important respects indeed, as we believe, become a bit more similar to one another, the world will never become uniform, be it Christian, Muslim, communist or liberal-democratic. Moreover, the absence of competing models of development will inevitably lead to stagnation. Christopher Hayes believes that 'we tend to view China as posing an alternative and threatening model for the future, one that's by turns seductive and repulsive, the source of envy and contempt. But after a while I wondered if we aren't in some way converging with our supposed rival. China has managed the transition from a repressive, authoritarian, impoverished country to an industrial, corporatist oligarchy by allowing a loud and raucous debate while also holding tightly onto power. Perhaps we are moving toward the same end from a democratic direction, the roiling public debate and political polarization obscuring the fact that power and money continue to collect and pool among an elite that increasingly views itself as besieged on all sides by a restive and ungrateful populace'.[60] Martin Jacques, placing emphasis on the cultural differences between Western and East Asian societies, recognizes nevertheless that 'indeed, an important characteristic of all Asian modernities, including Japan's, is their hybrid nature, the combination of different elements, indigenous and foreign'[61] and that 'we have moved from the era of either/or to one characterized by hybridity'.[62] David Brooks is of the opinion that 'if Asia's success reopens the debate between individualism and collectivism (which seemed closed after the cold war), then it's unlikely that the forces of individualism will sweep the field or even gain an edge' and that 'the rise of China isn't only an economic event. It's a cultural one. The ideal of a harmonious

[60] C. Hayes, 'The Great Leap', *The Nation*, 11 January, 2010.
[61] M. Jacques, *When China Rules the World. The Rise of the Middle Kingdom and the End of the Western World*, Allen Lane, 2009, p. 137.
[62] Ibid., p. 415.

collective may turn out to be as attractive as the ideal of the American Dream'.[63] Professor Barry Buzan from the London School of Economics observes that 'within China an effort is emerging to promote some of the principles from the Confucian order as a more collectivist, harmonious alternative to the conflictual individualism of most Western international relations thinking'.[64]

It is not only that liberal democracy is not as universal a model for the world as is believed by many in the West. It is also that in world politics size matters. The economic success of authoritarian Singapore, South Korea or Taiwan did not undermine the belief in the eventual triumph of liberal democracy not only because these countries indeed borrowed heavily from the West; they were also too small to serve as examples to follow. China is in a different category. Lord Peter Mandelson is, of course, right in observing that 'Europe and the U.S. need to recognize that China will not simply accept a model of global governance or multilateralism that it played no part in designing, or which it feels does not reflect the imperative of its growth and stability'.[65] Therefore, the calls that often come from the West that a stronger China will have to take on more responsibilities and behave like 'a responsible stakeholder', paraphrasing the then US Deputy Secretary of State Robert Zoellick,[66] sound a bit disingenuous, since a strong China will inevitably have its own, and often, though not necessarily always, different from Western, understandings of the concept of 'a responsible stakeholder'. Hugh White is right that 'we should not mistake China's reluctance to shoulder the burdens of leadership, as they are defined by Washington, for reluctance to exercise power in pursuit of its own agenda. From Beijing's perspective, Washington's definition of the responsibilities

---

63 D. Brooks, 'Harmony and the Dream', *International Herald Tribune*, 11 August, 2008.

64 B. Buzan, 'China in International Society: Is "Peaceful Rise" Possible?', *The Chinese Journal of International Politics*, 2010, vol. 3, p. 8.

65 P. Mandelson, 'We Want China to Lead', *International Herald Tribune*, 11 February 2010.

66 China's Role in the World: Is China a Responsible Stakeholder? Statement by Thomas J. Christensen, Deputy Assistant Secretary of State for East Asia and Pacific Affairs before the US-China Economic and Security Review Commission, August 3, 2006.

of leadership reflects American interests, not necessarily China's. China will not shoulder the burden of protecting the US-led international order where that does not suit its interests, but it will happily use its power to serve its own interests where it can. The Chinese are quite ready for prime-time, but they will sing their own song'.[67]

Stephanie T. Kleine-Ahlbrandt of the International Crisis Group (ICG), for example, produced a list of the requests Washington imposed on China regarding foreign policy issues such as adapting the Western approach to Iran's nuclear programme, to North Korea, to Afghanistan and to a host of other issues where American and Chinese interests overlap only partly (e.g., Beijing, like the rest of the world, doesn't want to see Iran as a nuclear-weapon power, but China has considerable economic interests in Iran, and for various reasons it 'lacks the West's sense of urgency about the Iran nuclear issue'[68]). Kleine-Ahlbrandt, however, writes that 'Beijing remains highly reluctant to take on more burdens – whether economic, political, or military – preferring to free-ride'.[69] But what about a possible Chinese list of requests to the United States' foreign policy that may include, for example, Washington's assistance towards a peaceful reintegration of Taiwan with China, or giving up on talking about China's human rights record, persuading the Dalai Lama to come closer to Beijing's vision of the future of Tibet, or inviting Beijing to become actively involved in the Middle East where China has considerable energy interests, or instead of increasing its military presence in the Far East withdrawing from the region? For many in the West such requests may sound preposterous, but so do some American requests, if looked at from Beijing. Politicians as well as peoples have to learn to see the world not only from their own perspective; they have to try to step as much as possible into the shoes of the Other. Dominique Moïsi makes a valid point in writing that the Americans will have to start to take into account the views of

---

[67] H. White, The China Choice: Why America should Share Power, Black Inc., 2012, (Kindle version), loc. 648.

[68] International Crisis Group. Asia Briefing No. 100, The Iran Nuclear Issue: The View from Beijing, 17 February 2010, p. 16.

[69] S. Kleine-Ahlbrandt, 'Beijing, Global Free Rider', *Foreign Policy*, 12 November 2009.

those who are becoming their equals, and that they will have to learn to understand and recognize other cultures.[70] So far, Washington has responded to a rising China by changing its strategic priorities. In November 2011 President Obama declared the Asia-Pacific region to be 'a top priority' of the US security policy. In June 2012, Leon Panetta, the American Secretary of defence, announced that by 2020 60% of the US navy, which would include six aircraft carriers, the majority of American cruisers, destroyers, combat ships and submarines, would be concentrated in that region.[71] Naturally, Beijing sees these moves as aimed at China, and who could believe that they are not. As Dr Yang Jiemian, the President of the Shanghai Institutes for International Studies, explained to me during our meeting on 20th July 2012, current Washington's 'pivot' to Asia is a delayed reaction to China's rise. Delayed, first, by 9/11 and the resulting wars in Afghanistan and Iraq, and then by the world financial and economic crisis, which started in the United States. If politically and economically Washington had already earlier (both under the G.W. Bush and Obama administrations) turned its attention to the Asia-Pacific region, in 2011–2012 also a military component followed.

The West, and especially Washington, needs a lot of wisdom and ironically Chinese-style patience to respond to China's 'peaceful rise'. Of course, equally important is the other side of the equation: whether the rising Dragon will always remain hidden, and keep a cool head, as Deng Xiaoping advised.

6. *FROM WESTERNIZATION TO SINIFICATION?*

Although Deng Xiaoping advised his countrymen to keep a cool head, maintain a low profile and to never take the lead while the same time aiming to do something big, it is doubtful that a country, which is increasingly becoming powerful both in absolute as well as in relative terms, will forever keep a low profile and refuse to take the lead. It is also doubtful that a strong and self-confident China will always keep a low profile. If the United States is a *status quo* power in

[70] D. Moïsi, *The Geopolitics of Emotion: How Cultures of Fear, Humiliation, and Hope Are Reshaping the World*, Doubleday Books, 2009 p. 185.

[71] www.bbc.co.uk/news/world-us-canada-18305750 (last visited 5 June 2012).

the sense that it seeks to maintain and consolidate its dominant position in the world (notwithstanding that by trying to export 'democracy', to, say, post-Soviet space or the Middle East, Washington is seeking to change these areas, but even these policies are aimed at consolidating American domination in these regions, i.e. their purpose is a purpose of a *status quo* power), China in that respect may indeed be seen as a revisionist power.[72] Of interest in this respect is an article by Chinese scholar Feng Yongping entitled *The Peaceful Transition of Power from the UK to the US*, who ends his historical study with the unmistakable conclusion: '[F]rom the perspective of China, which can be considered in a similar state to the United States at that time [i.e. when Washington at the end of the nineteenth century-beginning of the twentieth century peacefully took over from London the reins of world politics], the example of successful transition undoubtedly holds deep implications and provides a source for inspiration'.[73] One can be sure that such an idea does not inspire people in Washington. That is why, among other issues such as Taiwan, Tibet, Xingjian and the trade imbalance, references to China's democracy deficit and human rights violations may be used as an instrument to stop or slow down any potential transition of power in the world. In the balance of power world, a peaceful transfer of power has indeed been the exception. Moreover, the most recent U.S. national security strategies are based on the

---

[72] Barry Buzan, calling China a 'reformist revisionist' power, writes that '[A] reformist revisionist accepts some of the institutions of international society for a mixture of calculated and instrumental reasons. But it resists, and wants to reform, others, and possibly also wants to change its status. This sounds like the best description of China's positioning in contemporary international society' (Buzan, op. cit., p. 18). It is possible to agree with such characterisation of China's position in today's world, which certainly contains seeds of serious conflicts with Western powers whose interests and values have moulded the current international society. However, these potential conflicts become inevitable and unavoidable only if the West or China insist in full and uncompromising realization of their respective visions of the future of the world. Therefore compromises and acceptance of differences between societies as well as within societies are necessary for the avoidance of conflicts (see more about that in R. Müllerson, Processes of Dissimilation and Assimilation in Humankind's Evolution: Will E Pluribus Unum Replace Ex Uno Plures?, *The Chinese Journal of International Law*, 2010, Vol. 9, No. 2).

[73] Feng Yongping, 'The Peaceful Transition of Power from the UK to the US', *The Chinese Journal of International Politics*, 2006, No. 1, pp. 83–108.

assumption of continuing American economic and military superiority, and aim to help Washington shape the world and not to be shaped by it; no strategic competitor is allowed to rise.[74] If the US cannot find a way of accommodating China's rise (this doesn't mean that the America must inevitably accept 'the Beijing's consensus', but it cannot demand that China behaves according to 'the Washington consensus' either) then serious conflicts will be inevitable. Hugh White's recommendation that of the three options available for the United States in Asia (resisting China's challenge and trying to preserve Washington's dominant role in Asia, stepping back from its dominant role and leaving China attempting to establish its hegemony in Asia instead of the American one, remaining in Asia on a new basis allowing China a larger role but also maintaining a strong presence of its own), 'the best way for America to respond to China's growing power is to agree with China to share the leadership of Asia'.[75] And though, in White's opinion, such an arrangement would be very difficult to achieve, and even more difficult to maintain, he believes that this is the only way 'to avoid both the dangers of Chinese domination and the risks of rivalry' that is wrought with possible military conflict. 'The hope that America can maintain uncontested leadership in Asia is therefore as illusory as the fear that China will be able to dominate Asia in its place',[76] writes Hugh White.

For the first time in a long while, it is not primarily the Western democracies, which are set to define the future of our Planet. Dominique Moïsi believes that we may soon find that centralized non-democratic regimes like China are better prepared for economic crises than American style democracies.[77] However, taking into account the complex character of the current international system, and the fact that today it extends around the whole globe and is composed of too many actors – both governmental and non-governmental, it is doubtful that in contrast to previous international systems (like, say, the dual-hegemonic Cold War bi-polar

---

74 *The National Security Strategy of the United States of America*, March 2006, p. 43.

75 H. White, op.cit, loc. 1689.

76 Ibid., loc. 127.

77 D. Moïsi, op. cit., p. 8.

system dominated by the US and the USSR respectively) there will be any single centre, be it in the East or in the West, that could dominate the whole international system.

In some respects Beijing's behaviour as a leading state may even differ positively from the conduct of previous dominant powers. Firstly, there will be no return to colonialism, and therefore there will not be a new Chinese empire, like there have been British, Dutch, French or Russian. Secondly, Confucianism, in contradistinction to Christianity (or Islam for that matter) is not a proselytizing religion (if it can be considered at all as a religion). Western universalism and its attempts to turn all nations into liberal democracies are intellectually and emotionally, as we attempted to show above, based on Christianity's universal call and the European Enlightenment's legacy. A dominant China, even if forcefully advancing its interests, may not necessarily try to convert its neighbours, and especially Western liberal democracies, into Confucian autocracies. As Barry Buzan believes, '[U]nlike the universalist pretensions of American liberalism, "Chinese characteristics" points to a culturally unique way of doing things that is not necessarily relevant to those outside Chinese culture'.[78] China's history does provide us with a reasonable basis for optimism. The former Prime Minister of Australia (2010–2012) Kevin Rudd – a China specialist – has written that '[T]he China that I have studied over the decades is one that has not been in the business of invading other countries for more than 2,000 years. Nor has China sought to establish colonies around the world, even though its navigational skills and naval capabilities during the Ming Dynasty were considerably more advanced than those of countries in the west'.[79] This of course does not mean that the 'Chinese ways of doing things' will not influence other societies, especially those who are culturally and geographically close to the Middle Kingdom, but it seems reasonable to predict that China will not be obsessed with the idea of regime change in order to make the whole world look more like China.

There are grounds for believing that China will gradually become more open not only economically and socially but also politically,

---

[78] B. Buzan, op. cit., p. 21.

[79] K. Rudd, 'The west isn't ready for the rise of China', *New Statesman*, 11 July, 2012.

i.e. China will grow more democratic. There are two arguments in favour of such a view. Firstly, today's China is already very different from Mao's China, and secondly, as we have seen in the case of some East Asian and other countries (Chile, South Korea, Taiwan), economic modernisation does indeed has a tendency to lead to political reforms. However, some qualifications may be necessary. First, political change in China will come about not due to external pressure, which sometimes may even be counterproductive, but because of domestic reasons and impulses (bottom up public demands as well as top down reforms). Secondly, such reforms have to be cautious and gradual; any political 'shock therapy' will be disastrous not only for China but highly damaging for the rest of the world also. Thirdly, even if China becomes more politically open, it will be quite different from Western liberal-democracies. In contradistinction to its smaller East Asian neighbours, which in the process of modernisation have adapted from the West not only technological, financial and economic know-how, but also (often under pressure and in the case of Japan through decades of occupation) quite a few political institutions, China, due to its size, strength, successful reforms as well as pride in its glorious history, will go at its own pace, and will be less prone to borrowing from the West. Fourthly, a more open and democratic China will not necessarily be more accommodating towards the West; on the contrary, on some issues, especially on those 'non-negotiables' (Taiwan, Xingjian and Tibet being integral parts of China and probably also maritime delimitation disputes in the South China Sea) a more democratic China may well be even more assertive and less accommodative. It should not be taken for granted that the Chinese people, when given free choice, would decide on most issues as the American people do any more than the Chinese authorities would decide like the American government. Fifthly, a stronger China will mean that the so-called 'Beijing consensus' will have greater impact in different parts of the world than the 'Washington consensus' (due to the financial and economic crises this is already happening) and it would be more and more difficult to assert that a liberal-democratic future of the world will be preordained. Finally, there is nothing gloomy in this picture, and it does not at all mean that under Chinese pressure America, Great Britain, France or Estonia will have to introduce Politburos and start censuring the Internet. It has been the West, which due to its universalising Christian religion and the Enlightenment's legacy, as well as more recent colonial and post-colonial dominance, that has had a strong tendency and urge to westernise the whole world.[80] China's history and religion have not shown tendency or strive for making the rest of the world Confucian. But who knows?

---

[80] After the collapse of communism, only liberal democratic and Islamic extremists still have an ambition of creating a uniform world either in the form of world-wide liberal democratic system or building an Islamic Caliphate.

Chapter Four

REGIME CHANGES IN RUSSIA: GORBACHEV, YELTSIN AND PUTIN

1. UNDERSTANDING RUSSIA OR BELIEVING IN RUSSIA

For me, having lived, studied and worked for many years in Moscow, it is sometimes amazing how little Westerners, and I include here quite a few specialists and not only the man on the Clapham omnibus, as they put it in London, understand Russia. Usually everyone remembers Winston Churchill's characterisation of this big Eurasian empire as 'a riddle, wrapped in a mystery, inside an enigma'.[1] Those who are familiar with Russian culture, especially with her sublime poetry, may quote one of the nineteenth century greatest poets Fyodor Tyutchev, who wrote: 'One cannot understand Russia by reason,/ Cannot measure her by common measure,/ She is under a special dispensation – / One can only believe in Russia'. However, not all, who quote Churchill or even know Tyutchev's poetry, remember that the great old man of British politics did not stop with the words usually quoted. He continued and thought that perhaps at the end of the day there may have been a key to solving this riddle, and that key could well have been 'Russian national interests'.

Churchill's observations on Russia's national interests, as the key to understanding Russia's behaviour in her external relations, has to be taken seriously, though this observation necessitates an explicatory commentary: it was made, in my opinion, either too late or too early; at a time when Russia's continuity was interrupted by the Bolshevik's experiment, when there existed neither the Russian Empire nor the current Russian Federation, but the communist Soviet Union. The latter had rather peculiar understanding of national interests, if they at all could be called national interests. Let us explain what we have in mind.

[1] Winston Churchill, first lord of the admiralty, radio broadcast, London, October 1, 1939.—*Winston S. Churchill: His Complete Speeches, 1897–1963*, ed. Robert Rhodes James, vol. 6, p. 6161 (1974).

Some Western scholars have argued that, in contrast to Western colonialism and expansionism, economic considerations did not play a major role in Russian colonialism or expansionism; specifically, they have claimed that any economic motivation was practically absent in the Russian expansion into Central Asia.[2] However, for the foreign policy of Czarist Russia, economic factors certainly played a significant role, even if they were not always of immediate concern. Seymour Becker is right when he observes that Russia's aims, for example in the mid-nineteenth century Central Asia, were both political and economic.[3] Naturally, the same holds true for British interests in that region and elsewhere. It was not only that London was apprehensive lest it lose India to the Russians, who indeed were toying with the idea of moving much further south than the then limits of the Russian Empire[4] (which, in Central Asia, were finally established by the Anglo-Russian Convention of 1907), but London and Calcutta also tried to expand the markets for their goods as far northward as possible, and to restrict the southward penetration of Russian merchants to areas too close to the British Raj. Like London's foreign policy, Washington's foreign economic interests, i.e. the interests of American capital and businesses, have always played a determinative role. Stephen Kinzer makes the most valid point observing that 'spreading democracy, Christianising heathen nations, building a strong navy, establishing military bases around the world, and bringing foreign governments under American control were never ends in themselves. They were ways for the United States to assure itself access to the markets, resources, and investment potential of distant lands.'[5] Today we may also observe that Washington's ultimate aims, when promoting democracy in

---

[2] See, e.g., W.C. Fuller, *Strategy and Power in Russia 1600–1914*, The Free Press, 1992, p. 290.

[3] S. Becker, *Russia's Protectorates in Central Asia: Bukhara and Khiva, 1865–1924*, Harvard University Press, 1968, p. 13.

[4] Although today we may conclude that due to impenetrable Afghanistan interposing between the Russians descending from the north and the British advancing from the south neither could the Cossacks wash their boots in the Indian Ocean, nor could Sepoys water their horses in the Siberian rivers.

[5] S. Kinzer, *Overthrow: America's Century of Regime Change from Hawaii to Iraq*, Time Books, 2006, p. 34.

different parts of the world and effecting regime changes, are primarily economic. But in contradistinction to the United States, or to Czarist Russia for that matter, Soviet foreign policy did not, and even was not meant to serve economic interests; on the contrary, more often than not, Soviet foreign policy was a significant burden on its economy. Soviet expansionism was motivated primarily by political, military-strategic, and most importantly by ideological, considerations. Eastern European countries of 'peoples' democracy', which were firmly under Soviet control, and especially so-called 'countries of socialist orientation' (e.g., Cuba, Angola, Mozambique, Mongolia and Vietnam), with their Soviet imposed artificial, ineffective planned economies, were much more a burden on the Soviet economy than a source of any profit. However, for the Kremlin it was not profit, but the spread of socialist ideology and Soviet political influence that was the primary motivations of its foreign policy. Such differing accents between the foreign policies of the United States and the Soviet Union may be explained by differences in their socioeconomic systems – the former was, and is, a capitalist, market-oriented system; the latter was a totalitarian, ideologically and politically oriented system. Simplifying slightly, we may say that if the first makes money using all available means, including political and military tools, the second spends money in order to gain long-term political and ideological influence. After the collapse of the Soviet Union, with its utopian and warped ideology that believed in its mission to make, at the end of the day, the whole world communist and therefore often acted counterproductively to its real material interests by imposing its own ineffective political and economic systems on its client regimes in Eastern Europe, Asia, Latin America and Africa, whom Moscow supported and maintained while throwing away billions of dollars, Russia seems to have learned the lesson. Today she more or less tries to act in accordance with her genuine national interests (as they are understood by the Kremlin, of course), and it is more often the United States, together with its allies, who are carried by the ideological zeal of remaking the world (though if you scratch ideological slogans deep enough you will always discover tangible economic interests). However a small caveat may be necessary. Russia, as a country of state capitalism, sometimes subordinates the interests of her private capital to the interests of the capitalist state as a whole, as they are understood and defined by those in the Kremlin. If in Russia, *grosso modo* and with some exceptions, the Kremlin dominates Russian capitalists (what is good for the Kremlin, is good for Russia), in America, it is big business and financial capital that controls the White House and the Capitol Hill (what is good for Ford is good for America). As one of the profoundest thinkers of the past century John Kenneth Galbraith famously put it: 'Under capitalism man exploits man: under communism, it is just the opposite.'[6] However there is nowhere in today's world, with the exception of North Korea, actual experimentation of putting into practice distorted communism ideals. Today Galbraith's witticism characterises more accurately the differences, or their absence thereof in any important respect, between free market capitalism and state capitalism. Of course, here we only compare the accents and emphases of two aspects or facets of the national interests of different countries. Security, and primarily guaranteeing the physical security of the state from outside attacks, as well as subversions or other kinds of interferences, is intrinsically the number one foreign policy priority of any state. Without guaranteeing these values, economic interests cannot be secured either.

The attitude of Westerners towards Russia usually vacillates between admiration and deep suspicion and fear, though the latter usually prevails and the former, if we exclude classical Russian literature, music and ballet, is reserved for the policies of Presidents Gorbachev and Yeltsin. If Gorbachev's policies led to the dissolution of the Soviet Union – the nemesis of the United States and the West (for the Soviet people and the East and Central European nations this was, of course, liberation from a totalitarian system), Yeltsin's policies resulted in robber capitalism, the oligarchisation of Russia's economy and politics as well as a weakening of Russia's international positions.

Of course, there are quite a few Western experts who know and understand Russia well, and in this book we rely, *inter alia*, on their knowledge and wisdom. For example, Daniel Treisman, in his well

---

[6] Quoted from H.-J. Chang, *Bad Samaritans. Rich Nations, Poor Policies & the Threat to the Developing World*, Random House Business Books, 2007, p. 103.

researched and balanced book on Russia *The Return: Russia's Journey from Gorbachev to Medvedev*,[7] emphasises that he had consciously done his best 'to avoid two familiar styles of writing about the country' that seem to obscure more than they reveal about Russia. If one approach focuses on the darker side of the country and presents 'Russia as a land of deformity', the second approach 'is to turn mystical whenever Russia is mentioned'.[8] Treisman's book confirms that it is possible to understand even Russia, provided there is enough effort made and goodwill shown.

A prime, though a somewhat caricatural, example of the first category of works on Russia as mentioned by Treisman, is Edward Lucas' book *The New Cold War: How the Kremlin Menaces both Russia and the West* (Bloomsbury, 2007). I can understand why many Russian leaders in the rich tapestry of Russian history, where there is indeed too much red (though even in this respect Russia is not so unique at all), want to emphasise only the glorious victories, and see only the wrongs committed against Russia and not by her; being brought up in a closed society and brainwashed more than those who were lucky enough to be born into freer societies, their narrow viewpoints may be explained if not justified. Moreover, for politicians, and even more so for military leaders, an attempt to assess problems from all possible angles, and have a more sophisticated view of the world, may lead to political or military-strategic paralysis. Besides, while politicians are prisoners to their slogans, sound bites and pre-election promises to the electorate and lobby groups, military men are often overly instilled to the language of simple commands. Hence, there emerges a black and white picture of the world, and a vision based on the principle: 'those who are not with us are always against us'. However, I cannot comprehend how somebody who, like Edward Lucas, was educated at the London School of Economics and Political Science (LSE), cannot be more sophisticated and open-minded. Why a writer, journalist and academic, whose task should be to come as close to the truth as possible, while never hoping of course to reach it, would straighten one's narrative,

---

[7] D. Treisman, *The Return: Russia's Journey from Gorbachev to Medvedev*, Simon Spotlight Entertainment, 2010.

[8] Ibid., p. 2.

make it so mono-dimensional. Such views may be caused, in our opinion, by a combination of what can be called the three D's: Dislike, Disappointment and Dread. Dislike, because Russia has indeed all too often behaved like a big bully (though she is not the only, and certainly not the first, in this category); Disappointment, since notwithstanding 'the 1990s promises', she still refuses to become a 'normal' country and toe the line drawn up in Washington or Brussels; and Dread, because suddenly this 'abnormal' entity is once again, like the Phoenix, rising from the ashes and becoming more and more assertive in protecting her interests, as she understands them. Such an attitude towards Russia has not helped this big country become more liberal and democratic domestically, and especially not in showing her friendlier face externally. On the contrary, due to such an attitude and expectations, Russia has become more prickly externally, and prone to overreaction. Fear and hatred are not the most reliable political guides, since they tend to subordinate facts to preconceived ideas, i.e. to ideology. This was also noted by Barack Obama, who – when still a senator – wrote that while 'values are faithfully applied to facts before us, ideology overrides whatever facts call theory into question.'[9] In that respect, the advice of Daniel Deudney and G John Ikenberry is wise and pertinent: 'The democratic states should orient themselves to pragmatically address real and shared problems rather than focusing on ideological differences. Looking for alignments based on interests rather than regime type will further foreclose the unlikely coalescence of an antiliberal autocratic bloc.'[10] Unfortunately, this has not always been the case. On the contrary, as we are trying to show, while the two former communist giants – China and Russia – have started to carry out rather pragmatic policies globally, today it is the liberal democratic West, and especially Washington, whose foreign policy is increasingly guided by an ideology that overrides facts whenever they differ from preconceived ideas.

[9] B. Obama, *The Audacity of Hope. Thoughts on Reclaiming the American Dream*, Canongate, 2006, p. 59.

[10] D. Deudney and G. John Ikenberry, 'The Myth of the Autocratic Revival. Why Liberal Democracy Will Prevail', *Foreign Affairs*, January-February 2009.

2. COLLAPSE OF THE USSR AND THE EMERGENCE OF YELTSIN'S RUSSIA

The Soviet Union – a stable totalitarian state with some imperial characteristics – in 1991 disintegrated rapidly and rather unexpectedly. At the end of the 1980s, when Mikhail Gorbachev's reforms, expressed in the policies of *glasnost* and *perestroika*, had opened up the country both internally and externally, many people in the West as well as in the former USSR, believed (now, with hindsight, we may say rather naively) that it would be possible to, relatively quickly and painlessly, transform this closed totalitarian society into an open, democratic, market oriented country. Although in contradistinction to some other societies, including those which are currently undergoing regime changes, the Soviet Union as a whole had a highly educated population, including women, with almost 100% literacy, world class natural sciences, traditions of European high culture in literature, music, dance etc., as well as some other factors that are usually acknowledged as facilitators of democratic transformations. Unfortunately, this was not to be the case. The Soviet Union's disintegration was not only inevitable; for many it was quite a positive development, and not at all 'the greatest geopolitical catastrophe of the twentieth century', as President Vladimir Putin put it.[11] The Soviet Union was a doubly artificial entity: it was not only its ideology that was utopian, its geographic and ethnic composition, which was inherited more or less intact from the Russian Empire, had by the end of the twentieth century also become anachronistic.

Gorbachev's reforms were enthusiastically welcomed by many Soviets who felt let down with an order which had its roots in the ideology of Leninism–Stalinism, and which had brought immense suffering to the people. These were intellectuals who most enthusiastically welcomed Gorbachev's policy of *glasnost* (openness, transparency), and for whom it was like a gulp of fresh air in a stifling prison cell. I remember well how the population of Moscow in March 1989, in the elections for the Congress of People's Deputies (the highest legislative body, which under Gorbachev turned from a

---

[11] MSNNews, 25 April 2005 (http://msnbc.com/id/7632957, visited 16 June 2005).

rubber stamp into a discussion club), voted for Boris Yeltsin (around ninety per cent of the Muscovites cast their vote for him). This amazing result was a protest vote, because at that time Yeltsin was being harassed by Gorbachev – himself a reformer, but for whom Yeltsin was becoming a rival who, moreover, was starting to rock the boat captained by Gorbachev – and was vilified in that part of the mass media that supported Gorbachev. People were fed up with being told who to respect and who to denounce, and therefore voted for Boris Yeltsin. In the Soviet Mission to the United Nations in New York where, as a member of the UN Human Rights Committee, I cast my vote, the result was over ninety-five per cent for Yeltsin; this notwithstanding – or rather due to – the fact that the Soviet diplomats who worked in the mission, were told in no uncertain terms to guarantee an anti-Yeltsin result. However, this was a vote for freedom against an order that had prevailed for too many decades.

Yet, during an almost decade of rule (or non-rule) under Yeltsin, the situation changed dramatically. Unprepared, not thought through and poorly administered liberal economic and political reforms not only destabilized the country, but also discredited the very ideas of democracy, human rights and free markets – ideas so enthusiastically accepted at the end of the 1980s. When Boris Yeltsin, as advised by the World Bank, IMF, Washington and other experts, exercised 'shock therapy' on Russia, his anti-democratic behaviour (rule by decree instead of law, declaration of a state of emergency, rigging of the 1996 Presidential elections, by-passing, dismissing and finally shelling of the Parliament etc.) was if not exactly welcomed, then at least not frowned upon either by Washington. Serious people there well understood (as Pinochet's repression in Chile and other experiences in Latin America had proven) that economic 'shock therapy' and democracy are opposites; they cancel each other out; they both cannot simultaneously succeed. The harshest 'rebuke' came from Warren Christopher, the then Secretary of State in the Clinton Administration who stated that: '[T]he United States does not easily support the suspension of parliaments. But these are extraordinary times'.[12] Wang Hui, comparing the West's response to the Tiananmen

---

[12] N. Klein, *The Shock Doctrine. The Rise of Disaster Capitalism*, Allen Lane, 2007, p. 229.

tragedy and also to the West's reaction to Beijing's application in 1993 to host in China the 2000 Olympics with Boris Yeltsin's shelling of the Russian Parliament observes:

> This blatant enmity was shocking for Chinese society. It was also in October of that same year [1993] that the President of Russia, Boris Yeltsin, ordered a military attack and suppression of the legally elected Duma. This violent and anti-constitutional behaviour, undertaken by someone who had staked his reputation on rhetorical opposition to communism, not only exposed the grave crisis of Russian reforms – and particularly of the "spontaneous privatization process" promoted by American and other Western advisers – but also reflected the deep contradictions within Western, and particularly American, policies toward democracy and human rights, among other things, thus belying the extreme selfishness and anti-democratic character that lay at their core. American support for this violence was immediately compared to the American response to the Chinese violence of 1989.[13]

Today, the 'extraordinary times' are in the Middle East. The SCAF (Supreme Council of the Armed Forces) dissolved a democratically elected Parliament in Egypt, where the Islamist Muslim Brotherhood had a majority, and there was no criticism whatsoever either from Washington or Brussels. Indeed, when one deals with hard matters like oil, gas or the dismantling of one's strategic competitor – the 'evil empire', one cannot be stymied by considerations of 'soft' issues like democracy.[14] On a more theoretical note, it has to be emphasised that Western support for Yeltsin's attack on Parliament was a betrayal of some of the most fundamental liberal democratic principles for the sake of achieving that what was deemed to be good. Yeltsin was good because he was dismantling, or helping the West to dismantle, an evil system, while communist dominated Parliament was seen as bad since it was believed to cling to the old ways. Therefore, it was not only admissible but even necessary to set aside the procedural principles of democracy and fairness; it was acceptable, though regrettable, to use military force in order to guarantee the continuation of Yeltsin's pro-Western policies.

---

[13] Wang Hui, *The End of the Revolution: China and the Limits of Modernity*, Verso, 2011, p. 51.

[14] If I am ironical or cynical here, then only a bit; what I really do not like is hypocrisy, since its purpose is to fool everybody, often including the hypocrites themselves, since deception often starts with self-deception.

The famous Soviet dissident, who later became an Israeli Government Minister, Anatoly Sharansky, whose book *The Case for Democracy, The Power of Freedom to Overcome Tyranny and Terror* was allegedly read and admired by President George W. Bush, claims that '[W]hen freedom's sceptics argue today that freedom cannot be "imposed" from outside, or that the free world has no role to play in spreading democracy around the world, I cannot but be amazed. Less than one generation has passed since the West found the Achilles heel of the Soviet Union by pursuing an activist policy that linked the rights of the Soviet people to the USSR's international standing'.[15] Sharansky, in my opinion, makes serious mistakes in this assertion; Western efforts, and especially the attempts to promote democracy and human rights in the USSR played, if not a minor then at least a secondary role in the collapse of the Soviet Union (a somewhat greater effect may have had the intensified arms race forced upon the USSR by the Reagan Administration). Anatoly Sharansky may understandably exaggerate the effect of Western pressure on the Soviet Union on these matters, since he himself was freed from a labour camp and allowed to immigrate to Israel due to such pressure. One should not neglect this either. But for the country as a whole, the effect of this pressure was only cosmetic, and it benefited only a few individuals (for whom this may have been one hundred percent good). However, as the veteran Soviet Ambassador to Washington Anatoly Dobrynin (he served as Soviet Ambassador to Washington during the terms of six US presidents from 1962 until 1986) observes in his memoirs, Jewish emigration was sharply reduced in 1980 'mainly because of Carter's attack on human rights in the USSR' and that the Carter Administration's human rights policy 'did more harm than good' to human rights in the USSR.[16] This opinion, of a person who was intimate to the processes that led to the reform attempts of the communist system and finally to the collapse of the Soviet Union, should be given due weight. It has also been noted by some American authors that 'the most important

[15] N. Sharansky with R. Dermer, *The Case for Democracy, The Power of Freedom to Overcome Tyranny and Terror*, Public Affairs, 2004, p. 145.

[16] A. Dobrynin, *In Confidence: Moscow's Ambassador to America's Six Cold War Presidents*, New York, 1995, pp. 460, 389.

exaggeration of the US impact has been the belief that the Reagan administration's military build-up, support for anti-communist insurgencies, and confrontational rhetoric caused the Kremlin to retreat and reform.'[17] On the contrary, it was 'Gorbachev's gradual realization that Reagan would not use force to compel the Soviet Union to alter its system [that] helped him to overcome the climate of fear and take the risk of launching a destabilizing restructuring of the Soviet system'.[18] In this sense, it was not so much Reagan's missionary drive as much as his acceptance of the need for the United States and the Soviet Union to coexist, after Gorbachev had conveyed to the outside world his intention to reform the Soviet domestic system and change the Soviet Union's confrontational foreign policy, that facilitated the steps that Gorbachev undertook, and which finally led to the unravelling of the Soviet empire.

There is another topical point to be made about Anatoly Sharansky's views on matters of democracy and peace between Israel and the Palestinians. Sharansky writes that there cannot be any peace with the Palestinians until the Palestinian entity is not democratic. Therefore he is highly critical of two prominent Israeli politicians: Simon Peres and Yossi Beilin. The current Israeli President Peres had said on the matter that: 'I do not believe that democracy can be imposed artificially on another society'.[19] Beilin had similarly stated that 'if we wait until [the Palestinians] become democratic, then peace will wait for our great-grandchildren, not ourselves ... My first priority is to make peace with the Palestinians, I do not believe that it is up to me to educate them'.[20] Sharansky is a hawk, and believes chiefly in force, while Peres and Beilin, as Israeli politicians, are more or less dovish. The fact that the hawk seems to care more about democracy among the Palestinians than the doves leads me to suspect that any purity is suspect in the hawk's approach to democracy. Is he naïve, or is he opposed to any concessions to the Palestinians? He can hardly be a great believer in a democratic

---

[17] D.S. Foglesong, *The American Mission and the 'Evil Empire'*, Cambridge University Press, 2007, p. 195.
[18] Ibid.
[19] N. Sharansky with R. Dermer, op. cit., p. 154.
[20] Ibid., p. 183.

Palestine. Moreover, as the current developments in the Arab world indicate, the more democratic an Arab state, the tougher is its position on peace with Israel.

Alas, some states can exist only as autocracies, since when they liberalise they tend to disintegrate, and attempts by the world community or regional alliances to keep them together may only prolong the agony of the regime and increase the suffering of the people. This of course does not mean that the world community or regional alliances should encourage or contribute to the disintegration of states, as was the case with the manipulative international administration in Kosovo leading to its *de facto* independence from Serbia. The fate of the USSR, and maybe also the SFRY (the former Yugoslavia) testifies to this effect; today Iraq (a multiethnic society held together by a uni-ethnic state[21]) may well be on its way either to a more or less stable dictatorship, or to its disintegration into separate entities with equally questionable democratic credentials.

Because of its historical baggage, the transformation of the Soviet Union's successor states was certain to be a difficult and painful process; they had to radically change not only their economic and political systems, but also to dismantle an ideological basis, which in many cases left deep voids that became filled with nationalistic or religious ideas, often in their extreme forms. In some parts of the former USSR, for example the Baltic countries, due to a series of factors, among them their brief encounters with democratic ideas and practices between the two world wars, their relatively small size, and their proximity to the European Union (wrong are those who claim that in world politics geography does not matter; it certainly matters a lot, but as Ian Morris[22] and Robert Kaplan[23] have recently well shown, it matters differently at different periods of history and in different parts of the world), have witnessed relatively fast and painless democratic and market-oriented evolutions. However, if your neighbours are not Finland or Sweden, but are for example, states more akin to Afghanistan, the reform processes – be they political,

---

[21] J. Kurth, 'Coming to Order', *The American Interest*, 2007, vol. II, No. 6 , p. 60.

[22] I. Morris, *Why the West Rules – For Now: The Patterns of History and What They Reveal about Future*, Profile Books, 2011.

[23] R. Kaplan, *The Revenge of Geography: What the Map Tells Us About Coming Conflicts and the Battle Against Fate*, Random House, 2012.

economic and social – are much more difficult. Therefore, slightly paraphrasing an old proverb, we may say that 'tell me who are your neighbours and I will tell you who you are'.

These factors, together with their common historical heritage – both pre-Soviet and Soviet – have to be taken into account when one is assessing the process of reforms – their speed, success or failure – in different parts of the former Soviet Union.

Those who, from the outside, push for quick democratic reforms in societies that are not able to carry them through, i.e. in societies which do not have the economic, political and social capacities to rapidly implement such reforms, or whose historical baggage does not contain any seeds of liberalism, are either incompetent, or they are consciously trying to weaken states whose governments refuse to toe the line. Remarking specifically on Russia under President Yeltsin, Michael Cox, John Ikenberry and Takashi Inoguchi, for example, wrote that '[T]he causes of the failed transition [of Russia to democracy] are many. But the West cannot escape its fair share of the blame. It was especially foolish to demand the impossible and to believe one could construct a viable capitalism and American-style democracy together – the so-called "market democracy paradigm" – on the fragments left behind by Soviet communism. This was "panglossian complacency" of the highest order and was bound to end in tears. Put bluntly, Russia simply could not bear the weight that the West placed on it'.[24] However, in our view, it was not only 'panglossian complacency' (although for many both in the West and in Russia it certainly was) that contributed to the failure of Russian reforms. For some it was the conscious desire to enfeeble Russia, to turn it into a state that would toe the line and follow Washington's lead without questioning its wisdom, without attempting to pursue its own national interests, especially when the latter differ from interests of Western countries (particularly from those of the United States). Jeffrey Sachs has, with hindsight, recognised that at the beginning of the 1990s, when Russia's economy was undergoing 'shock therapy', 'many of Washington's power brokers were still fighting the Cold War. They saw Russia's economic collapse as geopolitical

[24] M. Cox, G.J. Ikenburry, Takachi Inoguchi (eds), *American Democracy Promotion*, OUP, 2000, p. 15.

victory, a decisive one that ensured U.S. supremacy'.[25] That was certainly so. Dick Cheney, who at the beginning of the 1990s was the United States Secretary of Defence, for example, openly encouraged the break-up of the Soviet Union, arguing that 'if democracy fails, we're better off if they are small'.[26] Therefore, as Daniel Treisman concludes, taking account of the humanitarian assistance that the West extended to Russia in the 1990s, as well as the loaned interest payments by Russia to Western countries, including the debts of the former Soviet Union, what Russia got from the West was minuscule. In his opinion, the amount of Western investments into Russia for the support of democracy was less that the cost of three B2 bombers.[27]

As Gorbachev's policies unwittingly led to the dismantling of the Soviet Union (for which the world and the peoples of many former Soviet republics should be thankful), this is the main reason of his unpopularity in Russia. With hindsight, it is possible to conclude that Gorbachev, as a leader of a superpower, and especially if we compare him with Deng Xiaoping, was a rather naive politician. Allen Lynch is right that 'Deng also understood China much better than Gorbachev did the Soviet Union'.[28] We would add that Deng also understood the world much better than Gorbachev, who believed that the West would embrace the reformist Soviet Union, help it integrate into the world community as one of the guarantors of a new world order based on the supremacy of international law where common values would prevail over narrow national interests, and all nations, in their external relations, would live in accordance with international law, and their domestic arrangements would conform to the principles of the Universal Declaration of Human Rights. Gorbachev did not understand that for leaders of powerful states, universal values are more often than not particular interests clad in lofty words (though they may sometimes sincerely believe in them, and feel genuinely offended if somebody doubts their sincerity).

One of the important differences between China's and the Soviet Union's reforms, and factors for their respective success and failure

---

[25] N. Klein, op.cit., p. 250.
[26] D.S. Foglesong, op.cit., p. 205.
[27] D. Treisman, op.cit., p. 297.
[28] A.C. Lynch, 'Deng's and Gorbachev's Reform Strategies Compared', *Russia in Global Affairs*, 24 June 2012.

that Allen Lynch analysis[29] was that the Soviet Union as a whole and its biggest part – Russia – was a European country and its intellectuals, i.e. its opinion makers, were essentially European in their outlook, and therefore they would not have supported a politically authoritarian model of economic modernisation. In China, on the contrary, intellectuals as a whole were supportive of Deng Xiaoping's model of economic modernisation under the Chinese Communist Party's leadership. At the end of his insightful article on the comparison of Deng's and Gorby's reforms, Lynch proposes an interesting, and in our opinion, useful counterfactual thought experiment that may be of more general interest.[30] What would have happened had Yuri Andropov, a former long-time KGB chief who became the Secretary General of the Soviet Communist Party after Brezhnev's death in 1982, been in better health and hadn't died in less than two years in office (Lynch is probably right that had Deng died soon after he started his reforms, China today wouldn't have been today's China) Lynch correctly, in our opinion, assumes that Andropov would not have relinquished the leading role of the Communist Party, and would not have initialised political liberalisation of Soviet society (not in his lifetime). Lynch is also right that Andropov garnered more authority not only among the political and military elite, but also among Soviet society at large (the clear exception being the Soviet intelligencia) than Gorbachev. And Andropov certainly was enough of a realist; having been at the head of the KGB for a long time, he certainly knew the real situation in the country better than most of the Soviet leadership, and most world leaders. Therefore, it is quite possible that Andropov's economic reforms would have borne fruit, and the Soviet Union would have existed for much longer than it did under Gorbachev. However, I doubt that the Soviet Union under Andropov would have been the same success story as China under Deng and his successors has been; the reasons for such a conclusion lie in the differences between the Chinese and Soviet societies (the USSR – a European society, China – an Asian nation; China - a more or less homogeneous society, the USSR – a multiethnic, multi-religious country; the USSR – an urbanised, industrially

29 A.C. Lynch, op. cit.
30 Ibid.

developed society, China at the end of the 1970s – basically a rural, agricultural society etc.) as well as the differences between the personalities of the two men. If Deng was a visionary pragmatist who well understood his people, Yuri Andropov was an ideologue, though cleverer, more knowledgeable and personally less corrupt than most of his colleagues, but nevertheless an ideologue who believed in the eventual superiority of the communist system, and whose worldview was not shaken but strengthened as a result of the Soviet suppression of the Hungarian revolt against communist rule and Soviet domination in 1956, when Andropov was the Soviet Ambassador to Budapest.

Yeltsin, in August of 1991, standing firm against the putschists, later used all the proper lexicon necessary to be liked by many in the West, but it was not as much democracy that emerged under Yeltsin (though elements of it were of course present) as the oligarchisation of society, and a process of plundering Russia's wealth.[31] That is why what is described in the West as a backlash against democracy under President Putin has to be seen in the context of what happened in Russia under Yeltsin, and to a great extent as a reaction to these processes. Adi Ignatius, the former *Wall Street Journal* bureau chief in Moscow, reminisced at the end of 2007 about Yeltsin's Russia of the 1990s in the following way: 'I retain three indelible images from that time. The first: the legions of Ivy League – and other Western – educated "experts" who roamed the halls of the Kremlin and the government, offering advice, all ultimately ineffective on everything from conducting free elections to using "shock therapy" to juice the

[31] The process of the pillaging of Russia has been well documented in Pavel Khlebnikov's book *Godfather of the Kremlin and the History of Pillage of Russia*, which in English translation carries the title *Godfather of the Kremlin: The Decline of Russia in the Age of Gangster Capitalism* (Harvest Books, 2001). In this book he showed how Boris Berezovsky, the Russian oligarch who now lives in the United Kingdom, made his first millions, and then used them, bribing and buying state officials to make his billions. Khlebnikov – an American journalist of Russian origin, who was the Russian Editor of Forbes – was gunned down in Moscow in July 2004 in what seemed to be a contract killing. In his articles and books he may have offended many influential people, including some oligarchs as well as Chechen militants. In 2003, he published a book, *Conversation with a Barbarian* (Moscow, Detective Press, 2003), in which he depicted in the most negative light one of the Chechen field commanders, Hozh-Ahmed Nukhayev, harshly criticized Chechen militants generally and made slighting remarks on Islam. In May 2006, a jury in Moscow acquitted the three Chechens who were accused of having murdered Khlebnikov.

economy to privatizing state-owned assets'.[32] As *Time Magazine* concluded in 2007, it is easy to see why the Russians today are looking for greatness and supporting Vladimir Putin 'after the humiliations of the 1990s, when Harvard M.B.A.s flooded Russia, preaching Western style democracy, only to let a small cabal of criminals bleed the country dry.[33]

The sudden and unprepared introduction of liberal reforms in Russia under Boris Yeltsin led to a chaos that resulted in nostalgia for order (*poryadok* in Russian and *ordnung* in German have been the words used to tighten the screws). Such nostalgia for past stability could be observed in many, if not in most (the Baltic countries being the only clear exceptions) post-Soviet states. Therefore, when President Putin, after the Beslan tragedy of 2004 where Chechen terrorists attacked a school in this Northern Ossetia's town, introduced a series of anti-democratic and anti-liberal political reforms, which moreover had nothing to do with anti-terrorist measures but were meant to construct a so-called 'vertical of power', the critical comments by Russian liberals, including the Russian Human Rights Ombudsman Vladimir Lukin, sounded very much like lone voices crying out in the wilderness. By then, Russians had generally had enough of Yeltsin era 'democracy' and experiments in free market 'shock therapy'.

3. *ON PUTIN'S AUTHORITARIANISM*

Anatol Lieven, a long-time Russian observer from the *New America Foundation*, now a Professor at *King's College, London*, who seems to comprehend Russia much better than most of his fellow citizens, has astutely observed, in writing about the prospects of democracy in Russia that:

> This [prospects of democracy in Russia] is indeed a problematic issue because the Russian president [Putin during his second term as President of Russia] has grown increasingly authoritarian. But U.S. expectations in this area are unrealistic. After all, the "democracy" that Putin has allegedly overthrown was, in fact, not a real democracy

---

[32] A. Ignatius, 'A Tsar is Born', *Time Magazine*, December 3, 2007-January 7, 2008, p. 42.

[33] Ibid., p. 60.

> at all but a pseudo-democracy ruled over by corrupt and brutal oligarchical clans. During the 1990s, the administration of Boris N. Yeltsin, under the sway of the oligarchs and the liberal elites, rigged elections, repressed the opposition and launched a bloody and unnecessary war in Chechnya – all with the support of Washington.[34]

Therefore, when Putin came to power in 2000, most people in Russia initially supported Putin's steps of 'strengthening the vertical of power', which of course was not a step towards democracy, but one whose purpose was in increasing stability, and at least at the beginning, and for a while after, contributed to the economic growth and well-being of the people (though the role of the high oil prices played a larger role than Putin's policies in raising the living standards of the Russian people). Richard Sakwa observes that 'while there are numerous points over which one may take issue with Putin's administration, the relentless negativity in which every action was perceived to be yet another brick in the edifice of an authoritarian order under construction in Russia is fundamentally mistaken. Russia's highly complex and undoubtedly contradictory process of re-establishing the authority of the state and the rudimentary notion of order was reduced to a single narrative of authoritarian restoration, and prepared the way for what many considered to be a reprise of Cold War confrontation.'[35] This misunderstanding of Russia's problems and predicaments, and a failure to understand that there is no fast track to democracy without backlashes (at best, two steps forward, one step back, paraphrasing Lenin), as mentioned by Professor Sakwa, alienated many in Russia, and made them sceptical of Western values and the sincerity of Western experts, the latter having advised Yeltsin and his ministers.

As a result of the transformations under President Yeltsin, in which the role of Western advisers was quite significant, Russia became weak, and not many Russians are thankful of that. That is why Yeltsin's successor, Vladimir Putin, a former KGB officer who limited democracy (if there was any democracy to limit in the first place; or as many Russians thought at that time, introduced some

---

[34] A. Lieven, 'Why are we trying to reheat the Cold War?' *The Los Angeles Times*, 19 March 2006.

[35] R. Sakwa, 'New Cold War' or twenty years of crisis? Russia and international politics', *International Affairs*, 2008, vol. 84, p. 249.

order into anarchy and chaos) during his first two terms as President of Russia (2000–2008) was genuinely popular in Russia. As two Russians wrote in the middle of Putin's second term as President in the *International Herald Tribune*: '[T]he United States finds much fewer supporters in Russia today than it did 15 years ago. Russian perceptions have changed dramatically, for domestic discourse, political stability and order have greater value than democracy. Democracy is often associated with the chaos, the collapse of the state and the material gains of the very few that occurred in the '90s'.[36]

The post-Soviet history of Russia moves in a circular fashion, or rather like a pendulum and there is certain logic to it. The following graph illustrates well a problem that is not idiosyncratic to Russia alone. This is a so-called J-Curve, a graphic tool applied in political sciences to illustrate the hazards of transformation of regimes from

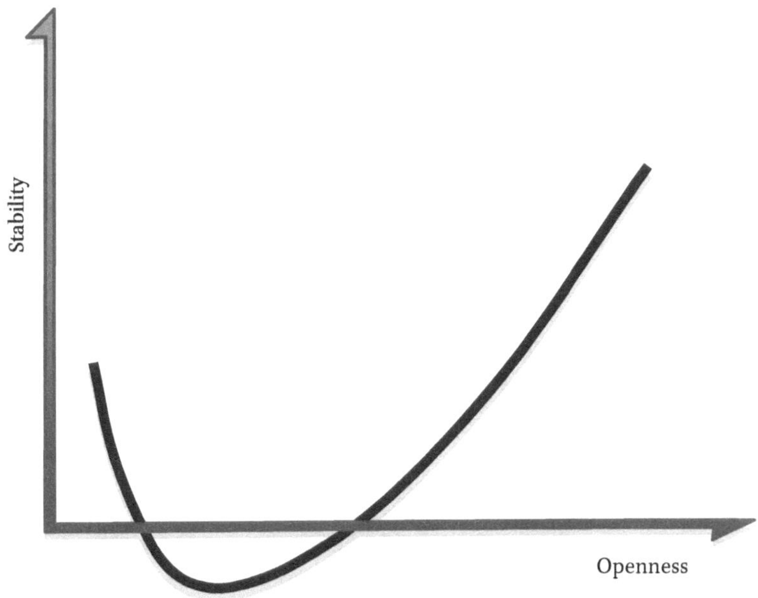

Representation of J-Curve.

36 I. Zevelev, K. Glebov, 'If you want democracy, don't push Putin', *The International Herald Tribune*, 13 March 2006.

authoritarianism or totalitarianism towards democracy.[37] The concept of J-Curve explains the nature and causes of the difficulties and pitfalls inherent in the process of a transition from closed into open societies. Some of them may not even survive such a transition (like the USSR and the former Yugoslavia, for example), but all multiethnic or multi-religious countries are especially prone to such a danger.

The vertical axis of the graph measures stability; the higher a country is on this axis, the more stable it is. On the horizontal axis, there is the measure of openness. The further to the right, the more open, free and democratic is a society. According to Ian Bremmer, 'movement from left to right along the J-Curve demonstrates that a country that is stable because it is closed must go through a period of dangerous instability as it opens to the outside world'.[38] Of course, it is not only the opening up of a country to the outside world that is wrought with potential of instability; internal liberalisation, like Gorbachev's policies of *glasnost* and *perestroika* in the former USSR, are even more, and not less hazardous. Putin's response to the instability and economic decline of Yeltsin's Russia was in accordance with the theory of J-Curve. In order to stop the economic downfall, put an end to disintegrative tendencies and restore stability, the authorities chose to climb up on the left side of the vertical axis, i.e. they tightened the screws and quite predictably also overreacted. Measures to prevent the fall into the bottom of the J-Curve may involve measures that curb individual liberties and even repressions. Therefore, it is preferable to move step by step to the right on the horizontal axis, i.e. not resorting to shock therapy. The simultaneous use of economic and political shock therapies would be especially dangerous; they seldom succeed.

4. *RUSSIA – NOT LOST TO DEMOCRACY*

Today Russia is not at all lost to democracy, though the mistakes of the 1990s, coupled with purposeful attempts to weaken the country

---

37 I. Bremmer, *J Curve: A New Way to Understand Why Nations Rise and Fall*, Simon & Schuster, 2006.

38 Ibid., p. 5.

and require it to follow Washington's lead have made Russia's path to democracy even more tortuous than it would have otherwise been. Of course the Kremlin has not been able to rise to the level of the challenges that the country faces. Ruslan Khestanov, the Deputy Editor-in-Chief of *Russky Reporter* has pointed out that '[I]n the formal terms of electoral procedures, a rollback from democracy would seem a reasonable enough statement. Competitive transfer of power is a reasonable distinguishing mark for democracy. On the other hand, a little knowledge of Russia's recent experiences would suggest otherwise. With such knowledge, there is little doubt that the chances of a stable democratic regime being established in Russia are much higher today than, say, at any time during the Yeltsin presidency'.[39] This view seems to indicate that the few steps backward after Yeltsin's chaos period may have been necessary in order to continue moving towards a more liberal and democratic order. It may indeed be so, though as the 2011–2012 protest movements indicated, democracy does not come about from above by fiat; it has to be actively demanded by the people. More than a decade of rule by Putin, first as President, then as Prime Minister and his third reincarnation as President of Russia in 2012, as well as four years of Dmitry Medvedev's warming of the throne, has forced many Russians to reconsider their scepticism towards democracy and freedoms. Sergei Karaganov, one of the proponents of state capitalism for certain societies, has expressed the view that 'there is not yet any definitive answers to the question whether "authoritarian capitalism" will be the final model of development for Russian or is it a step towards a more liberal model'.[40] In his opinion, the second option is plausible. However, do not expect Russian democracy to be a 'Western style democracy'. Whether it will be called 'sovereign', 'directed' or 'managed' or better simply democracy, it would be in any case different from the democracy that exists, say, in Western Europe; it will contain specific characteristics corresponding to the history, traditions, culture and even size of Russia. And it is especially important

---

[39] R. Khestanov, 'The path to democracy, Russian style', *Russky Reporter*, 27 February, 2008.

[40] S. Karaganov (ed.), *Russia and the World. A New Epoch of 12 Years that May Change Everything* (in Russian), Olymp, 2008, p. 55.

not to forget that it is left to the Russian people to decide what kind of democracy they want.

Today's Western concerns over democracy in Russia have an interesting angle, one that is present in Western policies *vis-à-vis* some other non-Western countries as well. Jonathan Dimbleby, for example, writes that 'for all their great virtues, the Russian people are not sleep-walking into this brave new world [he calls it Putin's crypto-fascism] but positively embracing it. So far from having democracy stolen from them, they consciously seek to give it away.'[41] If it were indeed so, if Russians indeed do not care at all about democracy, then would it be not only futile but unintelligent, arrogant and even undemocratic to wish for them what they do not want for themselves! The truth seems rather to be that many, and probably the majority of Russians increasingly care about democracy, but they do not necessarily understand democracy as most Westerners do, and more importantly, due to their history – both ancient and recent – they value stability, economic development and certain freedoms (e.g., the freedom to travel abroad, the freedom of information) which they now possess, but never enjoyed under the Soviet regime, higher than democracy. Dimbleby wrote that he returned from his journey to Russia 'more aware than ever before that the Russian people are not like "us". In a fundamental way they neither belong to the West nor share Western values.'[42] My conclusion, having travelled and lived not only in Russia but in also in many much more 'exotic' countries, is that people, in most cases are very much like 'us'. Such a conclusion requires, of course, that the concluder can, as a minimum, speak the language of the people he judges, shares their food, music and in general partakes in and understands their culture. Human beings are all quite similar. It is societies, due to their histories, traditions, political institutions and levels of economic development that are rather different.

There is no doubt that Russia needs to become more democratic, and one may well hope that the authorities, and foremost President Vladimir Putin, have received and understood the message

---

[41] J. Dimbleby, 'Seduced by a Smile', *The Sunday Times* (News Review), 24 February 2008, p. 2.

[42] Ibid., p. 1.

sent by the 2011–2012 protests, which were engendered by the rigged Parliamentary elections of December 2011, where the pro-Putin United Russia party won just under 50% of the vote (down from 64% in 2007) and the Presidential elections of March 2012. Democracy is demanded by, and necessary for the people of Russia. If before the anti-Putin demonstrations of 2011–2012 there may have been an impression that the majority of the Russian people may have indeed been content with 'authoritarianism with the consent of the governed',[43] as the system was sometimes called, since then the mood in the country has changed.

5. RUSSIA – TOO BIG TO PRACTICE BANDWAGGONING

It seems that the objectives of Washington's policy of advancing democracy and supporting 'colour revolutions' and different 'awakenings' and 'springs' in strategically or resourcefully important regions are twofold: if democracy, due to American efforts, takes root in said countries, they would hopefully become allies of Washington, if not for any other reason than being grateful for the support they have received from the US; however, if a country fails to build a sustainable democracy and even ends up in turmoil, it becomes a weak entity that does not threaten American or wider Western interests. Naturally, the first scenario is preferable but the second, from the point of view of US interests, is not a complete failure either (though weak or failed states may become hotspots of terrorism). This point was made by Anatol Lieven and John Hulsman who observed that 'among neoconservatives and liberal hawks, the desire to spread democracy can also take a form that is explicitly dedicated to the weakening or even destruction of other states, even when these are by no means full-fledged enemies of America'.[44] They added that 'too many American Democratists (i.e. those who believe in what the US National Security Strategies of 2002, 2006 and 2010 say about the export of democracy) base their approach to the world on the assumption that they know how best to run countries

---

[43] Trenin, op.cit., loc. 301.

[44] A. Lieven, J. Hulsman, *Ethical Realism. A Vision for America's Role in the World*, Pantheon Books, 2006, p. 104.

of which they know nothing and whose languages they don't speak – countries that quite often they have never even visited'.[45]

Sometimes there does indeed remains the impression that the West, and especially Washington, prefers to deal with weak or even unstable entities rather than face stable and strong but uncomfortable states that pursue their own interests (like the US itself naturally does), and do not always act according to the 'Washington consensus' (WC not only in the narrow economic-financial sense, but also in the wider philosophic-political sense) but prefer to adhere to, say, the 'Beijing consensus' (BC) or have their own parochial (no offence meant) understanding of their national interests. This does not mean that there is nothing good to the WC or that the BC is preferable to the WC; the point is that in today's globalising world there should be some consensus between the WC and BC, and a realisation that neither of them can be imposed on others. Nations, like individuals (and especially the young) tend to reject ideas and practices that they perceive as imposed on them, even if they are ultimately for their own good. The adage that the road to hell is paved with good intentions is truer in international relations than in any other field of human activity – far too many people assume that other societies are like us and have the same value systems. As Graham Greene's Thomas Fowler says about Alden Pyle, the quiet American: 'He was impregnably armoured by his good intentions and his ignorance.' Furthermore, Fowler had never known 'a man who had better motives for all the trouble he caused'. Most dangerous of all may be the desire, often even a missionary zeal, to make those who are different from us more like us. It is one of the characteristics of so-called 'soft power' that something has to be not only accepted voluntarily, but also has to be perceived as accepted voluntarily.

All the changes in both Russia's domestic and especially in its foreign policy (which has certainly become more assertive and independent), and Western reactions to these policies, has created a perception in Russia that the West, and especially Washington, indeed prefers to deal with a weak Russia which follows the Western lead. This inability to understand and accept that Russia has its own

---

[45] Ibid., p. 109.

interests and perceptions, and that they may differ from those of Washington or Brussels, is counterproductive to the development of mutually beneficial relations between Russia and the West. One would indeed be naïve, or believe others to be naïve, to imagine that Russia would not use its vast energy resources in order to promote its foreign policy aims. It would be like expecting the US to ignore its superior economic and military power in conducting its foreign relations. It would be like Madeleine K. Albright's questioning of Colin Powell: 'What's the point of having this superb military you're always talking about if we can't use it?'[46] No state, especially if it belongs or believes itself to belong to the category of great powers, and has possessed such leverages, has ever failed to use them to its own advantage.

An old friend of mine from my Moscow days, whom I have not seen for at least a decade, but who has meanwhile become Foreign Minister of Russia, Sergei Lavrov, has written that 'those who study Russia professionally (and not just Soviet studies), and are working out policy toward it, must understand that it would be naive to expect from us readiness to be content in the world with the role of one being led',[47] and that, 'Russia has acquired freedom to behave in accordance with its historical mission, that is, to be itself, and hence to make its full contribution to the common cause of maintaining international stability and harmony between civilizations at the critical stage of the formation of a new architecture of international relations'.[48] Although in these statements there are some unrealistic observations dictated, probably, by nostalgia for past glory, there are also grains of truth. Some countries, due to their history, size and potential as well as their perception of the world based on these factors, cannot be subject of bandwaggoning, following the lead of a hegemonic actor.

In the case of smaller countries, and depending on whether a country possesses the necessary preconditions for building sustainable democratic institutions, outside efforts may bear fruit, but in

---

[46] M. Dobbs, 'With Albright, Clinton Accepts New U.S. Role', *The Washington Post*, 8 December, 1996.

[47] Moskovskiye Novosti, 'Russia in Global Politics', *Moscow News*, 3 March 2006.

[48] 'Sixty Years after Fulton: Lessons of the Cold War and Our Time', *Rossiiskaya Gazeta*, 6 March 2006.

the absence of such necessary preconditions a country may end up, if not as a failed state, then at least as a failed experiment in democratisation. In the cases of China, as well as Russia, such attempts inevitably lead to confrontation. In his pre-election article on Russia's foreign policy in winter 2012, the then presidential candidate Putin wrote: 'We cannot be isolated, and we do not want to be isolated... ... At the same time, everything we do will be based on our own interests and goals, not on decisions other countries impose on us'.[49] This may be put too bluntly and undiplomatically, in a style typical of Putin, but the truth of the matter is that Russia is indeed too big to be led. This has to be understood; otherwise there would be misperceptions and conflicts. British expert Richard Sakwa wrote already some years ago: 'The international system today does not have a mechanism for integrating rising great powers. This applies to China, as well as to Russia and some other countries'.[50] We believe there is a deep truth in this short remark, which is not limited to countries as big as Russia or China. As Putin continued in his pre-election article, 'Russia has practically always had the privilege of pursuing an independent foreign policy and this is how it will be in the future'.[51] First, this is a response to Yeltsin's failed attempts to have Russia accepted by Washington as an equal, independent player who may have its own interests, different from those of the United States, but who nevertheless may be a partner of, and on good terms with, Washington. Secondly, this remark expresses the truth that nations react differently to attempts to 'civilise' them, to induce them to correspond to the dominant trend. Quite a few happily follow the lead, others do it grudgingly, while some become prickly, and rushing them becomes even more counter-productive. Thirdly, and from the Kremlin's perspective, attempts to always carry out independent foreign policy in an interdependent world are counter-productive. One of the shortcomings of Moscow's foreign policy has been its lack of flexibility, its inability to recognise that in a world where even Washington increasingly cannot always have its

[49] V. Putin, 'Russia and the Changing World', *Moscow News*, 27 February, 2012.

[50] R. Sakwa, 'New Cold War' or twenty years' crisis?, *International Affairs* 2008 v. 84, No 2, p. 255.

[51] V. Putin, op. cit.

way, ambitions that are not backed up by sufficient material and ideological resources, i.e. sufficient 'hard' and 'soft' power, do more harm than good to a country's interests.

In previous chapters we discussed how, in the eyes of many American politicians and experts, the world has to follow, as if by default, the road trotted by the Anglo-American nations – first by Great Britain, and then by the United States. Fyodor Lukyanov, responding to the question by a journalist, of why Russia had not followed Washington's lead, as Germany and Japan, for example, had done after they had been defeated in World War II, said that not only was Russia not defeated in a war, but that in the 1990s the West did not even attempt to use *vis-à-vis* Russia any policies akin to Marshall plan to integrate the country to the West. Now, in 2012, continued Lukyanov, 'we cannot follow the Anglo-Saxon policies since today nobody can be certain that they lead somewhere'.[52]

External pressure on Russia through Western support of and financial aid for Russian non-governmental organizations may also have been sometimes counter-productive. There is a bizarre situation in Russia – although tens, and in rare cases even hundreds, of thousands of people protested in various cities across Russia, notably in Moscow and St Petersburg against the policies of the Kremlin and called for more democracy and fairer elections, most of the leaders of these protest movements are considerably less popular in Russia than President Vladimir Putin or even Prime Minister Dmitry Medvedev. These leaders lack an internal domestic legitimacy that cannot be compensated for by external support and popularity. The latter may even do more harm than good. Robert W. Merry's astute analysis of the reaction in the Arab world, as well as in Russia and China, to the democracy-promoting efforts of American, or American funded, NGOs such as the National Democratic Institute (NDI) and the International Republican Institute (IRI), shows that in many cases their pushy and insensitive interference to promote change has been counterproductive.[53] He writes: 'But the arrogance of many of these people is almost guaranteed to be incendiary in target countries. Consider the words of Michael McFaul, once the

52 Interview with F. Lukyanov, 13 March 2012, *Argumenty i Facty*, 8 June 2012.
53 R. Merry, 'American NGOs Abroad', *The National Interest*, 2 April 2012.

NDI's representative in Russia. "We are not going to get into the business of dictating [Russia's] path [to democracy]", he said. "We are just going to support what we like to call 'universal values' – not American values, universal values'.[54] Further, Merry puts a most pertinent question: 'Who, one might ask, is the arbiter of such universal values, and how does one get appointed as crusader in their behalf'.[55] It does not help either that now Michael McFaul is the United States Ambassador to Moscow, appointed by President Obama. Robert Merry explains: 'For anyone trying to understand why this anger is welling up in those countries, it might be helpful to contemplate how Americans would feel if similar organizations from China or Russia or India were to pop up in Washington, with hundreds of millions of dollars given to them by those governments, bent to influencing our politics'.[56] This is not to say that many human rights NGOs, such as *Amnesty International* or *Medicine sans Frontier* or many others – both local and international, have not done and are not doing important work in improving the human rights situations in many parts of the world. I have worked with many of them and I admire their dedication and good will. However, for such work to be effective, not counterproductive, it has to be carried out with a profound understanding of the character of the target society, a knowledge of the balance of political forces in the country, its potential and limitations, and most importantly has to not be seen as arrogantly preaching to local people and governments to accept 'universal values' that are not only 'American values' (I sometimes wonder whether there can be any universal values that are not American values). Laurence Jarvik, in writing on developments in Central Asia that however have relevance for Russia as well, observes: 'Thus, traditional elites had an advantage over the Western-sponsored NGOs: they knew their society organically and were masters of how to balance different elements—whether clan-related, geographical, ethnic, business, political, or international'.[57] A recent adoption in

[54] Ibid.
[55] Ibid.
[56] Ibid.
[57] L. Jarvik,'NGOs: A 'New Class' in International Relations', *Orbis: Journal of World Affairs*, 2007, Vol. 51, No.2, p. 224.

Russia of the new law that regulates the activities of NGOs,[58] which obligate those NGOs who receive funding from abroad to register as 'foreign agents', with a requirement to publish biannual reports on their activities and have themselves submitted to annual financial audits is indeed, as it is often called, controversial. On the one hand, it gives the authorities an instrument to harass those organisations, especially human rights NGOs, which are critical of the authorities, and judging by earlier experience, the authorities will hardly fail to use (abuse) this law against such NGOs. On the other hand, knowing full well that there aren't any free lunches, and those who pay the piper also call the tune, and also judging by previous experience, one should not hold any doubts that those who pay (and often it is Western, especially American, taxpayer money) do attempt to change domestic and foreign policy in Russia (and as an ultimate aim – to effect regime change), i.e. to do what in the language of international law is called 'interference in internal affairs'. Of course, such an almost even-handed critique of those who are on the supply end and those who are on the receiving end does not help mobilise the masses against or for any cause. However, this is not our aim. There are too many who do exactly that. Our aim is to deconstruct lofty words to reveal the underlying interests of various players.

Western diplomats in non-Western countries, and often even NGOs, typically have contacts with leading elites, whom they as a rule do not respect, and sometimes even hate and despise,[59] as well as with those who are in radical opposition to the authorities, whom they usually like and support. In countries where there is a democracy deficit, or where elements of democracy are completely lacking, both of these categories of people are rarely representative of the majority of the population. Julia Sweig of the US Council on Foreign Relations has identified what she calls the '80/20 problem',[60] meaning that the United States, in its dealing with a particular country,

---

58 Russian Parliament Approves NGO 'Foreign Agents' Law, RIA Novosti, 6 July 2012, en.rian.ru/Russia/20120706/174436993.html.

59 See, e.g., Craig Murray's *Murder in Samarkand: A British Ambassador's Controversial Defiance of Tyranny in the War on Terror* (Mainstream Publishing, 2006).

60 J. Sweig, *Friendly Fire: Losing Friends and Making Enemies in the Anti-American Century*, New York, Public Affairs, 2006.

mostly relies on the English speaking elite – usually not more than 20 percent of the population (in my opinion, a very optimistic estimate that may be true in some former British colonies or in Europe but certainly not, say, in Russia or Central Asia where Russian in still the *lingua franca*). To better understand a country, it is absolutely necessary to communicate with representatives of the remaining 80 percent of its population – not only because of its numerical weight, but even more for the reason that this majority is more representative of the country than the 20 percent of governing or opposing elites. To understand a country and its problems, talking to people in the marketplace, to a taxi driver, to a barber or to those who work out with you in a local gym (and not to those who swim with you in the swimming pool of a five star hotel), often helps more than spending hours with government officials or members of a radical opposition though, naturally, one cannot and should not ignore them.

Outside influence on these matters, though never great or decisive, will have the desired effect if outsiders are not seen as giving unsolicited advice. The paradox of the process of promoting human rights and democracy abroad is that often, though not always, the less one outright talks about human rights and democracy, especially in countries like Russia or China, the more one may achieve in these fields; though in any case, in the absence of favourable internal conditions an outsider can achieve very little since external factors are usually secondary, though in certain circumstances they may play the role of that proverbial straw that 'breaks the camel's back'. This, of course, does not mean that one should not criticise Russia's, or China's for that matter, human rights records. However, if one wants to help achieve practical positive results, and not satisfy one's sense of self-righteousness or hope to promote regime-change, one should find ways doing that without antagonizing the authorities and the people. More often than not those whom Western organisations, especially those that are supported by or linked to Western (especially American) governments, actively prop up, enjoy little internal support. Western media attention on them (some of them especially like to provoke the authorities into arrests before Western TV cameras) may make them well known abroad, but at home their popularity may even decline because of it. Instead, drawing attention to the plight of those genuine human rights activists who are persecuted by the authorities is the right way to proceed. This of course means that one has to know the country well, as well as knowing who is who and what they stand for.

6. *RUSSIA AND ITS CLOSE NEIGHBOURS*

Vladimir Putin began his third presidency's foreign policy by emphasising the importance of Moscow's relations with its neighbours.[61] Although it is natural that Putin puts Russia's interest (as he and those who support him understand them), in its foreign policy generally, as well as in its relations with Russia's neighbours, first, the Kremlin is not going to revive the Soviet Union in any form, as some of Russia's neighbours assume (whether they seriously believe it or use such rhetoric to annoy Russia is another matter). Dmitri Trenin is right when he, after an extensive study of the foreign policy of post-Soviet Russia, concludes that 'Russia has abandoned the age-old pattern of territorial growth'[62] and that 'Abkhazia and South Ossetia were turned into military buffers, but only in extremis'.[63] The Kremlin's recognition of Abkhazia and South Ossetia as *de jure* independent states, though contrary to international law (notwithstanding that it was Georgia who initiated the military conflict in August 2008) and politically unwise (it alienated some of Russia's influential friends, like China or India, who otherwise would have welcomed Russia's tough response to Georgia), was Moscow's overreaction to Georgia's attack. The Russian leadership saw Saakashvili as an American proxy who was acting on behalf, and with the knowledge and encouragement, of Washington. They did not believe that it was Saakashvili – a bit of a loose cannon, who, having used his own initiative, decided to regain lost territories. This, combined with NATO's unwise and certainly prematurely eager responses to Saakashvili's and Yuschenko's (the then President of Ukraine) frantic efforts to join the Atlantic Alliance, caused Russia to create such buffer zones in the Caucasus, *de facto* controlling these two territories. Trenin continues:

---

[61] V. Putin, 'Russia and the Changing World', *Moscow News*, 27 February, 2012; S. Markedonov, 'Putin's Eurasian Aspirations', *The National Interest*, 29 May, 2012.
[62] D. Trenin, op.cit., loc. 2011.
[63] Ibid.

> Russia, however, is not the only post-imperial state in the former Soviet Union. In an ironic way, all the new states that have emerged from the USSR are also afflicted with elements of post-imperial, or in some cases, post-colonial, syndrome. This can be described as seeking to distance themselves from the former hegemon, attempting to create new national myths and write new suitable histories of their nations, and yet exhibiting many of the features usually associated with the Soviet Union, among them doublespeak, lack of serious debate, and intolerance.[64]

This is true. Too often the policies of some of Russia's neighbours in their hostility towards the former hegemon mirror, sometimes even in an exaggerated manner, the Kremlin's own policies towards these states. Therefore, one of the obstacles to a closer integration between the European Union and Russia (or Russia and the West as a whole) is the negative historical baggage that has become a bone of contention between Russia and some of those Central and Eastern European states that until recently were either parts of the USSR (e.g., Estonia, Latvia or Lithuania), or being *de jure* independent states, were tightly controlled from the Kremlin. On the one hand, Russia is reluctant to recognise the wrongs committed in the past against these peoples or denies any responsibility for Stalin's crimes, often claiming that the Russian people did not suffer less than other Soviet peoples (which is true but does not justify the policies of the state, whose successor Russia claims to be). On the other hand, these newly independent states – members of the European Union – often use every appropriate, and even inappropriate opportunity to pick on Russia, and are always ready to take steps that would annoy Moscow, be it education in the Russian language in Estonia or Latvia where sizable Russian minorities live, the attitude towards the building of a North Stream gas pipeline in the Baltic Sea, Georgia's and Ukraine's NATO membership, NATO's construction of a missile shield without Russia's participation, or even worse, justifying and honouring as freedom-fighters those who together with the Nazis and often in SS uniform fought against the Soviets in World War II. Whenever there is more than one policy option available and one of them is not to Russia's liking, the default policy of some of these states is to render their support to this option.

---

64 Ibid., loc. 348.

It seems that, for example, Poland has recently become much more grown up, mature, responsible and free from default policy positions dictated by a historical past. And this notwithstanding that it has historically been Poland that has particularly suffered from Russia (though since 2005 Russia celebrates 4th November as a 'Day of People's Unity' that is meant to commemorate, *inter alia*, the eviction of Poles from Muscovy in 1612). At the same time Moscow responds in kind, either using economic 'sanctions' against goods from these countries or failing to recognise the Soviet Union's wrongs against these peoples, and still maintains, contrary to overwhelming evidence, that Estonia, Latvia and Lithuania voluntarily adhered to the Soviet Union. This certainly does not make these countries more trustful of Russia.

Western European nations, or so-called 'old Europe', in the sense of the term used in 2003 by the then US Secretary of Defence Donald Rumsfeld, and France and Germany in particular, have failed to strike a balance and distinguish between a support for the justified grievances of these states and their unjustified prickliness towards Russia, and in some cases have even rather passively followed the lead of these countries in determining the European Union's policies towards Russia. Instead of trying to find something positive in the negative (e.g., the significant number of native Russian speakers in Estonia and Latvia and a knowledge of Russia, the Russian language and culture among ethnic Estonians, Latvians and Lithuanians are assets that could be utilised to the benefit of these countries) and act as a bridge between Western Europe and Russia, these countries have so far served more as roadblocks on the way to closer integration between Brussels and Moscow and contributed to the alienation of Russia from Europe.

Edward Lucas, as we wrote above, though extremely and mostly unjustifiably critical of all the aspects of the domestic and foreign policies of Russia, nevertheless writes of some of Russia's neighbours that 'the paradox is that these ill-governed, tetchy and intolerant countries are the front line that the West is trying to defend.'[65] However, as he believes, defending them is a crucial task, and

---

[65] E. Lucas, *The New Cold War: How the Kremlin Menaces both Russia and the West*, Bloomsbury, 2007, p. 209.

whenever these 'ill-governed, tetchy and intolerant' governments have disagreements with Moscow, it is always the latter that is in the wrong, as if Russia by definition can do nothing right.

Let us take the reaction of the West towards the August 2008 military conflict between Georgia and Russia, which we have already mentioned above. The initial, almost as if default, reaction of the political elites of most Western countries to this conflict well illustrates how ideology blinds the perception of reality. Practically all big Western mass media outlets declared that it had been Russia that had committed an unprovoked and naked act of aggression against small, defenceless and democratic Georgia. The presidents of Estonia, Lithuania, Ukraine and Poland and the Prime Minister of Latvia immediately flew to Tbilisi to express their support to Saakashvili. However, soon drops of doubt started to filter in. Even before the *Independent Fact-Finding Mission on the Conflict in Georgia*, established by the European Union and chaired by Swiss diplomat Heidi Tagliavini, published its Report, it had become recognised by some independent observers in the West that, in truth, it had been Tbilisi that had initiated the war.[66] Tagliavini's well-balanced Report correctly emphasised that all parties involved had contributed to the escalation of tension leading up to the war, and all of them had breached international law before, as well as during, the conflict. However, finding that 'the use of force by Georgia in South Ossetia, beginning with the shelling of Tskinvhali during the night of 7/8 August' was unjustifiable under international law,[67] it laid the blame for the initiation of a military conflict squarely on Saakashvili's doorstep. Had Russia's military response

[66] See, e.g., D. Bandow, 'Tbilisi's Baggage', *The National Interest Online*, 12.31.2008; The German *Spiegel* wrote already in November 2008: 'One thing was already clear to the officers at NATO headquarters in Brussels: They thought that the Georgians had started the conflict and that their actions were more calculated than pure self-defense or a response to Russian provocation. In fact, the NATO officers believed that the Georgian attack was a calculated offensive against South Ossetian positions to create the facts on the ground, and they coolly treated the exchanges of fire in the preceding days as minor events. Even more clearly, NATO officials believed, looking back, that by no means could these skirmishes be seen as justification for Georgian war preparations' ('Did Saakashvili Lie? The West Begins to Doubt Georgian Leader', *Spiegel International Online*, 09. 15. 2008).

[67] *Independent International Fact-Finding Mission on the Conflict in Georgia*, Report, Vol.I, September 2009, p. 22.

been proportionate to the initial attack (which it was not), and within the rules of international humanitarian law (which it was not either), it would have been lawful. However, even almost half a decade later there are those who are unable to see the complexity of the conflict, and almost as if by default continue to speak of Russian aggression against Georgia in August 2008.[68] This is not an innocuous bias. Daniel Treisman is right in that the biased anti-Russian reaction in the West to the Georgia-Russia 2008 war, which was initiated by the regime of Saakashvili, in Russia forced even the opponents and critics of Vladimir Putin to support Russia's response to the Georgian attack, and to develop serious doubts about the objectivity of the Western media and the sincerity of Western leaders. So, Mikhail Gorbachev, who has been rather vocal opponent and critic of Putin's governance of Russia, found that 'Russia had to respond. Accusing Russia of having committed an act of aggression against a "small and defenceless Georgia" is not only a masterpiece of hypocrisy; it is also an act of inhumanity'.[69] Such a confrontational approach towards Russia, reminiscent of the Cold War period when the allies were always right while opponents were wrong as if by definition, does not help these Russian neighbours become less tetchy, better governed and more tolerant. On the contrary, it would entrench them in their mistaken policies, and it may indeed be a step, if not towards a new cold war (which seems to be impossible),[70] then at least towards a cold peace that is in the interest of neither Russia nor Europe.

7. RUSSIA – PART OF EUROPE?

Russia is a European country, and the Russians are Europeans that have greatly contributed to European culture; even in Russia's

[68] A. Cohen, R. Hamilton, 'The Russian Military and the Georgia War: Lessons and Implications', United States Army War College. Strategic Studies Institute. Georgia Russia war, June 2011.

[69] D. Treisman, op.cit., p. 150.

[70] Fyodor Lukyanov correctly notes that 'Russia will never play a role of the Soviet Union and, as a consequence, a new Cold War is not possible' (F. Lukyanov, Interview to the Russian newspaper *ArgumentyiFacty*, *Argumenty i Facty*, 8 June 2012.

experimentation with communism there is something that can be traced back to the European Enlightenment's heritage. One of the most insightful Russian foreign policy analysts, the Editor-in-Chief of *Russia in Global Affairs,* Fyodor Lukyanov, has written that 'Russia simply has no alternative to the West. Culturally, psychologically and historically it has always been part of the Western world, despite its many unique features. Nobody in Asia thinks of Russia as an Asian power, even though three quarters of its territory are located in Asia (but three quarters of Russia's population live in its European part).'[71]

Russia has indeed had long and close links with the rest of Europe. Putin is right when he opines that 'Russia is an inalienable and organic part of Greater Europe and European civilization. Our citizens think of themselves as Europeans.'[72] It is encouraging both for Russia as well as for Europe that the Russian President emphasises this point. At the same time, due to its size, history as well as religion –Russian Orthodoxy – she presents a special case.

Nikolay Spasskiy, a Russian diplomat and historian, well articulates the prevalent attitude of Russia's political and business elites on the 'Europeanness' of Russia: 'In whatever way we may position ourselves as a centre of power in its own right – which is quite fair – Russia will be an integral part of greater Europe. However special our national history, including the key fact that the Renaissance, the Reformation and the Enlightenment barely scratched its surface, Russia took shape within the mainstream of the pan-Western and pan-Christian historical process. In their perception of the world Russians are Europeans. It's not worth trying to deceive ourselves. As we laugh at the current turmoil in Western Europe, in fact we laugh at ourselves'.[73] However, the two additional comments to this main thesis are equally significant. First, as Spasskiy writes, '[A]t the current historical stage neither Russia nor other key international players are prepared to consider an option that would assign to Russia the role of a junior partner of another, stronger state – like the role of

---

[71] F. Lukyanov, 'Uncertain World: Will Russia become part of the West?', *RIA Novosti*, 31 May, 2012 (http://en.rian.ru/columnists/20120531/173771631.html).

[72] Ibid.

[73] N. Spasskiy, 'The Decline of Europe and Russia's Future: Why we Need Lee Kuam Yee Style of State', *Russia in Global Affairs*, 23 June 2012.

Austria-Hungary in alliance with the German Empire, or Britain in alliance with the United States'.[74] Secondly, he opines: 'Cutting the long story short, we need a Lee Kuan Yew style of state – with inevitable adjustments, because we are not Chinese. A strong, robust and honest state. A wise one. And tough, if need be. The rest will come'.[75] If we now cut this long story short it would read something like this: Russia is a European nation, though with her own idiosyncratic history; she is too big and ambitious to practice bandwaggoning; more than anything else, Russia at this moment needs a strong state *à la* Lee Kuan Yee while the rest (e.g., democracy) can wait.

In some ways, Russians, as representatives of a former superpower, which is, once again, attempting to regain its lost 'greatness', are indeed closer to Americans than to the Western Europeans. This means that in many ways Russian society is rather different from other European societies, and this has to be taken into account when we speak of the prospects and nature of democracy in Russia, or her closer integration with European institutions. Consequently, Russia's integration into the wider Europe presents some real difficulties that, nevertheless, are not insurmountable in a case where all sides fully understand the potential benefits of closer cooperation and integration and try to leave history for historians. For that to become reality, both Russia and Europe have to change their policies, though the greater changes should be expected from Russia since they concern not only her foreign policy, but her domestic politics as well. Until Russia decisively curbs corruption and indeed becomes more democratic (I don't see any contradiction in my argument that Russia has to become more democratic for the sake of the Russian people as well as for the sake of its closer integration with the rest of Europe, and my claim that Western criticism of Russia's internal institutions is often insensitive, harking back to the past and therefore sometimes even counterproductive), its closer integration into Europe is difficult. And Russia, in contradistinction to many other countries that the West has attempted to democratise and liberalise (e.g., Afghanistan, Iraq and some other Middle Eastern countries),

---

[74] Ibid.
[75] Ibid.

has indeed the potential to become, in some important respects, more like Western European countries, but would maintain an identity that would always make her different from most other European societies. At the same time, until the West changes its perceptions of Russia, the reality of relations between Europe and Russia does not change either. Dmitri Simes and Paul Saunders write: '[W]ith all the uncertainty about Russia, it may be helpful to focus on what the country is not. First and foremost, Russia is not a country governed by a messianic ideology and is neither intrinsically antidemocratic nor anti-Western. Secondly, however, Russia is not a nation of altruistic do-gooders upon whose support the United States can rely when its interests and priorities differ from Washington's.'[76]

Today's economic, political as well as military strategic realities are such that Europe and Russia need each other, though many political leaders, both in Europe as well as in Russia, have not yet been able to recognise this need. Notwithstanding declarations from both sides that the Cold War has ended and that NATO and Russia are no longer enemies, the behaviour of both parties too often bears witness to the contrary. Or rather, though both NATO and Russia (at least their most reasonable representatives) seem to genuinely understand that the other side does not present either an imminent or even realistically foreseeable military threat (though there are some Russian generals, as well as political and military leaders in some NATO countries, in particular the US and some Eastern and Central European states, who think, speak and act differently), some of their practical policies testify to the effect that they have serious doubts as to whether such a state of affairs is sustainable. Therefore, both sides seem to be preparing for worst-case scenarios and thereby, if not hastening the realization of such scenarios, then at least creating an ambience of a lack of confidence between the West and Russia. For example, if NATO's nuclear shield in Europe is indeed only meant to protect the American European allies from missiles launched by rogue states or terrorist groups, both today as well as in the foreseeable future, and is in no way even potentially directed

[76] D. Simes and P. Saunders, 'The Kremlin Begs to Differ', *The National Interest*, November/December 2009.

against Russia, then NATO has failed to persuade more actors than just Russia that this is the case. Many independent and impartial observers have remained unconvinced by the lack of concrete proofs. Can NATO guarantee that these systems can never be used against Russian missiles? Of course not! Russia, in turn, reacts nervously (and often, as in the case of the Georgian attack on South Ossetia in August 2008, it overreacts) when NATO moves closer to the Russian border (as with the possibility of Georgia's and Ukraine's NATO membership), and her behaviour often expresses mistrust and hostility towards NATO, and especially towards the United States. Russia threatens to undertake steps, like deploying *Iskander* missiles in the Kaliningrad exclave in response to NATO's missile shield, which make Russia's neighbours nervous. Dmitri Trenin writes that Russia's 'strategic bombers and ships practicing off Venezuela were designed to put the U.S. government in an uncomfortable position of watching the foreign power play in its backyard. Even though this "toy" show of force did not impress many people in the United States and won Moscow no friends, from the Kremlin perspective, it was worth it; an important point had been made'.[77] However, there was hardly anything positive in the point made by the Kremlin; it was clearly an awkward attempt to punch above one's weight. Then, Putin did not attend the May 2012 G-8 meeting in the United States, sent Prime Minister Medvedev in his stead, and ignored the opening of the London Olympics, despite being a keen athlete himself. Indeed, Prime Minister Vladimir Putin attended the opening ceremony of the 2008 Beijing Olympic Games, though his stay was cut short by the Georgian attack on its runaway territory of South Ossetia. Dispatching Medvedev in his stead to London is not a step that would improve relations with these important Western democracies (though later Putin attending judo competitions together with the British Prime Minister David Cameron).

Fyodor Lukyanov writes:

> The current difficulties in Russian-U.S. relations are hard to formulate: Putin has to understand that Obama is not George W. Bush. The world sees Obama as the polar opposite to Bush, but this is not so obvious to

77 Trenin, op. cit., loc. 539.

> the new Russian president. Putin does not trust the United States as a matter of principle, but not because of his Soviet background or KGB training. The reason is more to do with his relations with Bush during his first two presidential terms. According to Putin, who was initially pro-American, instead of gratitude, the Bush administration responded to his moves toward rapprochement with the United States in 2000–2002 by launching an aggressive expansion into the post-Soviet space, withdrawing from the 1972 ABM Treaty, announcing plans to deploy BMD [ballistic missile defence] elements near Russia's border, and setting a course for global hegemony.[78]

After 9/11, Putin indeed made a serious bid for an 'alliance with the Alliance', using the expression coined by the then US Ambassador to Moscow, now Deputy Secretary General of NATO Alexander Vershbow.[79] Immediately after the attack on the United States Putin offered his full support to the United States, and Russia worked closely with Washington on political, logistical and intelligence matters. And the Kremlin still continues to cooperate with the United States and NATO on Afghanistan. For example since 2009, Russia has allowed Afghan-bound NATO transport through its territory as an alternative to convoys through Pakistan, which were subject to militant attacks, and in 2012 it allowed its airport facilities in Ulyanovsk (Vladimir Lenin's birthplace in the Volga river) to be used as a transit point for shipments of non-lethal supplies to and from Afghanistan by air, rail and road.[80]

What are these important factors that necessitate a much closer cooperation and even integration between Europe and Russia than we have hitherto seen? First of all, it is Russia's need of Western European know-how, experience and investments that will all have a beneficial impact on the corruption-ridden economic life of Russia, while Europe needs access to Russia's markets and natural resources, especially energy. Secondly, as Washington turns its attention more and more, and understandably so, to the Pacific region, Europe needs ever more than before a friendly Russia, closely integrated, on

---

[78] F. Lukyanov, Putin and Washington: Is Conflict Inevitable? *Russia in Global Affairs*, 10 May, 2012.

[79] Trenin, op. cit., loc. 1512.

[80] G. Briansky, 'Putin signals support for NATO Afghan supply hub', 11 April 2012, *Reuters* (http://www.reuters.com/article/2012/04/11/us-russia-putin-nato-idUSBRE83A0WO20120411).

its doorstep. European nations can only lose from having unfriendly relations with Russia. Although Europe and Russia are no longer enemies and do not threaten one another, they have both failed to properly and convincingly communicate this to each other. Such a rapprochement between Europe and Russia must not be, and need not be, carried out on account of, or as a counter-balance against, any other centre of power, especially against Washington and Beijing. Russia certainly needs stable and sustainable good-neighbourly relations with China, and Washington and its European allies will continue closely cooperating, including within NATO (though, notwithstanding all the statements of Alliance's leadership, it is becoming increasingly obvious that NATO has not found a proper role in the post-bi-polar world). Yet, to move towards such cooperative arrangements, Europe, NATO and the United States, on the one hand, and Russia, on the other, will have to come to an understanding that they are not only foes at the present, but that they need not be potential enemies in the foreseeable future. This, notwithstanding many declarations to the contrary, is not yet perceived by the parties.

Relations between the West and Russia need not be as edgy and confrontational as they are today. Although there is no cold war, a kind of 'cold peace' that does not allow the realisation of the potential for cooperation (I would emphasise, in many areas, including international security, such cooperation is a must and not at all impossible) between the West and Russia has the potential for a deterioration of relations between them. Such a state of affairs between the West and Russia is mainly due to the perceptions, stemming from a past that both sides cling to, and that have a strong impact on present day realities. If one perceives the other side as a strategic rival, or even a foe or a potential enemy and acts upon such perception, then of course we have a case for a self-fulfilling prophecy. For example, Mitt Romney, the then Republican American Presidential candidate, commenting on the outcome of the meeting of the American and Russian presidents in Seoul in March 2012, said: '[R]ussia, this is, without question, our number one geopolitical foe'.[81] Although this

---

[81] http://www.acus.org/new_atlanticist/americas-number-one-geostrategic-threat.

was said in the heat of a presidential electoral campaign, such irresponsible statements and visions harking back to the past, if not determine, then at least have a negative impact on, the future relations between these two countries. Another, more general reason that we discussed in many parts of this book, is the West's desire and attempts to make non-Western societies more like themselves. Reading and watching Western media, one may conclude that not being a Western style liberal democrat is a kind of moral disability, which, like homosexuality in quite a few Muslim countries, has to be, if not punished, then at least cured. For example, in July 2007 *The Economist* wrote: 'Viktor Chernomyrdin, Russia's Ambassador to Ukraine, is no Western style democrat. Nor does this (now wealthy) founder of Gazprom and ex-prime minister pretend to be'.[82] In this assertion, there seems to be the assumption that not being a Western style democrat, or not even pretending to be or trying to become one is something abnormal and reproachable.

So, there is both the need and potential for closer cooperation between the West and Russia, and for the closer integration of Russia within European structures. Whether this need is met and potential realised depends on both sides. However, as Fyodor Lukyanov insightfully observes:

> But these are all assumptions based on the expectation that political players will follow rational considerations and act expediently. However, modern politics is full of examples of leading players making colossal blunders – either out of arrogance, complexes, dogma or misunderstanding one's own interests. The unpredictable, rapid changes that characterize global politics in the 21st century are accompanied by the unexpected reawakening of instincts from a distant past, in which relations between countries can backslide into old-fashioned realpolitik and considerations of prestige can override all else. The defining characteristic of the transitional period in which we live is uncertainty. We know not where we are headed – forward, to a new political morality, or backward, to ossified principles enforced by high-tech weapons. Anything is possible at this point.[83]

---

[82] The Economist, July 7th-13th 2007, p. 39.

[83] F. Lukyanov, 'Uncertain World: Will Russia become part of the West?', *RIA Novosti*, 31 May, 2012 (http://en.rian.ru/columnists/20120531/173771631.html).

Chapter Five

DEMOCRATIC PEACE THEORIES AND REGIME CHANGE

1. THEORY AND POLITICS OF DEMOCRATIC PEACE

Current regime changes (the so-called Arab Spring and Colour Revolutions in some of the former Soviet republics) raise interrelated issues of international relations (IR) theory and international law. Among these issues are democratic peace theory (DPT) and its role in supporting or justifying policies which are guided mainly by economic and strategic interests, external assistance or encouragement of regime change, and the use of force for humanitarian purposes [i.e. humanitarian intervention or responsibility to protect (R2P)] as well as interference, militarily or otherwise, in internal conflicts on behalf of either governments or opposition.

One of the arguments in favour of the promotion of liberal democracy all over the world is the belief in so-called 'democratic peace theories', which have their philosophical groundings in Immanuel Kant's 1795 essay *Perpetual Peace: A Philosophical Study*. In 1964 American sociologist Dean Babst published an article *Elective Governments – a Force for Peace,*[1] where he, using Quincy Wright's classical work *A Study of War,* in which Wright had analysed major wars since 1480 to 1941, concluded that the existence of independent states with elective governments, i.e. democracies, greatly enhances the chances of maintaining peace.[2] Until the end of the Cold War Kant's philosophical treatise was treated as a masterpiece of abstract philosophy that had little to do with the real world, while very few remembered or referred to Babst's article.

There was some revival of interest in the topic in the 1980s, when several authors claimed that the absence of wars between democracies or liberal states is both a fact in international relations and

[1] D. Babst, 'Elective Governments – a Force for Peace', *The Wisconsin Sociologist*, 1964, No. 3, pp. 9–14.

[2] Ibid., p. 14.

empirical law of IR theory. So, Rudolf Rummel concluded his article on the topic with the statement that 'violence will occur between states only if at least one is non-libertarian'.[3] Jack Levy even wrote that 'the absence of war between democracies comes as close as anything we have to an empirical law in international relations'.[4] The 1990s, marked by the dissolution of the Soviet Union and a new wave of democratisation in Eastern and Central Europe, saw an exponential increase of interest in the ideas expressed in those works. A new IR theory (theories) emerged – that of Democratic Peace Theory (DPT). The gist of this theory is the assertion that as democracies do not wage wars against one another, the more democracies there are in the world, the less there is the chance of a military conflict breaking out.[5] Or as President Clinton put it at the level of practical politics: 'Ultimately the best strategy to insure our security and to build a durable peace is to support the advance of democracy elsewhere'.[6]

DP theories are part of liberal IR theories, which, in contradistinction to Realist theories, which believe that conflicts, and especially military conflicts, between states are inherent in and stem from the anarchical nature of international society and do not depend (or depend little) on internal characteristics of states, pay close attention to the nature of states, to their domestic features.[7] Christopher Layne, an adherent to Realist IR theory, writes that DP theories and Realism part company on a crucial point: '[T]he former holds that changes within states can transform the nature of international politics. Realism takes the view that even if states change internally, the structure of the international political system remains the same. As systemic structure is the primary determinant of international political outcomes, structural constraints mean that similarly placed

---

[3] R.J. Rummel, 'Libertarianism and International Violence', *Journal of Conflict Resolution*, 1983, Vol. 27, No. 1, p. 29.

[4] J.S. Levy, 'Domestic Politics and War', *Journal of Interdisciplinary History*, 1988, Vol. 18, No. 4, p. 662.

[5] see, e.g., B. Russsett, *Grasping the Democratic Peace: Principles for Post-Cold War World*, Princeton University Press, 1994; M. Doyle, *Ways of War and Peace*. New York: W.W. Norton, 1997.

[6] President Clinton's State of the Union Message, January 1994 http://www.presidency.ucsb.edu/ws/index.php?pid=50409#axzz1ss6W8zdb.

[7] R. Cooper, The Post-Modern State and the World Order, Demos, 1996.

states will act similarly, regardless of their domestic political systems'.[8]

Usually it is the following explanations that are given to statistical studies that, in the opinion of adherents of DPT, prove their theories. Firstly, as democratically elected governments are accountable to their electorate and as it is the people who bear the brunt of all wars, democracies are naturally more peace-loving than non-democracies. Secondly, as democracies resolve their domestic problems and disputes not by means of arms, but through discussion and compromise, they extrapolate these procedures to their external relations. Sometimes these two interrelated, but nevertheless different, explanations are called (1) the role of institutional constraints, i.e. the checks and balances embedded in democratic institutions and the constraining role of public opinion as the factors making democracies more peaceful and (2) the role of normative effects meaning that democratic norms and cultures applicable domestically are externalised to also cover relations between states. Finally, it has been argued by some that as democracies are wealthier, they have more to lose from wars than those who are less well-off.

Dyadic DP theory, supported by most adherents of DPT, suggests that democracies don't fight each other, while monadic DP theory, which has fewer adherents, supposes that democracies are generally more peace-loving. Dyadic DP theories explain that as democracies are open and trust each other, they see other democracies as following the same logic; their external contradictions are resolved like domestic disagreements – through discussions, compromises and concessions. As non-democracies are opaque, as internal discontent in such societies is either suppressed or explodes in violent revolts, it is not possible to trust non-democratic regimes; like methods of domestic politics in democracies, their ways of doing politics at home are also externalised. Although all these explanations should be usable, in principle, to also support monistic theories of DP, i.e. theories which claim that democracies not only don't wage wars against each other, but that they rarely wage wars also against non-democracies (or at least, if they fight non-democracies, they do not

[8] C. Layne, Kant or Cant: The Myth of the Democratic Peace, International Security, (1994), 19:2, 12.

initiate those conflicts), monistic theories have fewer supporters since they so obviously contradict reality. Even mature liberal democracies have waged wars against non-democracies, and not always has the initiative of such conflicts come from the part of non-democracies.

2. PROBLEMS WITH DEMOCRATIC PEACE THEORIES

Intuitively, and after comparing the European continent of today with its relatively recent past, one may indeed give credence to DP theories. European history is as bloody as the history of any other continent, and due to its dominant role in the twentieth century, twice in that century have European wars dragged other peoples in, transforming its internal conflicts into two world wars. Since 1945, however, the Western part of Europe has indeed enjoyed peace. Although the democratic nature of today's France and Germany, for example, may not be the only factor that makes a military conflict between them virtually unimaginable and even absurd, it seems to definitely be a contributing factor to the solid peace between these erstwhile enemies. The same applies to many other pairs of European states.

There are, however, several serious problems with DP theories, even within the European context. First, statistical data used to prove DP theories relates to a relatively short period of time; the very phenomenon of the democratic state is fairly recent. Democracy is a relative latecomer to the world, especially if we limit democracies to so-called mature or liberal democracies and do not go as far back as to Ancient Greece. James Lee Ray observes that 'the majority of democratic states that have ever existed have emerged during the Cold War' and because this 'historic epoch may prove idiosyncratic with respect to relationships among democratic states; only time will tell whether the large number of democratic states that have emerged in recent years will fight wars against each other in the absence of a serious threat from the Soviet Union'.[9]

---

[9] J.L. Ray, 'Does Democracy Cause Peace?', *Annual Review of Political Science* (N.W. Polsby ed.), CA Annual Review Inc., 1998, pp. 37–38.

It is indeed true that most democracies emerged or matured during the Cold War. They all belonged to the same – Western – camp of the bi-polar world and felt threatened by their communist rival (the presence of several liberal democracies, like Austria and Finland, that did not belong either to NATO or the EEC does not change the overall picture). This, naturally, made conflictual potential of intra-camp relations secondary and not vital to their interests, compared to the main threat, i.e. the military as well as ideological threat from its rival – Eastern – bloc. Related to this factor, or even part of it, is the role of a unique single overwhelmingly powerful leader in the Western bloc – the United States of America. Washington played the role of a Big Brother that not only guaranteed the security of the smaller members of the Western bloc from outside threats, but also kept order within the camp, though it is necessary to emphasise that the 'smaller brothers' succumbed to Washington's leadership much more voluntarily than their Eastern bloc contemporaries yielded to Moscow's authority and control. However, Tony Smith is right when he writes that '[I]n conceptual terms, the chief failure of DPT is that it does not acknowledge the role of a hegemonic leader in creating, protecting and expanding the zone of democratic peace'.[10] Indeed, there was a uni-polar and hegemonic peace within one of the parts of the bi-polar world. The presence of a totalitarian adversary, whose threat was not only military but also ideological, certainly played a role in liberal democracies' submission to the will of a protector, who acted as a kind of Leviathan for that part of the world – the so-called first world. The domestically democratic United States has been and remains internationally hegemonic. This factor, on the one hand, contributed to the democratic peace practice within the camp of mature democracies during the Cold War period, but on the other, the same factor explains why Washington as a hegemonic power behaved, and continues to behave, quite aggressively in its external relations towards those beyond the camp of mature liberal democracies following Washington's lead. Even today the 'hard face' of the Enlightenment's legacy, which is morally neutral and whose purpose may not only be liberation but also domination, has a tendency that

---

10 T. Smith, 'Democratic Peace Theory: From Promising Theory to Dangerous Practice', *International Relations*, 2011, Vol. 25, No. 2, p. 154.

Martti Koskenniemi has defined as a 'hegemonic struggle to make one's partial view seem like the universal preference'.[11]

Robert Cooper, who distinguishes between pre-modern, modern and post-modern states, believes that the United States, whose domestic structures and processes are relatively similar to those of European post-modern states, conducts itself externally as a modern state which behaves like states that follow Machiavellian principles and *raison d'état* have always behaved.[12] Observing that outside Europe, it is Canada (one could probably add Australia and New Zealand) that corresponds to the criteria of a post-modern state, Cooper writes: '[T]he USA is the more doubtful case since it is not clear that the US government or Congress accepts either the necessity and desirability of interdependence, or its corollaries of openness, mutual surveillance and mutual interference to the same extent as most European governments now do'.[13] Such a dissimilarity between the United states and other liberal democracies is explained by the global role Washington plays, which Cooper politely calls 'the knowledge that the defence of the civilised world rests ultimately on its shoulders',[14] but which a more impartial or critically minded observer may consider as the role of a hegemonic power acting in the belief that its values are universal and its interests may clash with the interests of other nations only when the latter are non-democracies guided by narrow self-interest. However, the problem with this logic is, as Robert Cooper himself states, that 'hegemony is no longer acceptable in a liberal world that values human rights and self-determination'.[15] This was written in the 1990s, when China and other non-Western nations were not as strong and assertive as they are today in the second decade of the twenty first century, and when financial and economic crisis did not loom on the horizon. Any hegemony is even less acceptable in a contemporary world that is moving further towards multipolarity and diversity

---

11 M. Koskenniemi, 'International Law in Europe: Between Tradition and Renewal', *The European Journal of International Law* (2005), vol. 16, No 1, p. 119.

12 R. Cooper, 'The Post-Modern State', in *Reordering the World: The Long-Term Implications of September* 11, The Foreign Policy Centre, 2002, p. 12.

13 Ibid., p. 29.

14 Ibid.

15 R. Cooper, *The Post-Modern State and the World Order*, Demos, 1996.

within political regimes and economic models. A globalised world is simply too big to be governed from one hegemonic centre.

Today's Europe consists of mature liberal democracies, and indeed, the potential for armed conflict between them is not very realistic. Although the democratic nature of European states seems to be, at least intuitively, one of the factors that exclude the use of force or even the threat of force between them, there are other factors as well. The most important among them is the fact that not only are European states post-modern states, but that the European state-system is, what Robert Cooper calls, a post-modern state system.[16] This international system, to which Western and now also Central and Eastern European states belong, is characterised, in Cooper's words, by the breakdown of distinctions between domestic and foreign affairs; mutual interference in (traditionally) domestic affairs; not only a formal rejection of the use of force for resolving disputes among themselves, but the impossibility of foreseeing realistic scenarios for such use of force; the growing irrelevance of borders; security based on transparency, openness and interdependence.[17] European liberal democracies not only have similar domestic political and economic systems as well as *grosso modo* shared history (mostly bloody), but they have also created a unique international system where Realist principles (anarchy, concerns for relative power, prisoners' dilemma etc.) either do not apply at all, or play only a secondary and subordinate role. Here, the structure of the international political system, of which Layne speaks, hasn't remained the same; it is not any more anarchic, or at least as anarchic as the whole international system or other regional international systems. The European international system has radically changed; indeed, we may say that instead of remaining Hobbesian, it has become rather Kantian. However, this does not mean that democracies, even *vis-à-vis* other democracies, act in a similar fashion outside such an international system. Moreover, the European international system could hardly be replicated globally, at least in the foreseeable future. Can anyone be sure that even if a rapidly rising China were to become more and more democratic it would also

16 Ibid., p. 42.
17 Ibid.

increasingly have relations with the United States akin to those between France and Germany or Holland and Spain? There is more than one reason why it is authoritarian rulers rather than democratically elected governments who can more easily resolve certain conflictual situations peacefully (e.g., through bribery, by means of dynastic marriages, or a weaker party retreating fearing inevitable defeat). Of course, this does not mean that a world of authoritarian states would be more peaceful than a world of democracies; certainly not. However, it means that even if a world of democracies were possible, it may not necessarily be more peaceful. Moreover, proponents of DPT understand democracy as a Western style liberal democracy that is, as we discussed above, a rather limited vision of possible future political arrangements. There is something significant in Ido Oren's statement that 'the democratic peace claim is not about democracies *per se* as much as it is about countries that are "America like" or of "our kind". The apparently objective coding rules by which democracy is defined in fact represent current American values'.[18]

That there is a hegemonic struggle going on in the world is obvious and beyond any doubt. Globally, there is still only one hegemonic power – the United States; acting sometimes unilaterally, often together with its allies. One of President G.W. Bush's aids explained to Ron Suskind how reality is created in today's world: 'We're an empire now, and when we act, we create our own reality. And while you're studying that reality – judiciously, as you will – we'll act again, creating other new realities, which you can study too, and that's how things will sort out. We're history's actors ... and you, all of you, will be left to just study what we do.'[19] This statement is not only arrogant but also illusionary, since Washington's ability to control and guide events is increasingly diminishing, and may have characterised the rather short unipolar moment[20] that followed the demise of the

---

[18] I. Oren, 'The Subjectivity of the "Democratic" Peace: Changing U.S. Perceptions of Imperial Germany', *International Security*, 1995, Vol. 20, No. 2, p. 1.

[19] R. Suskind, "Faith, Certainty and the Presidency of George W. Bush", *The New York Times Magazine*, 17 October, 2004.

[20] C. Krauthhammer, 'The Unipolar Moment', *Foreign Affairs*, 1990/1991, Vol. 70, No. 1, pp. 23–33.

Soviet Union. Though the manner in which Bush's aid put it is an expression of extreme arrogance combined with some ignorance and naivety, many intelligent and knowledgeable Americans think quite similarly. In summer 2012, for example, in *International Herald Tribune* a piece by Yale law professor John Fabian Witt, *The Legal Fog between War and Peace*, where the author among many interesting and rather knowledgeable comments on the use of unmanned drones also writes: 'Inside the United States Government lawyers like Jeh C. Johnson in the Pentagon and Harold Koh in the State Department, along with hundreds of other lawyers in the Justice Department, the White House and elsewhere, are creating new systems for regulating the targeting process'.[21] I personally know well and hold in great esteem Professor Harold Hongju Koh – the current State Department Legal Adviser, who – I am sure – does not think that he, even if together with his colleagues from the State, Defence and Justice Departments of the United States, are creating international legal rules for targeting (and Professor Witt's article is about international law). Harold is too clever and professional for that. But if Professor Witt does not mean by 'and elsewhere' the foreign, defence and justice ministries of China, Russia, France, Germany, Brazil and many other countries, which have not delegated to the United States government the onerous task of producing international law for the whole world, his comment – in substance, though not in tone – differs little from what President G. Bush's aid had told Ron Suskind. Such a mindset is not harmless and though it may sometimes indeed help create new realities, they often have nothing in common even with what Washington intends to create.

Yet, when some regional powers such as China in the South China Sea or Russia in the Caucasus claim to have their own special spheres of interest close to their borders, the global hegemon immediately cries wolf: in today's world there should not be any place for spheres of interest; there are only universal values and interests, and their content (free market, democracy, secularism etc.) is defined by the West. However, there is also a serious problem with this soft and

[21] J.F. Witt, 'The Legal Fog between War and Peace', *International Herald Tribune*, 10 June 2012.

humane facet of the Enlightenment's legacy when used as an export item. Though there are more than just a handful of Western educated or influenced people in many non-Western countries who cry out for liberties and democracy, in practice their sought revolutions often end in chaos, frustration, reversals to dictatorships or the emergence of failed states. Why so?

Even if Western values are, in principle, universalisable, not all societies are ready for an immediate introduction to them. Sometimes such medicine is too strong, and instead of curing the patient it may kill them. How things end up depends on many variables. Samuel Huntington has identified the following conditions that are favourable for the consolidation of emerging democracies: 1) the experience of a previous effort at democratisation, even if it had failed; 2) relatively high levels of economic development; 3) a favourable international political environment, with outside assistance; 4) early timing of the transition to democracy, relative to a worldwide "wave," indicating that the drive to democracy derived primarily from indigenous rather than outside influences; and 5) the experience of a relatively peaceful rather than violent transition.[22] Thomas Carothers does not consider such, or other, factors as preconditions but rather as core 'facilitators or nonfacilitators' that would make democratisation 'harder or easier'.[23] It would be possible to agree with such an approach if one were to add that some combinations of such 'nonfacilitators' make democratisation impossible, at least for the time being. It is important to note that democratic reforms in societies that have not had any, or have had little previous experience with democracy are a most serious business and cannot be approached slightly. Democratic institutions, if introduced from the outside without being called for domestically, as Jürgen Habermas observes, 'disintegrate without the initiatives of a population *accustomed* to freedom'.[24] In the export-import business

---

[22] S. Huntington, *The Third Wave. Democratization in the Late Twentieth Century*, University of Oklahoma Press, 1993.

[23] T. Carothers, 'The "Sequence" Fallacy', *Journal of Democracy*, 2007, vol. 18., No. 1, p. 24.

[24] J. Habermas, *Between Facts and Norms, Contributions to a Discourse Theory of Law and Democracy*, Polity Press, 1996, p. 130.

of democracy it is necessary to bear in mind that democratisation has to be demand-induced, not supply-stimulated. Only if there is a strong desire among a people to build democratic institutions as well as at least a minimum of material and cultural preconditions can the supply side play a positive role. Otherwise its role will be destructive, and in contradistinction to what Joseph Schumpeter's theory of 'creative destruction'[25] predicts, there is little creative in such destruction.

Further, if we exclude the Cold War period due to its 'idiosyncratic' nature, the statistical picture of DPT becomes much more confusing. As there is no consensus on the criteria for democracy, for some authors certain wars were fought between democracies, while other theorists discount them. For example, Bruce Russett did not consider the 1812 war between Britain and the United States as a war between two democracies since Britain, in his opinion, did not become a democracy until the Reform Bill of 1832.[26] Christopher Layne, in analysing four case studies of 'near misses' where democracies almost went to war against each other (Britain and the United States in 1861 over the Trent incident; Britain and the United States in 1895–1896 over the Venezuela–Great Britain border dispute; the British-French struggle to control the Upper Nile and the Fashoda incident of 1898; and the Franco-German Ruhr crisis of 1923), finds that the reasons why none of these crises, (where the pairs of democracies were ready to resort to arms), exploded in an armed conflict, are much better explained, not by arguments of DP theory, but by the conclusions of Realist theory: the weaker party always succumbed, thereby shunning an imminent military conflict.[27] Christopher Layne also makes an important point, observing that '[T]he greater the external threat a state faces (or believes it does), the more "autocratic" its foreign policymaking process will be and the more centralized its political structures will be'.[28] To formulate

[25] J. Schumpeter, *Capitalism, Socialism and Democracy* (3d edition), Harper Perennial, 1984.

[26] Russett, *Grasping the Democratic Peace*, p. 16.

[27] C. Layne, 'Kant or Cant: The Myth of the Democratic Peace', *International Security*, 1994, Vol. 19, No. 2, pp. 5–49.

[28] Layne, op. cit., p. 45.

this observation as a principle, we may say that it is not democracy (or not primarily democracy) that leads to peace, but that peace is, in the longer run, conducive to the emergence and sustainability of democracy. Moreover, foreign policy-making, even in liberal democracies, is less open and less subjected to parliamentary control than domestic policy-making. It was so a hundred years ago, i.e. in the run up to the First World War, when, say, 'even in democratic France, the executive enjoyed unfettered power in the realm of foreign policy',[29] and when '[I]n the realm of foreign policy, France and Britain were no more and no less democratic than the Second Reich'.[30] It is so today, even in mature democracies and especially in the United States, where the use of the political questions doctrine and other mechanisms make certain that foreign affairs are less prone to legislative and judicial supervision than domestic affairs. Recent developments such as the drone attacks in Pakistan, Yemen and other places, as well as acts of cyber warfare in the form of *Olympic Games* or *Stuxnet*[31] have raised issues of executive powers *vis-à-vis* the legislative branch. As Malou Innocent writes, '[B]ased on a broad theory of executive power, President Obama, and possibly his successor, has the authority to target people for death – including American citizens – without a semblance of transparency, accountability or congressional consent'.[32] This accurate remark, due to a tiny but significant detail, deserves a small diversion. This is a reference to 'American citizens', who together with non-American citizens are the targets of assassination. There seems to be visceral, almost subconscious, assumption that while it may be OK to target non-Americans, American citizens deserve special, enhanced, protection. Such an attitude, if not directly contrary to international law (the principle of non-discrimination), is in a sure way leading to its breaches in concrete circumstances. Moreover, it does not enhance

---

[29] Ibid., p. 42.

[30] Ibid., p. 43.

[31] D.E. Sanger, 'Obama Order Sped Up Wave of Cyberattacks Against Iran', *International Herald Tribune*, 1 June 2012; D.E. Sanger, *Confront and Conceal: Obama's Secret Wars and Surprising Use of American Power*, Crown, 2012.

[32] M. Innocent, 'Yemen, Drones and the Imperial Presidency', *The National Interest*, 4 June 2012.

American 'soft power'; one may be tempted to argue that Washington may target its own citizens but has to leave citizens of other countries alone.

In addition, democratic governments are as skilful as non-democracies in manipulating public opinion to prepare it for the use of force if initiated by them. As we will discuss in detail in the next Chapter, whenever there is an intensive as well as sustained media attention on a conflict with special emphasis on the crimes committed by one side, there are usually two possible reasons. First, it may indeed be one of those rare cases when there is only one villain in town with a few cynical self-interested manipulators supporting him. Secondly, and this happens quite often when a 'regime change' is in preparation, sustained attention to a conflict and the singling out of one main culprit while others are depicted either as innocent victims or even freedom-fighters, usually means a prelude and preparation for the use of 'all necessary means' for a regime change. Moreover, the argument that democracies do not easily go to war because in democracies it is the people, i.e. the electorate who bear the burden of military conflicts with their pockets and even with their lives, is only partly true. Below we will discuss problems with financing war efforts. Here, it is necessary to underline that Western democracies, especially the United States, which are military-technologically far more advanced than both their potential and actual foes, and often use against them only airpower (and even in that case, increasingly use unmanned drones), have tens or even hundreds of times less casualties than their enemy's combatants, and even civilians.

3. *IMMANUEL KANT AND THE XXI CENTURY WORLD*

In his essay on 'Perpetual Peace' Immanuel Kant laid out six preliminary steps (conditions) towards perpetual peace. None of them have lost their relevance, though some of them may be quite unrealistic taking into account the political realities of both Kant's and today's world. One of these was that governments should not borrow to finance wars. This preliminary condition indeed colludes, in a significant way, with ideas of democracy and peace. Taxation, which most people may not be especially fond of, is one of the cornerstones of democracy. The slogan 'no taxation without representation' may be reversed to 'no representation without taxation'. Take, for example, Saudi Arabia or other energy rich autocracies. The absence of taxation or very low taxes serve as a kind bribery that the authorities use to keep the population, which does not have much or any say in the affairs of the state, content. Such oil or gas rich kingdoms in the Middle East or other autocrats such as those in Turkmenistan, who do not tax their citizens, instead bribe the population using profits from plentiful natural resources.

In this context, one interesting and peculiar development were the George W. Bush era tax cuts, enacted at a time when the United States became almost simultaneously engaged in two serious wars in Iraq and Afghanistan. Earlier American administrations had used taxation to finance wars. During the Second World War a 'highly progressive tax system' was enacted in the United States.[33] It was observed by the Urban Institute in the US that 'like the events of December 7, 1941, the attacks of September 11 triggered a strong "rally round the flag effect" as Americans readied themselves for the sacrifices of war. Unlike Pearl Harbour, however, there was virtually no talk in the wake of the September 11 attacks of a need to increase taxes in order to mobilize for war. Just as earlier leaders appealed to Americans' sense of patriotism to raise taxes, some politicians used the same tack to argue for cutting them during the wars in Afghanistan and Iraq. One commentator wrote in an April 2003 op-ed: "by keeping tax rates too high and 'sacrificing' economic growth, we don't help the war effort, we hinder it; we don't get more revenue, we get less." Earlier generations may have witnessed debates over the right form and magnitude of tax increases for fighting wars abroad, but so solid a rejection of the increases, the authors conclude, is truly unprecedented in American history'.[34] By borrowing, instead of taxing, the Bush administration not only passed the economic burden of war from this generation to further generations, but also secured the consent to its war efforts from the current generation. It was a kind of bribery to the current generation at the

33 J. Stiglitz, *The Price of Inequality*, p. 4.

34 Urban Institute: Bush-Era Tax Cuts Depart From History of America War Finance, http://www.urban.org/publications/901162.html (visited 17 March 2012).

expense of future generations. And it goes without saying that such financing of wars is contrary to Kant's preconditions for perpetual peace. It also contradicts one of the tenets of democracy – the financial burden of today's wars, especially if these are wars of choice, not wars of necessity, should not be passed on to future generations. Moreover, as the greatest American judge Oliver Wendell Holmes put it, '[T]axes are the price we pay for civilization'.[35]

4. ON THE WAR-PRONENESS OF SOME DEMOCRATISING STATES

In the context of studying current regime changes in different parts of the world, DP theories have to face some other challenges as well. First, several experts have argued that though it may be true that mature liberal democracies have not fought wars against one another (recalling that, as we saw, the phenomenon of mature liberal democracy is a recent occurrence), authoritarian or totalitarian states usually go through a dangerous transition to democracy, and historical evidence from the last 200 years has shown that in this phase countries become more war-prone, not less, and they do fight wars with other democratic or democratising states. Partly, this is due to the fact that democratisation is often accompanied by a rise in nationalism, sometimes in its extreme forms.[36] Will Hutton is wrong when he believes that 'democratizing countries are less vulnerable to both internal and external conflicts'.[37] The truth is usually just the opposite. Only mature democracies are intrinsically more stable; democratising countries very often have to transverse the dangerous J-Curve, as we discussed in the Chapter on the difficulties of a democratic transition in Russia.

Secondly, the fact that mature liberal democracies have not fought wars against one another does not at all mean that they do not act bellicosely *vis-à-vis* non-democracies or fledgling democracies. It

---

[35] http://www.quotes.net/quote/4027.

[36] see, e.g., E. Mansfield, J, Snyder, 'Democratization and War', *Foreign Affairs*, May/June 1995; J. Snyder, *From Voting to Violence: Democratization and National Conflict*, W W Norton & Co. Ltd., 2001.

[37] W. Hutton, *The Writing on the Wall: China in the 21st Century*, Little, Brown, 2006, p. 185.

has been emphasized by some authors that democratic peace theory has its 'dark side' – the propensity for democracies to be more aggressive towards non-democracies or fledgling democracies.[38] Washington's military adventures against democratic Iran under Mohammad Mosaddegh in 1953, the democratic Chile of Salvador Allende in the 1970s and in a host of other situations shows that it is not so much democracy or its absence that determines whether peace or war prevails, as whether a particular state behaves as expected by its more powerful neighbour; or if we extrapolate this to global affairs, whether its behaviour is in accordance with Washington's expectations or more generally, with the expectations of those who belong to the Euro-Atlantic alliance. Finally, even if we were to assume, against all the doubts and odds, that all societies would eventually become liberal democracies, rivalries over limited resources, over who will lead and who will have to follow, as well as a host of other potential sources of conflict will remain. This is not only because democratising states may constitute serious security threats, but also because attempts to democratise that which is not democratisable (and it is not important whether this be in principle or only for the time being) is an even bigger threat. Besides the ambiguities and pitfalls in relying on actual policies in democratic peace theories, the proactive promotion of liberal democracy, especially by means of military force, has several other dangers. Christopher Hobson has made an extremely pertinent observation: 'Any early celebrations were distinctly premature, however, as ideas related to DP soon emerged as a central justification – and potential motivation – in the "freedom agenda" of the Bush administration, which manifested itself most explicitly in the coercive democratization of Iraq. Rather than being a "force for peace", DPT scholarship became implicated in a deeply divisive and costly war'.[39] Indeed, attempts to impose DPT may well lead to wars whose results have nothing to do with democracy.

---

[38] A. Geis, L. Brock, H. Miller (eds.), *Democratic Wars: Looking at the Dark Side of Democratic Peace*, Palgrave, 2006.

[39] C. Hobson, 'Roundtable: Between the Theory and Practice of Democratic Peace. Introduction', *International Relations*, 2011, Vol. 25, No. 2, p. 147.

Our ability to predict the future trends in social development is rather limited. Every big social plan has turned out to be a kind of utopia. All historical attempts to radically alter societies have resulted in more significant unexpected and unwanted consequences than foreseen and desired ones. One of the most scathing criticisms of the Bush's administration's efforts to spread democracy in the wider Middle East came from the neo-conservative author Andrew Sullivan, who had earlier supported the 2003 war against Iraq: 'The final error was not taking culture seriously enough. There is a large discrepancy between neo-conservatism's scepticism of government's ability to change culture at home and its naiveté when it comes to complex, tribal, sectarian cultures abroad'.[40] It is indeed amazing how quickly and with how little doubt the American political elite embark on radical transformations of foreign societies, especially if we compare all this with ineptitude and sluggishness of the same elite in resolving a host of urgent domestic issues, such as reforming the ineffective and unjust healthcare system, or effectively responding to the banking crises. For example, Joseph Stiglitz observes that '[E]conomists marvel at our health care sector and its ability to deliver less for more: health outcomes are worse in the United States than in almost all other advanced industrial countries, and yet the United States spends absolutely more per capita, and more as a percentage of GDP, by a considerable amount. We've been spending more than one-sixth of GDP on health care, while France has been spending less than an eighth. Per capita spending in the United States has been two and a half times higher than the average of the advanced industrial countries'.[41] In comparison with the near impossibility of resolving health care problems at home, the democratisation of Afghanistan, Iraq and the wider Middle East seems to be a much easier task. Is it really so? Such a rhetorical question hardly needs an answer.

Those who rely on DPT to promote democracy in the world have to remember that Kant's philosophy is permeated with the idea of not using war as a means to promote historical change. He wrote:

---

40 A. Sullivan, 'What I Got Wrong about the War', *Time*, 5 March 2006.

41 J. Stiglitz, *The Price of Inequality*, p. 97.

'No attempt should be made, however, to realize this idea precipitously through revolutionary methods, that is, by violent overthrow of a previously existing imperfect and corrupt government ... Instead, the idea should be attempted and carried out through gradual reform according to fixed principles'.[42]

DPT theories have contributed to justifications of several foreign interventions. In their book *The War over Iraq* Lawrence Kaplan and William Kristol, starting from the premise that 'democracies rarely, if ever, wage war against one another', conclude that 'the more democratic the world becomes, the more likely it is to be congenial to America'.[43] Such a conclusion cannot be justified theoretically because of its intellectual fallacy; equally, practice also testifies that in some cases the counter argument may be truer: the more democratic an entity becomes, the less it may be ready to follow an American lead.

---

[42] I. Kant, *Metaphysical Elements of Justice* (*Rechtslehre from Metaphysics of Morals*), Macmillan Library of Liberal Arts, 1965, p. 129.

[43] L. Kaplan, W. Kristol, *The War Over Iraq: Saddam's Tyranny and America's Mission*, Encounter Books, 2003, p. 104–5.

Chapter Six

HUMANITARIAN INTERVENTION, CIVIL WARS AND REGIME CHANGE

1. USE OF FORCE AND HUMANITARIAN CONCERNS IN 'MODERN' AND 'POST-MODERN' INTERNATIONAL SOCIETIES

It is, of course, possible to argue over whether it is democracy that brings about peace, or *vice versa* that it is peace that is conducive to the progress of democracy, but the general correlation between these phenomena is indeed positive, i.e. one usually reinforces the other. However, as we have seen above, sometimes attempts to expand the circle of democracies not only lead to the breaches of peace, but even endanger the very phenomenon they are meant to promote, i.e. democracy. As a result, there is neither democracy nor peace. Therefore, as well as for a host of other reasons, international law, and rightly so, prohibits both the use and threat of military force even if its aim is the promotion of democracy. The prohibition of the use of force is one of the few imperative (*jus cogens*) norms of international law, from which states cannot derogate even with mutual consent. Although it may be surprising, it is nevertheless true that the prohibition of the use of force in international relations became a legally binding norm relatively recently. As a legal principle it started its evolution after World War I and matured as a result of World War II; it was enshrined in the United Nations Charter and its importance has not diminished since, notwithstanding its overly frequent breaches. As the International Court of Justice put it in the *Nicaragua case*, '[I]f a State acts in a way *prima facie* incompatible with a recognized rule, but defends its conduct by appealing to exceptions or justifications contained within the rule itself, then whether or not the State's conduct is in fact justifiable on that basis, the significance of that attitude is to confirm rather than to weaken the rule'.[1] Although some academics

---

1 Case concerning military and paramilitary activities in and against Nicaragua (Nicaragua v. United States of America), ICJ Decision of 27 June 1986, para. 186.

have claimed that due to the inefficiency of the UN collective security system the Charter prohibition of the use of force has become redundant,[2] no state has made such a claim. While justifying their own transgressions states are usually 'appealing to exceptions or justifications within the rule', and when condemning the use of force by others, they confirm their own adherence to the principle.

The problem is, however, that the principles of sovereign equality between states, the non-use of force and non-intervention in domestic affairs (as they are enshrined in the United Nations Charter, in respective UN General Assembly resolutions and numerous other documents), and the principle of respect for and protection of human rights as it has developed since 1945, *partly* reflect values of different international societies. The Charter principles prohibiting the use of force in international relations and especially non-interference in domestic affairs are the crown jewels in the progressive development of the Westphalian or modern international society, while the principle of respect for and protection of human rights, including the right of peoples to self-determination and minority rights, *in a way* rocks the very foundations of that society. I would like to emphasise that I have used the word *partly* when writing about the distinctions in the values of different international societies and I have used the words *in a way* when referring to possible conflicts between the norms governing these different international societies – the traditional Westphalian and today's post-Westphalian or post-modern international society. These principles may indeed clash in their interpretation and application, but they all aim at the protection of real and important values and interests. Louis Henkin, for example, wrote that 'Article 2(4) is the most important norm of international law, the distillation and embodiment of the primary value of the inter-state system, the defence of state

[2] See, e.g., T. Franck, 'Who Killed Article 2(4) or Changing Norms Governing the Use of Force by States', *The American Journal of International Law*, 1970, Vol. 64; but see also L. Henkin, 'The Reports of the Death of Article 2(4) Are Greatly Exaggerated', *The American Journal of International Law*, 1971, Vol. 65. Unfortunately, both of these two great American international lawyers – good friends and colleagues of mine – are not with us anymore.

independence and state autonomy'.[3] However, later he admits that 'international human rights law reflects a major derogation by the international system from its commitment to basic state values–autonomy and impermeability'.[4]

The principles prohibiting the use of force and interference in domestic affairs have been among the main legal guarantors of the sovereignty of states and the inviolability of their territorial integrity. This means that they have emphasised the sanctity of two out of three elements of statehood[5]–authority and territory–while neglecting the third one – population (i.e. human beings). However, the evolving law regulating the use of force cannot ignore the development of the international law of human rights, including the right of peoples to self-determination and the rights of ethnic and religious minorities. The international law of 2013 cannot be the same as the international law of 1945. The interpretation of the Charter norms on use of force has to correspond to the changes in international society as well as in international law. Kofi Annan, the then UN Secretary-General, in emphasising that 'the central message of the UN Charter "with its call for justice and promise for peace, is as strong as ever", at the same time, also warned: 'clearly we cannot meet challenges of the new millennium with an instrument designed for different circumstances of the middle of the twentieth century'.[6] It is interesting to point out that in his Annual Report to the General Assembly on 20th September 1999, Kofi Annan emphasised that 'the Charter is a living document' and 'nothing in the Charter precludes recognition that there are rights beyond borders'.[7]

---

3 L. Henkin, *International Law: Politics and Values*, MartinusNijhoff Publishers, 1995, p. 113.

4 Ibid. p. 203.

5 The Montevideo Convention on the Rights and Duties of States of 1933 in its Article 1 stipulates: 'The state as a person of international law should possess the following qualifications: (a) a permanent population; (b) a defined territory; (c) government; and (d) capacity to enter into relations with the other states'. This Article of the Convention that never entered into force is usually quoted as reflecting customary international law requirements for statehood.

6 Address to the Council on Foreign Relations, New York, 22 April 1997 (SG/SM/6218).

7 Press Release SG/SM/7136, 20 September 1999.

After the Second World War and to a great extent due to the atrocities committed before and during the war, the international human rights movement gained momentum. What states do within their borders and how they treat their people are no longer their internal affairs. An episode in the history of the League of Nations, described, *inter alia,* by René Cassin,[8] well illustrates the extent to which international society has changed since the 1930s. In September 1930 Mr Franz Bernheim, a Jew from Upper Silesia, appeared before the Assembly of the League of Nations in Geneva complaining of the persecution of Jews by the Nazis. He accused the Nazis of having committed, *inter alia,* the crimes of arson, rape, massacre and the profanation of synagogues and Jewish tombs. These acts, outrageous and condemnable in any situation, had, moreover, taken place in the context of the existence of the German-Polish Convention of 1922 on the protection of minorities in Upper Silesia. The response by the representative of Germany, the Minister of Propaganda and Information Joseph Goebbels, to the question of the plight of minorities in Upper Silesia was as follows: 'We are a sovereign nation and therefore all said by this person is none of your business. We treat our socialists, our pacifists, and our Jews as we consider it necessary and we are not subject to any control by mankind or the League of Nations'.[9] The Nazis got away with this arrogant and overt challenge to the competence of the League. The League of Nations in its resolution avoided any condemnation of Germany and only reminded in polite terms that states are expected to treat their minorities better.

Since then, things have changed considerably. Human rights have ceased to be an internal affair of the state. In the first half of the 1990s the two *ad hoc* international criminal tribunals were set up to try those who were accused of having committed war crimes, crimes against humanity, and acts of genocide in the former Yugoslavia and Rwanda (The International Criminal Tribunal for the Former

---

[8] R. Cassin, 'L'Homme sujet de droit international et la protection des droit de l'homme dans la societé universelle', *Etudes an l'honneur de George Scelle*, Paris, 1950; see also M. Mazower, 'The Strange Triumph of Human Rights, 1933–1950', *The Historical Journal*, 2004, vol. 47, No. 2.

[9] Quoted from M. Bettati, *Le droit d'ingerérence*, Odile Jacob, 1996, p. 18 (my translation from French).

Yugoslavia – ICTY and the International Criminal Tribunal for Rwanda – ICTR). In the summer of 1998 the Statute of a permanent International Criminal Court (ICC) was opened for signature in Rome and on the 14th March 2012 the Court found its first defendant, Thomas Lubanga Dyilo of the Democratic Republic of Congo guilty of war crimes.[10] Although these trends are still quite fragile (and they may even be reversible), they certainly do not fit well into the traditional framework of Westphalian international society, within which the League of Nations dealt with minority issues.

In November 1998 the Law Lords of the British House of Lords found in the *Pinochet* case, using the words of Lord Nicolls, that 'international law has made plain that certain types of conduct, including torture and hostage taking, are not acceptable conduct on the part of anyone. This applies as much to heads of state, or even more so, as it does to everyone else; the contrary conclusion would make a mockery of international law'.[11] The Law Lords found that General Pinochet, as a former head of state, was not immune from criminal prosecution in the United Kingdom's courts. International law no longer recognises that acts such as torture, murder and hostage taking are acts that can be performed 'in the official capacity of head of state'.[12]

Some governments treat their people, either as a whole or often some subset of them, in such a way that the population rises in revolution to overthrow it, or sometimes a repressed and discriminated against segment of the population seek secession, i.e. separation, from the whole. It would not only be morally wrong but also politically reckless for the world community not to take any interest in such situations, and international law should provide for extreme responses to extreme situations. In the aftermath of the Cold War and in response to the increasing number of internal conflicts

---

[10] ICC-01/04-01/06, The Prosecutor v. Thomas Lubanga Dyilo.

[11] *Regina* v. *Bartle and Commissioner of Police for Metropolis and others* ex parte *Pinochet* (on appeal from a Divisional Court of the Queen's Bench Division, 26 November 1998.

[12] *Regina* v. *Bartle and Commissioner of Police for the Metropolis and others* ex parte *Pinochet* and *Regina* v. *Evans and another and the Commissioner of Police for the Metropolis and others* ex parte *Pinochet*, Judgement of the House of Lords, 24 March 1999.

(Somalia, Haiti, the former Yugoslavia etc.), the UN Security Council started considering a number of such conflicts as threats to international peace and security (sometimes correctly, in other cases stretching the concept almost to a breaking point as, for example, in Haiti in the 1990s), since otherwise the main security body of the United Nations would not have jurisdiction over humanitarian catastrophes. In a few cases, the Security Council not only made a finding based on Article 39 of the Chapter (that a situation, which was created by or which involved massive human rights violations, constituted a threat to international peace and security) but also authorised states 'to take all necessary means' (a euphemism authorising the use of military force) to put an end to such threats and to the humanitarian crises that had caused the Security Council to act. However, in other cases, having confirmed that a situation represented a threat to international peace and security, the Security Council stopped short of such authorisation [e.g., Resolution 688 (1991) on Northern Iraq and 1199 (1998), 1203 (1998) on Kosovo]. Then, what became known as 'coalitions of the willing' took the initiative and used military force to allegedly enforce such resolutions.

There have been various justifications for such uses of force, both legal and moral. So, the Independent International Commission headed by Judge Richard Goldstone called the 1999 NATO operation against Serbia 'illegal but legitimate'.[13] Although the Commission was the first to phrase it in such a way, the approach in itself was not completely new. Previously in 1973, in the aftermath of the Indian intervention in Eastern Pakistan (now Bangladesh), Thomas Franck and Nigel Rodley took more or less the same stance in writing that: '[U]ndeniably, there are circumstances in which the unilateral use of force to overthrow injustice begins to seem less wrong than to turn aside. Like civil disobedience, however, this sense of superior "necessity" belongs in the realm of not law but of moral choice, which nations, like individuals, must sometimes make weighing the costs and benefits to their cause, to social fabric, and to themselves'.[14]

---

[13] See, Richard Goldstone et al., *The Kosovo Report: Conflict, International Response, Lessons Learned,* Independent International Commission on Kosovo (New York: Oxford University Press, 2001).

[14] T. Franck, N. Rodley, 'After Bangladesh: the Law of Humanitarian Intervention by Military Force', 67 *American Journal of International Law* (1973), p. 304.

Professor Franck made a similar comment more than a quarter of a century later in an article entitled *Break It, Do Not Fake It*, observing that 'NATO's action in Kosovo is not the first time illegal steps have been taken to prevent something palpably worse. Law gives those taking such illegal but necessary action several well-established strategies'.[15] In his view, the best strategy would be 'to proffer the most expiating of the special circumstances that ordained their moral choice'.[16] Bruno Simma, analysing the Kosovo conflict, believes in the same vein that sometimes 'imperative political and moral considerations may appear to leave no choice but to act outside law'[17] since 'legal issues presented by the Kosovo crisis are particularly impressive proof that hard cases make bad law'.[18]

However, some international lawyers are of the view that in certain situations, when the UN Security Council has certified the existence of a humanitarian crisis as threatening international peace and security, the use of military force to protect human rights, i.e. humanitarian intervention, may be not only legitimate but also lawful. Sean Murphy, for example, wrote regarding the creation of no-fly zones and 'safe havens' for Kurds in Northern Iraq – Operation Provide Comfort:

> The lack of global condemnation of the interventions was most likely not based on a perception that states have a unilateral right to intervene for humanitarian purposes. Rather, it was based on a perception that authority to intervene for those purposes emanated in some fashion from Security Council authorisation. ... On the other hand, it could be attributable to an acceptance of humanitarian intervention by a state or states acting on their own initiative subsequent to a Security Council identification of a threat to peace and security from a widespread deprivation of human rights, even where the Security Council does not expressly authorise intervention.[19]

Such an interpretation is like a halfway house towards the recognition of the right of states to humanitarian intervention. There is a

---

15 T. Franck, 'Break It, Do Not Fake It', 78 *Foreign Affairs* (July/August 1999), p. 118.

16 Ibid.

17 B. Simma, 'Nato, The UN and the Use of Force: Legal Aspects', 10 *European Journal of International Law* (1999), No. 1, p. 22.

18 Ibid., p. 14.

19 S. Murphy, *Humanitarian Intervention*, University of Pennsylvania Press, 1996, p. 195.

Security Council confirmation of threats to international peace and security stemming from a severe humanitarian crisis, and willing states can act, either individually or better yet collectively, to put an end to the crisis even without express Security Council authorization. Still, there are also those who consider that states can act militarily in cases of severe humanitarian crises even without any Security Council involvement. So, Tony Aust, at the time a Legal Counsellor to the United Kingdom Foreign and Commonwealth Office, informed the Foreign Affairs Committee of the British House of Commons in December 1992 that: 'Resolution 688 recognised that there was a severe human rights and humanitarian situation in Iraq and, in particular, in northern Iraq; but the intervention in northern Iraq "Provide Comfort" was in fact, not specially mandated by the United Nations, but the states taking action in northern Iraq did so in exercise of *customary international law principle of humanitarian intervention*' [emphasise added RM].[20] In answering questions about the legality of humanitarian intervention under international law Mr Aust said: 'There is no agreement in the sense of rules which have been laid down by any international body, but the practice of states does show over a long period that it is generally accepted that in extreme circumstances a state can intervene in another state for humanitarian reasons. ... International law in this field develops to meet new situations and that is what we are seeing now in the case of Iraq'.[21]

Often NATO's bombardment of Serbia over Kosovo in 1999, code-named *Operation Allied Force* (or *Operation Nobel Anvil*, as code-named by the US), has been cited as an example of a successful military operation whose aim was the protection of human rights. The British Labour party leader, Ed Miliband, speaking in a debate on British military intervention in Libya, told the House of Commons on 21 March 2011 that 'by taking action in Kosovo we saved the lives of tens of thousands of people.'[22] In his 22 April 1999 speech

---

[20] *The Expanding Role of the United Nations and its Implications for the UK Policy: Minutes of Evidence*,Hearing Before the Foreign Affairs Committee of the House of Commons, Sess. 1992–93, 2 December, 1992, p. 84.

[21] Ibid., p. 92.

[22] www.publications.parliament.uk/pa/cm201011/cmhansrd/cm110321/debtext/110321-0001.htm.

in Chicago,[23] when NATO's *Operation Allied Force* was in full swing, the then British Prime Minister Tony Blair put forward five requirements to be met in order for an intervention on humanitarian ground be justified: First, are we sure of our case? War is an imperfect instrument for righting humanitarian distress; but armed force is sometimes the only means of dealing with dictators. Second, have we exhausted all diplomatic options? We should always give peace every chance, as we have in the case of Kosovo. Third, on the basis of a practical assessment of the situation, are there military operations we can sensibly and prudently undertake? Fourth, are we prepared for the long term? In the past we talked too much of exit strategies. But having made a commitment we cannot simply walk away once the fight is over; better to stay with a moderate numbers of troops than return for later with larger numbers. And finally, do we have national interests involved? The mass expulsion of ethnic Albanians from Kosovo demanded the notice of the rest of the world. But it does make a difference that this is taking place in such a combustible part of Europe.

There is no reference to international law or the role of the Security Council among these requirements, though Blair is a lawyer by education and had even worked for a while as a barrister. As NATO's 1999 Kosovo operation too often serves as an example and justification for other operations, including the 2011 NATO operation against Qaddafi in Libya (though the Libya operation had the blessing of the Security Council), it is deserving of closer scrutiny.

2. *THE KOSOVO CASE REVISITED*

For the beginning I must admit that I myself cautiously supported the NATO Operation Allied Force against the Federal Republic of Yugoslavia over Kosovo, and presented legal justifications for it.[24] However, since then there have been some revelations and further

---

23 Tony Blair's speech, 'Doctrine of the international community', delivered at the Economic Club, Chicago, 22 April 1999, http://www.number-10.gov.uk/output/Page1297.asp, accessed 6 Sept. 2005.

24 See, e.g., R. Müllerson, *Ordering Anarchy: International Law in International Society*, MartinusNijhoff Publishers, 2000.

developments that have undermined the alleged humanitarian purity of NATO's Kosovo operation. And this is unfortunate since, as we will try to show below, there are situations when military intervention to protect people from their own government (or from the absence of any effective government) may be necessary even in the absence of Security Council authorisation, and, as we will discuss in this Chapter, there have indeed been interventions not authorised by the Security Council that have put an end to severe humanitarian crises. So, what was wrong with NATO's operation against the Federal Republic of Yugoslavia (President Slobodan Milošević) over Kosovo? What should be avoided so as not to discredit this extreme concept (extreme in the sense that it can be used only in extreme circumstances, and even then as an extraordinary measure), which may nevertheless sometimes be needed?

First, it was the propaganda campaign to demonise one party and the victimisation and sometimes even glorification of the other party. NATO's spokesperson Jamie Shea particularly excelled in this respect, as someone who became known as NATO's 'spin doctor'.[25] While the atrocities of the Serbian side were all meticulously reported (and there no doubt were such atrocities), sometimes even exaggerated, and any doubts as to the who and the how were ignored, the parallel acts of the Kosovo Albanians, especially the KLA fighters, which often mirrored and sometimes even exceeded the Serbian atrocities, were usually downgraded or received only limited coverage in mass media. And this was done notwithstanding that shortly prior to the operation President Bill Clinton's special envoy to the Balkans, Robert Gelbard, had described the KLA as, 'without any questions, a terrorist group'.[26] The KLA had long been engaged in 'tit-for-tat attacks with Serbian nationalists in Kosovo, using reprisals against ethnic Albanians who "collaborated" with the Serbian government, and bombing police stations and cafes known to be frequented by Serb officials, killing innocent civilians in the process. Most of its activities were funded by drug running, though its ties to

---

[25] See, e.g., L. Cooper, M. Pal, 'Lectures from Spin Doctor: A NATO strategist's position at a top British university', *Open Democracy*, 30 June 2011.

[26] Council on Foreign Relations. Terrorist Groups and Political Legitimacy (http://www.cfr.org/terrorism/terrorist-groups-political-legitimacy/p10159).

community groups and Albanian exiles gave it local popularity'.[27] The then UK Foreign Secretary, Robin Cook, told the House of Commons on 18th January 1999, i.e. only a couple of months before the NATO operation: 'On its part, the Kosovo Liberation Army has committed more breaches of the ceasefire, and until this weekend was responsible for more deaths than the security forces. It must stop undermining the ceasefire and blocking political dialogue.'[28] Later it was revealed by Gabriel Keller, a deputy head of the Kosovo Verification Mission (KVM), that: '... every pullback by the Yugoslav army or the Serbian police was followed by a movement forward by [KLA] forces [...] OSCE's presence compelled Serbian government forces to a certain restraint [...] and UCK [i.e. KLA] took advantage of this to consolidate its positions everywhere, continuing to smuggle arms from Albania, abducting and killing both civilians and military personnel, Albanians and Serbs alike.'[29] However, such revelations from people who knew what was going on on the ground were drowned by a sea of information (misinformation), in many cases true but oftentimes exaggerated, aimed at discrediting the Serbian side.

The second factor that undermines the purity of the humanitarianism at the heart of NATO's Kosovo operation is the so-called 'Rambouillet Agreement', presented in February 1999 to Belgrade and to a delegation of Kosovo Albanians in the Chateau Rambouillet in France. The latter expressed their consent with the text of the Agreement while Belgrade rejected it. This rejection was a crucial step leading to the war. However, could anyone have realistically expected Belgrade, or any other sovereign state for that matter, to accept such an agreement? Appendix B of the Agreement, being an integral part of it, provided, *inter alia*, that 'NATO personnel shall enjoy, together with their vehicles, vessels, aircraft, and equipment, free and unrestricted passage and unimpeded access throughout the FRY (Federal Republic of Yugoslavia that at that time comprised of

---

[27] Ibid.

[28] www.publications.parliament.uk/pa/cm199899/cmhansrd/vo990118/debtext/90118-06.htm.

[29] *Masters of the Universe?: NATO's Balkan Crusade* (Tariq Ali ed.), Verso Books, 2000, p. 163.

Serbia and Montenegro) including associated airspace and territorial waters. This shall include, but not be limited to, the right of bivouac, manoeuvre, billet, and utilization of any areas or facilities as required for support, training, and operations'. Furthermore, the authorities in the FRY were obligated to 'facilitate, on a priority basis and with all appropriate means, all movement of personnel, vehicles, vessels, aircraft, equipment, or supplies, through or in the airspace, ports, airports, or roads used'.[30] It was an ultimatum requesting unconditional surrender, something that no state that was not defeated in a war would have accepted. In a commentary released to the press, the former United States Secretary of State Henry Kissinger declared that: 'The Rambouillet text, which called on Serbia to admit NATO troops throughout Yugoslavia, was a provocation, an excuse to start bombing. Rambouillet is not a document that an angelic Serb could have accepted. It was a terrible diplomatic document that should never have been presented in that form'.[31] Lord Gilbert stated in the House of Lord of the British Parliament: 'I think the terms put to Milošević at Rambouillet were absolutely intolerable; how could he possibly accept them? It was quite deliberate'.[32] One can only conclude that it was not as much the humanitarian concerns as the wider intransigence of President Milošević of Yugoslavia that was the main cause of NATO's bombardment of the FRY in 1999. As John Norris, Strobe Talbott's Director of Communications during the Kosovo crisis, wrote, 'it was Yugoslavia's resistance to the broader trends of political and economic reform – not the plight of Kosovar Albanians – that best explains NATO's war. Milošević had been a burr in the side of the transatlantic community for so long that the United States felt that he would only respond to military pressure'.[33] Therefore Kosovo was not an operation with singularly humanitarian objectives, but as a regime change operation with geopolitical purposes and implications.

---

[30] US Department of State.Rambouillet Agreement (Interim Agreement for Peace and Self-Government in Kosovo), http://www.state.gov/www/regions/eur/ksvo_rambouillet_text.html.

[31] *Daily Telegraph*, 28 June 1999.

[32] Select Committee on Defence. Minutes of Evidence, June 2000.http://www.publications.parliament.uk/pa/cm199900/cmselect/cmdfence/347/0062005.htm.

[33] J. Norris, *Collision Course. NATO, Russia, and Kosovo* (Foreword by Strobe Talbott), Praeger, 2005, p. xxiii.

NATO's Kosovo operation, which many Western politicians and experts refer to as an example to be followed in order to save lives in, for example, Libya or Syria may, however, serve also as a different, mush more negative, precedent. German journalist Alexander Rar writes that in the aftermath, in Russia NATO lost prestige even among many liberally minded people, and they started to profess doubts in democracy as a form of political regime.[34] Even more disturbing may be another effect of NATO's operation, exposed by Rar: 'Many Russians suddenly lost their antipathy towards use of force by their own country. They sincerely started to believe that if the civilized West is not averse to violence, then Russia with her existential problems simply has to do the same'.[35] Later, in this Chapter, we will see how Russia used arguments related to the concept of R2P (responsibility to protect) that is a slightly modified, though wider and not necessarily linked to the use of military force, version of humanitarian intervention.

Finally, an additional fly in Kosovo's anointment was what happened later, after the years of manipulative administration of Kosovo by the international community, including the United Nations and the European Union. The recognition of the independence of Kosovo by the majority of Western states, notwithstanding a clause in all Security Council resolutions on Kosovo both before NATO's invasion [Res. 1199 (23 September 1998), Res. 1203 (24 October 1998)] as well as after the invasion [Res. 1244 (10 June 1999)], emphasised the importance of guaranteeing the territorial integrity of Yugoslavia. For example, Resolution 1244 reaffirmed 'the commitment of all Member States to the sovereignty and territorial integrity of the Federal Republic of Yugoslavia and the other States of the region, as set out in the Helsinki Final Act and annex 2'. Notwithstanding all these clauses most NATO and EU member states recognised the declaration of independence of Kosovo, which, in turn, made for the Kremlin easier to recognize the two Georgian break-away provinces as independent states. This, together with other such *gung ho* approaches to international law, contributed to the undermining of

---

34 A. Rar, *Vladimir Putin – The Best German in the Kremlin*, Moscow, Algoritm, 2012 (Russian translation from German), p. 174.

35 Ibid., p. 175.

the foundations of the latter. The Advisory Opinion delivered by the International Court of Justice on 22nd July 2010 stating that Kosovo's declaration of independence 'did not violate general international law', though formally correct, is anodyne in content, and potentially explosive in its consequences. Even if I were to declare my house with its small plot of land in Tallinn independent from Estonia, I would not be in breach of general international law since international law simply does not deal with such matters. However, if a neighbouring state were to recognise my extravagant declaration, it would certainly violate general international law; this would be a clear-cut interference in the internal affairs of my country.

3. *RECOGNITION OF KOSOVO, ABKHAZIA AND SOUTH OSSETIA*

One recent contentious issue discussed by politicians, diplomats as well as academics has been the attitude towards the independence of Kosovo on the one hand, and South Ossetia and Abkhazia on the other. Quite a few international lawyers, condemning the recognition of independence of the Georgian break-away territories (Abkhazia and South Ossetia) by Russia, as well as several of other states, have at the same time welcomed Kosovo's independence from Serbia, and *vice versa*, those welcoming the independence of Abkhazia and South Ossetia deny that Kosovo has any right to independence, oblivious of any irony in their attitude.

There is no doubt that there are a lot of factual differences between what happened and what is going on today in these two mountainous regions – the Balkans and the Caucasus. In many respects, all cases are unique. Lawyers know all too well the saying that 'hard cases make bad law' and one may well want to add to that that unique cases do not make any law at all. However, in international relations, all cases of any significance are hard cases, and it is only the hard cases that can produce law for hard cases. Moreover, in the domain where international law functions, where no more than 200 states, hugely differing as to their size, power, political regimes and other characteristics, operate, all situations are also markedly more unique than those taking place in relations between individuals and legal persons within a particular state; that is why in international society most situations are relatively more unique than cases covered by domestic law. Therefore, in international society just a few cases tend to serve as precedents that may make, undermine, change or modify legal norms. If all the more or less significant developments and situations in interstate relations were seen as unique, having nothing in common, international law would become not only a theoretical but also a practical impossibility.

However, states, especially the more powerful ones, more and more frequently, by referring to the uniqueness of circumstances they are acting upon as well as to the purity of their own motives, incomparable with the self-serving intentions of their opponents, consider that their behaviour *vis-à-vis* certain situations or certain states should not serve as a precedent. For example, Condoleezza Rice, the then US Secretary of State, claimed that situations in the Balkans and the Caucasus had nothing in common: 'I don't want to try to judge the motives, but we've been very clear that Kosovo is *sui generis* and that that is because of the special circumstances out of which the breakup of Yugoslavia came'.[36] However, her Russian counterpart, Sergei Lavrov, in justifying the recognition of South Ossetia and Abkhazia by Kremlin as independent states, was equally clear. Although not referring to Kosovo's recognition as a precedent, he may well have had Kosovo in mind when he talked about the legality of recognising the breakaway Georgian territories. Yet, the Russian Foreign Minister, like Condoleezza Rice, claimed that 'the recognition by Russia of Georgia's Abkhazia and South Ossetia as independent states does not set a precedent for other post-Soviet break-away regions .... There can be no parallels here.'[37] The main problem with Rice's as well as Lavrov's certainties that there are no parallels between these and other cases, and that neither case can serve as a precedent for other situations is how to persuade, for example, the Transdniestrians, Armenians of Nagorno-Karabach and the host of other separatist movements that Kosovo, Abkhazia

[36] 6 March 2008, Briefing by Secretary Rice en route to Brussels, Belgium (www .usembassy.org.uk/ forpo1244/html).

[37] Abkhazia, S. Ossetia no precedents for other rebel regions – Lavrov", RIA Novosti, 18 September 2008 (en.rian.ru).

and South Ossetia are so unique, so *sui generis* that they cannot serve as precedents for others.

Differences, or parallels for that matter, are often only in the eye of the beholder. Whether certain situations, facts or acts can serve as precedents depends to a great extent on whether one is interested in seeing them as such. Too many people too often act upon their ideologies, beliefs and prejudices, not upon facts; or rather, the latter are interpreted in the light of preconceived ideas. All these secessionist conflicts and situations, notwithstanding their many differences, have something quite essential in common: there is always a group of people who, being part of a bigger political entity but distinguishing themselves from the whole, want to secede from the rest in order to form an independent state or become a part of another political entity. In this essential respect, say, Quebec in Canada, Nagorno-Karabakh in Azerbaijan and Abkhazia or South Ossetia in Georgia are all in the same boat, and if they refer to their uniqueness, it is only to show that they deserve independence more than anybody else. When the Quebecois claim their right to independence, they refer to the fact that their distinct culture and language are flourishing, that they have effective democratic governmental institutions and other positive achievements, which, in their view, serve as a basis for Quebec's independence. Other secessionist movements, on the contrary, emphasize the lack of such achievements and believe that only through secession can they achieve those characteristics that, as they suppose, are denied to them by oppressive alien regimes.

4. THE LIBYA CASE

Already in 2005, Secretary of State Condoleezza Rice, speaking in Cairo, commented that 'for sixty years, my country, the United States, pursued stability at the expense of democracy in this region here in the Middle East—and we achieved neither.'[38] The meaning of these words was that it was time to set new priorities; instead of a stability that had hitherto worked but was reaching a tipping point, it was

[38] N.K. Gvosdev, R. Takeyh, '*Triumph of the New Wilsonism*', *The National Interest*, January-February 2012.

better to harmonize with the emerging trend and support democracy movements in the Middle East. Nevertheless, in 2007, the late Tom Lantos, Chairman of the House Foreign Affairs Committee, argued: 'I am very proud of America's success in convincing Qaddafi to become a decent citizen of global community. … Our engagement with Qaddafi and the prosperity it has brought to Libya serves as a model to countries currently sponsoring terror or compiling weapons of mass destruction. They should know that they, too, can come in from the cold'.[39] What had changed since 2007, and why less than five years later did the United States support the overthrow of Gaddafi notwithstanding that he had just 'become a decent citizen of global community'? As always in complicated cases, there is more than one answer to this question. However, the main reason behind the change of heart by Washington lies in its coming to the understanding that the Middle East had reached a tipping point after which it would become impossible to rely on autocrats, who had hitherto served America's interests well, notwithstanding all the uncertainties and apprehensions that Islamic democracy could bring. Of course, there was also the rather naive belief that Washington would be able to ride the tiger i.e. that following the developments, Washington and its allies could channel the emerging trends in direction favourable for American strategic and economic interests. That is why Western capitals found it safer to abandon their old (in the case of Qaddafi, newly found) friends. However, it is important to note that even before the coming of the Arab Spring, the United States and some other Western countries were acting as hedge funds do, i.e. they were hedging their bets. While these governments were working with and relying on Middle Eastern dictators, various Western organizations, including government funded ones, groomed bloggers and activists from Arab countries in, for example, Serbia and the United States.[40]

If the wars in Iraq (the 2003 invasion or the so-called 'second Gulf War') and Afghanistan were, if not inspired then at least partly

---

[39] Quoted from N.K. Gvosdev, R. Takeyh, 'Triumph of the New Wilsonism', *The National Interest*, 2012, January 4.

[40] http://www.wikileaks.ch/cable/2010/01/10CAIRO99.html; T. Ramadan, *The Arab Awakening: Islam and the New Middle East,* Allen Lane, 2012, pp. 7, 22.

justified by the arguments of DP theories, NATO Operation Unified Protector in Libya in 2011 had the hallmarks of humanitarian intervention. In his 28th March 2011 speech at George Washington University on NATO's military operation against Gaddafi's Libya, President Barak Obama declared that America had a responsibility to stop the looming genocide in the Libyan city of Benghazi.[41] The 2011 NATO Libya operation, in contradistinction to the Kosovo operation, had the blessing of the UN Security Council and therefore was arguably lawful.[42] We use the word 'arguably' since like in several other UN Security Council sanctioned interventions, the practicalities and consequences of intervention went beyond what was mandated in the Council's resolution. An operation justified by the protection of civilians turned into a war against the regime of Colonel Gaddafi, leading to its overthrow. James Pattison, for example, writes: 'Indeed, the rhetoric of several of the coalition leaders, who in various speeches have argued that Qaddafi must step down, suggest that the perceived success of the intervention will be measured primarily by whether Qaddafi's reign is ended.'[43] This means that the primary aim was not humanitarian but regime change. Later, not only the 'usual suspects' China and Russia, but also the Arab League, which had requested the establishment of no-fly zones to protect the civilians, criticised NATO's actions, which had gone beyond what the League had requested.[44] Amr Moussa, the then Secretary General of the Arab League declared in March 2011, when NATO's Operation United Protector was in full swing: 'What is happening in Libya differs from the aim of imposing a no-fly

---

[41] http://abcnews.go.com/Politics/libya-president-obama-makes-case-intervention/story?id=13244178#.TwlNfW9MsVc.

[42] The Security Council Resolution 1973 authorized 'Member States that have notified the Secretary-General, acting nationally or through regional organizations or arrangements', to take 'all necessary measures ... to protect civilians' and for that end to establish no-fly zones (S/RES/1973 (2011).

[43] J. Pattison, 'The Ethics of Humanitarian Intervention in Libya', *Ethics & International Affairs*, 25, No. 3 (2011), p. 274.

[44] 'La Ligue arab, la Russie et la Chine critiquent l'intervention', *Le Monde*, 20 March 2011 (http://www.lemonde.fr/afrique/article/2011/03/20/la-ligue-arabe-la-russie-et-la-chine-critiquent-l-intervention_1495991_3212.html); 'Arab League Condemns Broad Western Bombing Campaigns in Libya', *Washington Post*, 20 March 2011 (http://www.washingtonpost.com/world/arab-league-condemns-broad-bombing-campaign-in-libya/2011/03/20/AB1pSg1_story.html).

zone ... what we want is the protection of civilians and not the shelling of more civilians'.[45]

Even if the regime had consented to carrying out reforms and stopping repressions, this would not have been enough, either for the opposition in Libya or for their external supporters. Such an attitude from their external supporters made the opposition even more intransigent and uncompromising. Their aim was no longer to achieve reforms or to end the looming humanitarian crisis, but power. Like in the run-up to the 1999 Kosovo operation by NATO, in the case of Libya, as Tariq Ramadan observes, 'Western media were quick to propagate sombre account of the repression in Libya and a *sanitized version of the opposition* (emphasis added R. M.)',[46] while Amnesty International commented: 'Western media coverage from the outset presented a very one-sided view of events, portraying the protest movement as entirely peaceful and repeatedly suggesting that the regime's security forces were unaccountably massacring unarmed demonstrators who presented no security challenge'.[47] Once again we see that the demonization of the one side and the victimization or heroization of the opposing side should be treated, if not as a *prima facie* evidence that preparations for interference are underway, then at least it should cast doubt on the sincerity of calls that something has to be done.

In societies not used to democracy and not having any liberal traditions, political processes usually follow a winner-takes-all structure. Neither the authorities, nor the opposition are used to compromise. If the opposition feels that their uncompromising, maximalistic demands have found external support, they become even more intransigent, even more uncompromising. The authorities, at the same time, know well that if they lose power, they will lose also their wealth, liberty and possibly even lives. They know and understand well opposition's potential for revenge and its 'prudent' policies of eliminating any potential threat to their power once they

---

45 Ibid.

46 T. Ramadan, *The Arab Awakening: Islam and the New Middle East*, Allen Lane, 2012, p. 35.

47 'Amnesty Questions Claim that Gaddafi Ordered Rape as Weapon of War', *The Independent*, 24 June 2011.

attain it, since more often than not opponents of the regime, when in power, use the same methods as the authorities they have overthrown. Aaron David Miller's comment that 'the Arabs are much better at acquiring and fighting over power than they are at sharing it'[48] may be generalised; it is applicable to many societies beyond the Arab world.

In his 2000 Millennium report Kofi Annan, the then Secretary General of the United Nations, noted that the concept of humanitarian intervention 'might encourage secessionist movements deliberately to provoke governments into committing cross violations of human rights in order to trigger external interventions that would aid their cause'.[49] This comment applies not only to secessionist movements. Alan Kuperman has called this a 'problem of moral hazard', meaning that protection against a risk encourages risk-taking.[50] As Kuperman shows, the threats of force against Serbia over Kosovo emboldened the KLA (Kosovo Liberation Army) fighters and encouraged them to use even greater violence against ethnic Serbian civilians in Kosovo in order to provoke the Serbs to overreact, thereby forcing the West to use force to protect Kosovo Albanians. This was what eventually happened. And it is not only secessionist movements that may find encouragement in the threats of outside actors to use force against regimes that misbehave. Equally, opponents of dictators like Gaddafi in Libya and al-Assad in Syria have used the same tactics.

However, even if we agree that NATO's mission in Libya was a mission creep and that it went beyond the Security Council's mandate leading to a externally assisted change of regime, an important question remains: is it at all possible to protect a population from repressive governments without overthrowing or helping remove such governments from power? Perhaps they even deserve to be overthrown? David Rieff, a journalist who specialises in humanitarian issues, wrote in the *New York Times Magazine*: 'Use any euphemism you wish, but in the end these interventions have to be about

[48] A.D. Miller, 'The Stalled Arab Spring', *The National Interest*, 8 June 2012.

[49] K. Annan, 'We the peoples': the role of the United Nations in the twenty-first century, A/54/ 2000, 27 March 2000, para. 216.

[50] A. Kuperman, 'The Moral Hazard of Humanitarian Intervention: Lessons from the Balkans', *International Studies Quarterly*, 2008, Vol. 52, Issue 1, pp. 49–80.

regime change if they are to have any chance of accomplishing their stated goal.'[51] It may well be so that in some of these rare situations, when an intervention on humanitarian grounds may be justified, regime change is inevitable. But it seems that all too often, for the intervening states it is more important to get rid of the incumbent ruler than to protect human lives. So, Jon Western and Joshua Goldstein wrote about NATO's Libya operation: 'No sooner had NATO launched its first air strike in Libya than the mission was thrown into controversy – and with it, the more general notion of humanitarian intervention. Days after the UN Security Council authorized international forces to protect civilians and establish a no-fly zone, NATO seemed to go beyond its mandate as several of its members explicitly demanded that Libyan leader Muammar al-Qaddafi step down'.[52] Although regime change may occur, be inevitable or even necessary for a successful and sustainable military interference on humanitarian grounds, there are circumstances in which uncompromising insistence on a regime change intensifies the conflict, and leads to an even greater loss of life. That the main aim was regime change, not the protection of people, was even clearer in the case of Syria than in the case of Libya.

5. *THE SYRIA TRAGEDY*

Comparisons of mass media reports from Syria in 2012 with reports of western media from Kosovo in 1998–1999 and from Libya in 2011 are quite obvious and disturbing. Regime change efforts are usually accompanied by attempts of demonization of the target regime and 'angelization' of opponents of the regime. Paul Pillar in his article 'Wiping Out' published in *The National Interest* writes how President Sarkozy of France accusing President Bashar al-Assad of Syria of wanting 'wipe Homs from the map like Gaddafi wanted to wipe Benghazi from the map'[53] had distorted statements used by those dictators. Neither Gaddafi, notwithstanding all his eccentricity and

[51] D. Rieff, 'Humanitarian Vanities', *The New York Times Magazine*, 1 June, 2008.

[52] J. Western, J.S. Goldstein, Humanitarian Intervention Comes of Age, Foreign Affairs, 2011, November/December.

[53] P.R. Pillar, 'Wiping Out', *The National Interest*, 22 April, 2012.

bloodthirstiness, nor Bashar al-Assad had promised to 'wipe out' anybody.

In Syria, the repressive Government was using force, sometimes targeted, often indiscriminate, against its own people. That much was clear and very few, besides the al-Assad regime, would deny that. TV channels and newspapers in the whole world concentrated for months their attention on regime's atrocities. Almost everyone who watched TV or read the news felt that something had to be done to put an end to the violence committed by the Government of Syria. However, moral outrage, caused by the atrocities committed and channelled by the media, even if justified and just, also blinds. Not only are the important details lost. Even more importantly, instead of putting an end to the humanitarian catastrophe, such outrage may help fuel the conflict. And as in every war, it is the truth that is the first victim.

There is no doubt that, like in other Arab countries, the revolt against the Assad regime was a response to the decades of repression. However, it is not only that. The devil is not only in the details but it is also in the context. So is it with Syria and here the analysis of the political context and answers to the question *cui prodest* help if not better target the moral outrage then at least find immediate as well as long-term solutions to the crisis. Such an analysis also reveals that Alexander the Great's method of untying the Gordian knot works much better in the physical than in the human world. These are human beings that are tied in a knot that has to be disentangled and therefore threats to use military force only enflame the conflict, to say nothing about loss of lives in case of an actual external intervention.

Syria is a multi-ethnic and multi-religious country where the Alawi Shia minority has ruled for decades over a society with Sunni Muslim majority. I addition, there is a significant Christian minority comprising of Armenians, as well as Arabs. Ethnically the country is even more colourful: Arabs, Armenians, Kurds, Circassians and others. In all the neighbouring Arab countries (with the exception of Iraq), on the contrary, these are Sunni majorities that rule over, *inter alia*, Shia minorities. And then, of course, there is the elephant in the room – a big ambitious Shia Iran, whose ally or client the Assad regime certainly is. In the context of the geo-political rivalry in the

Middle East and from the point of view of conservative Arab monarchies, the second best to the 'cutting off the head of the snake' (a Saudi euphemism for attacking Iran) would be the biting off its tail (performing a regime change in Syria). Does this not indicate that in the Syrian context the Arab Awakening has been highjacked by geopolitical games? Isn't it rather strange that together with the United States and European democracies, these are the Gulf's autocracies Saudi Arabia, Bahrain and Qatar that are the most vocal critics of Assad regime's atrocities (and no doubt atrocities there were committed)? Wasn't it Saudi Arabia, that less than a year before the crisis erupted in Syria, helped to put down the popular revolt in Bahrain, where the Sunni minority regime rules over the majority Shia population? Is there indeed anybody who would believe, even discounting the Saudi anti-human rights intervention in Bahrain, that the Saudi Kingdom is concerned about human rights and democracy in another Arab country? As Bahrain is the base for the US Fifth fleet, Washington remained silent about its ally's misbehaviour. Moreover, the rebels were mostly Shia Muslims, i.e. Iran's co-religionists, and their success may have further strengthened the position of Iran in the region. This, after the folly of the Western invasion in Iraq in 2003, which at the end of the day benefited Iran, would have been too much to bear for those who fear and hate Iran. So, it seems that for several regional players the talk about human rights violations in Syria has been a cover for the Sunni-Shia or the Arab-Iranian rivalry in the Middle East. Then, there is no love lost between Israel and Assad's regime, though the former should be apprehensive lest any post-Assad regime turn out to be even more anti-Israeli than the regime of the current secular autocrat. Al Qaeda leader Ayman al-Zawahri, in a video recording posted on the Internet, urged Muslims around the region to help Syrian rebels.[54] Ban Ki-moon, the UN Secretary General, believed that the 10 May 2012 terrorist attack in Damascus that killed at least 55 people and wounded hundreds must have had al-Qaeda behind it.[55]

---

[54] http://www.telegraph.co.uk/news/worldnews/middleeast/syria/9151413/Syria-funerals-held-for-Damascus-bomb-victims.html.

[55] UN chief blames al-Qaeda for Syria bombing, Aljazeera, 18 May, 2012 http://www.aljazeera.com/news/middleeast/2012/05/201251827299973.html.

This is a geo-political context to the genuine humanitarian catastrophe in Syria and this has to be kept in mind when deciding how to end the bloodshed. What about military-strategic and legal issues of the Syria conundrum? The Syrian Army has been using heavy weaponry by either directly targeting civilians and civilian objects in rebellious cities or by using indiscriminate force against the opponents, both armed and unarmed. In legal terms such acts, whatever the intent and depending on the context, are either war crimes or crimes against humanity. The precise legal qualification depends on what may be called legal niceties, i.e. whether there is an internal armed conflict (civil war) or 'simply' a situation of internal disturbances, riots or rebellion. On 15 July 2012, the International Committee of the Red Cross (ICRC) declared that there is a civil war going on in Syria. Although such a conclusion by the ICRC, or any other body for that matter, would hardly have an effect on the situation on the ground, it may have significant legal consequences. First, this means that for the purposes of possible prosecution of those, who perpetrated atrocities in such a conflict, international humanitarian law applies. This is in terms of *jus in bello*. Secondly, as we will discuss in detail later, it is prohibited for third states to give military assistance to any party in a situation of an internal armed conflict, i.e. civil war. Hence, it would be in breach of international law not only to supply arms to the rebels (e.g., to the Free Syrian Army), but also to the al-Assad regime. This is in terms of *jus ad bellum*. UN Secretary General Ban Ki-moon acted in accordance with international law when he 'reiterated his opposition to the further militarization of the conflict [in Syria] and called on *all states* to stop supplying arms *to all sides* in Syria'[56] [emphasis added].

The al-Assad regime has *prima facie* committed war crimes and crimes against humanity. However, the opposition seems to be guilty of the same categories of crimes. For example, one should ask: why didn't the Syrian Army simply march into these rebellious areas to suppress the peaceful resistance to the regime, arrest the leaders of the opposition and do whatever dictators usually do? Why were

---

[56] http://www.silobreaker.com/un-chief-urges-end-of-arms-supplies-to-syria-5_2265940386843197711; RIA Novosti, 30 August 2012.

heavy artillery and tanks used to advance into Homs and other cities, and to fight in Damascus or Aleppo? Obviously, because there was somebody, who was fighting back from these civilian quarters. Because there was a so-called Free Syrian Army, and it was acting not out of the deserts and mountains of the countryside, but from those rebellious neighbourhoods. They operated amongst the civilians and civilian objects; from there they were fighting the advancing Syrian Army. However, shouldn't they know that a regime like al-Assad's doesn't care about the lives of innocent civilians caught in the crossfire, or that by positioning themselves in the vicinity of civilians and civilian objects they were also committing war crimes (if we assume that there was an internal armed conflict)? Fighting in the close vicinity of civilian objects and civilian population, as they were, whatever their intention, and actually using the latter as a human shield, is indeed a war crime. Certainly, it is not the first time that a weaker opponent utilized the foreseeable bloody response of a ruthless regime in order to generate sympathy for its cause, to demonize and delegitimize the regime, with the ultimate aim of bringing into being an external intervention on its behalf.

For those who care more about innocent lives than geo-political games and regime-change (and there is no doubt that sooner rather than later there will be one in Syria too) it would have been necessary to call for all armed groups to cease using force. Condemning only the Government and calling for a regime change has shown the opposition that they need not make any compromises; this has made them even more intransigent. Professor Flynt Leverett of Penn State University was right that 'Annan's efforts [the former UN Secretary General acted as the UN-Arab League peace envoy to Syria] were undermined by the US ... and to some degree he undermined himself by buying into the argument that you should stipulate at the outset that President Assad needed to go, which meant that there couldn't really be a serious political process'.[57]

Acting upon hopes for absolute power makes the opposition uncompromising that, in turn, may lead to more civilian casualties and the spiral of violence would go on and on. One would be naive

---

[57] 'Has Syria become the UN's proxy battlefield?' Inside Story, Al Jazeera, 3 August 2012.

in believing that even if the UN Security Council would unanimously call Bashar al-Assad to go, that he would do exactly that. Especially, knowing well how Colonel Qaddafi of Libya ended his days. Al-Assad could not quit even if he personally wanted to go since his fate is closely tied to that of his retainers. At the same time, any intervention on behalf of the opposition, and even 'simply' arming them would not only have been counterproductive (remember that it was Saudi Arabia that in the 1980s armed the Mujahidin's in Afghanistan, including Osama bin Laden, to 'kick Soviet's ass'), but it would have also clearly been in violation of international law (about military interventions in cases of riots and civil unrests at the invitation of governments and the prohibition of intervention in civil wars see further in this Chapter). Some may think that these are outdated norms that put state sovereignty and non-interference above humanitarian concerns. In some situations, like the one in Rwanda in 1994, humanitarian concerns would surely outweigh imperatives of state sovereignty. Yet, in order to decide what kind of situation we are in, we shouldn't let moral outrage blind our vision. On the other hand, Russia's continuing supply of arms to a Government in a civil war situation in Syria was equally unlawful, notwithstanding previous agreements between Russia and Syria on the trade in weapons. Hence, Moscow's claims that it was only interested in upholding international law also rang hollow. As Dr Yang Jiemian, the President of the Shanghai Institutes for International Studies, during our 21 July conversation in Shanghai explained it to me, it was only China that had acted on principle, when vetoing the three Security Council draft resolutions on Syria supported by Western powers. China, differently from Russia and other involved states, does not have any special interests in Syria. On the contrary, China has significant economic interests in the GCC (Gulf Cooperation Council) countries, which all support the opposition to al-Assad's regime. Hence, Beijing's opportunistic interest would be, as Dr Yang opined, to align itself with those states, which call for the regime change in Syria. However, China puts adherence to the principle of non-interference in internal affairs above such opportunistic concerns. Whether one takes or leaves such an explanation depends on one's worldview (also dictated, at least partly, by one's interest), but one should not brush it simply aside.

Those who fight bad guys are not necessarily good guys. As the Dean of Johns Hopkins School of Advanced International Studies Vali R. Nasr put it, '[Th]e fight is much more about the implications for redistribution of power between communities in Syria than it is about constitutionalism and democracy'.[58] What is going on in Syria is not struggle for democracy but the fight for power. Of course, without simplifications, without demonization of one side and the heroization of another, and a black and white vision of a conflict, the mobilizing effect of the picture would be seriously weakened. This may be one of the reasons why those who advocate or contemplate invasion (or the regime and its few allies defending its uncompromising stance) feel the need to present such black and white picture. However, if history teaches us something it is that such simplifications and acting upon black and white visions later return to haunt us. If this all sounds too cynical, one has to remember that we are dealing with regional and global power politics where the hypocrisy of both local actors (the government as well as opposition) and major players is all-pervasive. Whenever one speaks on behalf of humanity, it is always safer to double-check: aren't there behind the moral indignation, lofty words and calls for action hidden motives, other less inclusive interests at play? And if after such a double-check we indeed find that, for example, the Saudi monarchy together with its Gulf allies as well as other major players have nothing but the rights and interests of the Syrian people – Sunni and Shia, Muslims and Christians, Armenians and Circassians – in mind and that the Assad regime, notwithstanding all the efforts of domestic opponents and external actors to find a political solution to the conflict, is not able and willing to stop the bloodshed, then the world community may indeed use all necessary means to topple the only bad guy and his retainers in Syria. However, without openly discussing the particular interests of various Syrian factions as well as those of external players, it would be difficult to implement the most urgent tasks: putting an end to the bloodshed, securing access to

---

58 B. Gwertzman, 'What Syria's Power Struggle Means', interview with Vali R. Nasr, *Council for Foreign Relations* (http://www.cfr.org/syria/syrias-power-struggle-means/p28432).

humanitarian assistance for those in need, and starting a political process where all sides should be ready for compromises.

Then, once again, like in the cases of Iraq, Afghanistan or Libya, Western political leaders and supporting them journalists and academics are speaking of a future democratic, even liberal Syria. Those who know and love tennis would want to address such leaders with the famous words American tennis star John McEnroe usually reserved for umpires: 'You cannot be serious, man'. Joshua Landis correctly observes that 'if anyone tell you they are going to build democracy in Syria, don't buy it'.[59] Among factors that make any democracy building efforts in Syria even more difficult than in some other Arab countries, besides the level of economic development of the country, traditions or the lack of them, and the ethnic and religious divides in the country, Landis also mentions the median age of the population (21 years in Syria). He refers to the research by Richard Cincotta of the Stimson Centre in Washington DC, who having studied social and political revolutions in various countries between 1972 and 1989 and focusing on the age structure of countries, had found that countries with a median age of 30 or just under or over (if the median age is over 35 there aren't any revolutionary situations) have good chances for sustaining their democratic achievements.[60] The lower the median age, the more difficult would it be to have a successful and sustainable democratic regime change.

In the Arab Spring, like in many other significant developments, local, regional and global factors become intractably interlinked and concentrating only on one of them gives a limited and wrong picture. So far, we have emphasised the importance of local differences since they are often neglected when Western, especially American, observes look at the world. However, it would be equally wrong to lose sight of the bigger picture. Therefore, the events in the Middle East have to be seen also in the light of the changing balance of power in the world as a whole. During the Cold War era, the Middle East was an important region where Washington and Moscow vied

---

[59] J. Landis, 'Stay out of Syria', *The Foreign Policy*, 5 June 2012.

[60] S. Reardon, 'Egypt: Arab Spring could be wasted in youthful nations', New Scientist, 17 May 2012 (http://www.newscientist.com/article/mg21428653.800-egypt-arab-spring-could-be-wasted-in-youthful-nations.html).

for primacy in terms of their respective economic, strategic and ideological interests. Now the elephant (or rather the dragon), though still hidden behind the talk about democracy, human rights or war on terror (from the Western perspective) as well as Deng Xiaoping's advise for his successors to remain free of ambition and never claim leadership (from the Chinese perspective), is China and its increasing presence also in the Middle East. Tariq Ramadan is right that '[F]ar removed from celebration of democratic values, a genuine economic and ideological war is being waged throughout the Arab world, in Africa and Asia' and that 'the rise of strong, multifaceted competition has put the markets of the Western multinationals in danger'.[61] This is the context in which the Arab Awakening, notwithstanding its regional and local causes and idiosyncratic determinants of success and failure, is taking place; not taking this context into account would indeed be like groping a trunk of the elephant without seeing the rest of the animal.

6. *HUMANITARIAN INTERVENTION AND REGIME CHANGE: SOME GENERALISATIONS*

For the protection of a population against genocide or crimes against humanity to be effective and sustainable, there usually has to be a change of the government that ordered the acts of genocide to be committed, condoned them, or was unable to stop them. However, one of the problems is that in many cases when the Western or the world communities insisted on regime change, there was no genocidal situation where the authorities slaughtered innocent civilians but there was rather an internal conflict in which all the parties carried out atrocities, and the scale and seriousness of these atrocities depended not on who was more and who was less vicious, but on who was stronger and better equipped. At the same time, in the clearest case of governmental genocide – Rwanda of 1994 – it was not the world community that put an end to the genocide carried out on behalf of the Hutu led Government, but the fighters of the

[61] T. Ramadan, *The Arab Awakening: Islam and the New Middle East*, Allen Lane, 2012, p. 61.

Rwandan Patriotic Army (RPA) – the armed wing of the Patriotic Front of Rwanda (RPF) led by Paul Kagame.

There have been three significant, relatively large-scale and successful foreign invasions that have put an end to massive human rights violations which may be characterised either as genocide, crimes against humanity or war crimes, though quite interestingly and even understandably, none of the invading states referred to humanitarian concerns as the only or main reason or justification for their actions. The overthrow of the regimes of Idi Amin in Uganda in 1979, the ousting of Pol Pot in the same year in the so-called Democratic Kampuchea, and the Indian 1971–72 intervention in Eastern Pakistan, which all put an end to massive crimes against the civilian populations, all also ended up with a change of the regimes that had committed those atrocities (in the case of the Indian intervention it led to the breakup of Pakistan and the creation of a new state in Eastern Pakistan – Bangladesh). None of these interventions was sanctioned by the United Nations and the intervening states preferred to refer to self-defence as the justification instead of 'purely humanitarian concerns'.[62] Naturally, in all these cases, besides the humanitarian issues, there were other concerns and interests present, if not dominant, though none of these military operations could be qualified as actions of self-defence. There is something significant in the fact that these three large-scale, successful foreign military interventions, which were responses to genuine humanitarian catastrophes (even if not justified by references to them) and put an end to those catastrophes, were carried out by non-Western nations. One of the reasons for their success in the sense of the sustainability of the main results of their interventions (the end of mass atrocities and not democracy building) may have been in that after overthrowing bloody dictators (Idi Amin and Pol Pot) and putting an end to Islamabad's repressions in Eastern Pakistan, the intervening states did not attempt to put in place pro-Western or

[62] In December 1971, immediately after the Indian intervention had started, the Indian Ambassador to the UN declared: '[W]e have on this particular occasion absolutely nothing but the purest of intentions: to rescue the people of East Bengal from what they are suffering' (UN Doc. S/PV.1606, 4 December 1971, p. 86). Soon, however, the Indian Government denounced this statement of its Ambassador and referred to the right of self-defence instead.

Western-sounding and Western-looking governments, and did not carry out nation building exercises with the aim of widening the circle of liberal democracies in the world.

This observation seems to corroborate the point that generally people deserve the governments they have, though no nation, obviously, deserves a government that commits genocide or crimes against humanity. It would not be necessary, in that respect, to distinguish between genocide and crimes against humanity since the distinction between these two most serious international crimes is not in their relative gravity or scale but rather in legal definitions (the crime of genocide requires a special intent to destroy, in whole or in part, a specific national, ethnic, racial or religious group). Therefore, it may be difficult to qualify the crimes of non-discriminatory bloody dictators such as Stalin or Pol Pot as genocide, which in no way diminishes their gravity.

However, several warnings are necessary. Foreign meddling may lead to the formation of a government (political system or regime) that does not correspond to the characteristics of society and is not therefore sustainable. External actors usually use their own yardsticks to measure the suitability of political elites to govern target countries: the more Western they look and sound, the better. However, in most non-Western countries such leaders are usually the least suitable to govern their people; the absence of domestic legitimacy cannot be compensated by external support. Ahmad Chalabi, whose efforts and lies contributed to the March 2003 American led invasion of Iraq, did not even get a chance to lead the country, the support he enjoyed among some influential American politicians notwithstanding, while Hamid Karzai has been a disaster for Afghanistan. Therefore, the acceptance of Christopher Layne's recommendation that '[T]he United States must avoid future large-scale nation-building exercises like those in Iraq and Afghanistan and refrain from fighting wars for the purpose of attaining regime change',[63] though made to serve the interests of the United States, would also benefit countries like Afghanistan or Iraq.

[63] Ch. Layne, 'The (Almost) Triumph of Offshore Balancing', *The National Interest*, 2012, 27 January.

Most governments, be they liberal democratic or authoritarian, do not constitute threats to their neighbours, and even less so for far away nations. The character of the regime is in most cases secondary to its potential to be a threat to international peace and security. For example, the potentially explosive situation between Armenia and Azerbaijan does not stem from the nature of the governments in power in these states; nor is it in any way determined by the national characteristics of Armenians or Azeris (though many Armenians are convinced that if the Azeris were more civilised they would understand the Armenian arguments, and many Azeris believe that if only the Armenians were more humane there would be peace in the region). The issues, which has already led to bloodshed and may once again explode in an all-out war in the Southern Caucasus, belong to the category of unresolved territorial disputes, to different interpretations of the right of peoples to self-determination and respect for territorial integrity (these differing interpretations are not due to any intellectual or emotional differences between the Armenians and the Azeris; they reflect concrete practical interests of the parties).

Although there is some truth to the saying that domestic repression and external aggressiveness are the two sides of the same coin, it is not true in all cases. Taken without qualification this would be a Nazi-centric interpretation of history. In Nazi Germany, internal repression and external aggression indeed not only occurred at the same time but fed on each other. The creation of the universal, United Nations based, human rights protection systems as well as the European human rights mechanisms were responses to the Nazi atrocities both in Germany and beyond. Even today we see that North Korea and Iran, both led by repressive regimes (in the case of North Korea much more so), the first through its nuclear weapons tests and aggressive policies in the region; the second by not being transparent and honest enough with the IAEA and whose leaders make unacceptable statements about Israel, as well as their shared support of organizations that utilise terror tactics, also constitute threats to international peace and security. However, the intransigence of Washington and Israel *vis-à-vis* Iran, and their position of not being content with simply having a non-nuclear weapons Iran, but attempting to humiliate Teheran and eventually generating regime change in the country, have also been counterproductive. American nuclear physicist Yousaf Butt has written that 'the sanctions are not about Iran's nuclear program. They are aimed at regime change … Conditions for lifting sanctions go way beyond anything having to do with Iran's alleged nuclear weapons program. No matter what Iran does with its nuclear program, they will remain in place. The situation may – intentionally or not – become a prelude to war'.[64]

Yet, there have been xenophobic dictatorships that have closed themselves to the outside world and haven't caused much trouble abroad. Sometimes, these are democratic governments that may be quite tolerant at home, which in their missionary zeal have disruptive influences on international relations. Their efforts to 'enlighten' other nations and bring them freedoms that they believe to be universal may destabilise not only the target countries but also endanger regional peace and security.

There are at least two reasons why some democracies may also have an unsettling impact on other states specifically and on international relations generally. Firstly, the United States – the most powerful liberal democracy (and there is no doubt that the US is democracy whatever its faults) – and its closest allies have had quite a disruptive effect through their misconceived and incompetent attempts to promote democratic values in regions where there were no fertile grounds for such values to take root. The disastrous results of such policies can be most vividly seen in Afghanistan and Iraq, but they also spectacularly failed when applied to 1990s Russia. Nor have they been unalloyed blessings in the cases of the 'colour revolutions'. Secondly, and sometimes entwined with the first reason, is the fact that democratic governments are answerable to their electorates, which by itself is, of course, a very positive phenomenon. However the interests of those electorates, and especially the most influential segments of them, which through lobbying and financial contributions to politicians determine foreign policy options, often differ considerably from the interests of other nations, be they democratic or not. Economic and security interests have played and continue to play decisive roles in international relations. The bigger and

64 Y. Butt, 'Are Sanctions a Fatwa on Iran?', *The National Interest*, 13 January 2012.

the more powerful a state, the further it casts its shadow. As the balance of power in the world as a whole and in specific regions changes from time to time, conflicts become almost inevitable. The issue is how to resolve them – through compromise and accommodation, or through coercion and violence.

7. FROM HUMANITARIAN INTERVENTION TO R2P OR 'OLD WINE IN NEW BOTTLES'?

The twenty first century started with an attempt to reformulate and rephrase the concept of humanitarian intervention in terms of responsibility to protect (R2P). First, the *International Commission on Intervention and State Sovereignty* elaborated this idea in its report in 2001 *The Responsibility to Protect.*[65] Then the idea was developed by the *High Level Panel on Threats, Challenges and Change* in its report *A More Secure World: Our Shared Responsibility*[66] in 2004. Further, there came the report of the United Nations Secretary General *in Larger Freedom: Towards Development, Security and Human Rights for All,*[67] and finally, the concept found its expression in the UN General Assembly 2005 Outcome Document.[68]

Firstly, it is necessary to underline that none of these documents creates legally binding rights and obligations. Secondly, though using different terminology and emphasising different aspects of the problem, in substance they did not add much to what was already known. Neither did they clarify the most controversial issues on which discussions had been, and continue to be held. For example, there was not, and there still is not, any doubt that every state is responsible for the protection of the rights of its citizens (this obligation stems from numerous universal and regional human rights

---

[65] International Commission on Intervention and State Sovereignty, the Responsibility to Protect, available at <http://www.iciss.ca/report-en.asp>.

[66] A More Secure World: Our Shared Responsibility, Report of the High-Level Panel on Threats, Challenges and Change, UN Doc. A/59/565, at 56–57, para. 2 01 (2004), available at <http:ll//www.un.org/secureworld/report. pdf>.

[67] In Larger Freedom: Towards Development, Security and Human Rights for A ll, Report of the Secretary-General, U N Doc. A/59/2005, paras.1 6–22 (2005), available at <http://www.un.org/largerfreedom/contents.htm>.

[68] 2005 World Summit Outcome, GA Res. 60/1, paras. 1 38–39 (Oct. 24, 2005).

documents as well as from customary norms of international law) and that if a state commits acts of genocide, war crimes, ethnic cleansing or crimes against humanity it bears responsibility for these acts under international law. Moreover, those individuals, be they heads of states or governments or the highest military officers, who are personally responsible for such acts, bear criminal liability under international law. What is not clear, and what none of these documents clarifies, is the question: is it lawful for individual states or international organisations to use military force in order to protect the nationals of foreign countries in the territory of a foreign country, if their own government commits acts of genocide, crimes against humanity, ethnic cleansing or war crimes against its own people or is unable or unwilling to protect its people in cases of such crimes committed on its territory by any other party?

It was the *Commission on State Sovereignty and Intervention* that in 2001 attempted to go furthest in allowing the use of military force in certain circumstances, even without the Security Council's authorisation. The Commission developed five criteria of legitimacy for intervention (just cause, right intention, last resort, proportionality of means, and reasonable prospect of success[69]) applicable both to the Security Council and states. In these criteria we see a kind of revival of the old idea of 'just wars' that was prevalent when natural law concepts reigned in international legal literature, before positivist approaches started to prevail and the use of military force became outlawed in international law. The furthest the Commission went on the road towards legitimising use of military force without the Security Council's authorisation is in the following two paragraphs of the Report:

> 6.39 The first message is that if the Security Council fails to discharge its responsibility in conscience-shocking situations crying out for action, then it is unrealistic to expect that concerned states will rule out other means and forms of action to meet the gravity and urgency of these situations. If collective organizations will not authorize collective intervention against regimes that flout the most elementary norms of legitimate governmental behaviour, then the pressures for

---

[69] International Commission on Intervention and State Sovereignty, The Responsibility to Protect, paras. 4.18, 4.32–48.

> intervention by ad hoc coalitions or individual states will surely intensify. And there is a risk then that such interventions, without the discipline and constraints of UN authorization, will not be conducted for the right reasons or with the right commitment to the necessary precautionary principles.
>
> 6.40 The second message is that if, following the failure of the Council to act, a military intervention is undertaken by an ad hoc coalition or individual state which does fully observe and respect all the criteria we have identified, and if that intervention is carried through successfully – and is seen by world public opinion to have been carried through successfully – then this may have enduringly serious consequences for the stature and credibility of the UN itself.[70]

These propositions are not and are not meant to be legally binding norms, but rather warnings to the Security Council that if it does not act, others may react and the Council may lose its exceptional position and authority under international law.

Addressing the UN Human Rights Commission in April 1999, the then Secretary General of the United Nations Kofi Annan emphasised: 'Emerging slowly, but I believe surely is an international norm against the violent repression of minorities that will and must take precedence over concerns of State sovereignty'.[71] Later, when speaking of Kosovo in Stockholm, he said: 'There is emerging international law that countries cannot hide behind sovereignty and abuse people without expecting the rest of the world to do something about it'.[72] Speaking in The Hague on the occasion of the centennial of the first Hague Peace Conference, the Secretary-General, once again, stressed the need to act through the Security Council. At the same time, he expressed his belief that 'unless the Security Council can unite around the aim of confronting massive human rights violations and crimes against humanity on the scale of Kosovo, then we will betray the very ideals that inspired the founding of the United Nations'.[73] In autumn of the same year, in his article in *The Economist* Kofi Annan wrote that 'in cases where forceful intervention does become necessary, the Security Council–the body charged with

70 Ibid, paras. 6,39; 6,40.
71 Press Release SG/SM 6949, 7 April 1999.
72 *Financial Times*, 26 May 1999, p. 2.
73 Press Release, SG/SM/6997.

authorising the use of force under international law–*must be able to rise to the challenge* [emphasis added]'.[74] Two days later, in his address to the General Assembly, the Secretary General warned: 'The Charter requires the Council to be defender of common interest, and unless it is seen to be so–in the era of human rights, interdependence, and globalisation–there is a danger that others could seek to take its place'.[75]

It seems to be possible to draw the following three conclusions from these statements of the former Secretary-General: (1) Although the United Nations has to be 'respectful of the sovereignty of States', in cases of massive human rights violations and crimes against humanity, humanitarian concerns must prevail over state sovereignty; (2) The role of the Security Council, and the United Nations as a whole, should be central in dealing with extreme humanitarian catastrophes threatening international peace and security; (3) However, the Security Council, and especially its permanent members, have to act responsibly and 'unite behind the principle that massive and systematic violations of human rights conducted against an entire people cannot be allowed to stand'.[76] The world community has to rely on the Security Council on issues involving the use of force, but it can do so only if the Council and its permanent members act with the utmost sense of responsibility. If the Council neglects its responsibility, other institutions may have to fill the void.

However, notwithstanding the report of the *Commission on State Sovereignty and Intervention*, the cautious statements of Kofi Annan and other documents mentioned above that were adopted later foreclose any interventions on humanitarian grounds unauthorised by the United Nations Security Council. Alex Bellamy's conclusion that 'as agreed by world leaders in 2005, R2P does not countenance non-consensual military force without the authorization of the Security Council and does not set out criteria for the use of force beyond the four threshold crimes [i.e. genocide, crimes against

74 *The Economist*, 18 September 1999.
75 SG/SM/7136, 20 September 1999.
76 Ibid.

humanity, ethnic cleansing and war crimes] and the idea that the Council should assume responsibility in cases where the host state is "manifestly failing" to protect'.[77] Therefore, Carsten Stahn is justified in calling R2P partly 'Old Wine in New Bottles'.[78]

How relying on various interpretations of R2P may backfire can be seen in the situation Gareth Evans found himself. Being an ardent supporter of the concept of R2P as well as a co-chair of the International Commission on Intervention and State Sovereignty, Evans – the former Foreign Minister of Australia – encountered difficulties in explaining why Russia was wrong in August 2008 when invoking the R2P concept as justification for the Kremlin's response to the Georgian attack on Tskinvhali, the capital of South Ossetia.[79] He was forced to admit that 'in the absence of UN Security Council approval, there is no legal authority for an R2P-based military intervention'. And he added: 'The 2005 General Assembly Outcome Document makes it clear that any country or group of countries seeking to apply forceful means to address an R2P situation – where another country is manifestly failing to protect its people and peaceful means are inadequate – must take that action through the Security Council'.[80] And Evans is certainly right that 'the sense of moral outrage at reports of civilians being killed and ethnically cleansed can have an unintended effect of clouding judgement as to what is the best response, which is another reason to channel action collectively through the United Nations'.[81] The point is not whether Russia correctly invoked the R2P concept (in any case, it was only secondary in the Kremlin's justifications of its military response), and as Gareth Evans correctly points out, Russia's response was 'manifestly excessive', i.e. disproportionate to the Georgian attack. The point is that depending on political, economic and strategic interests as well as ideological proclivities, states use various concepts in their own

---

77 A.J. Bellamy, 'The Responsibility to Protect and the problem of military intervention', *International Affairs*, 2008, Vol. 84, No. 4, p. 638.

78 C. Stahn, 'Responsibility to Protect: Political Rhetoric or Emerging Legal Norm?', *The American Journal of International Law*, 2007, Vol. 101, p. 111.

79 G. Evans, 'Russia, Georgia and the Responsibility to Protect', *Amsterdam Law Forum*, 2009, Vol. 1, No. 2.

80 Ibid.

81 Ibid.

self-interest. Moreover, as Alex de Waal comments on Gareth Evans' and Samantha Power's enthusiastic support of the concepts of R2P and humanitarian intervention, '[I]n the face of "evil", the idealists tend to turn righteous and forget to ask important questions about what they want to achieve and how'.[82] More often than not less sharp instruments than military intervention or a dogged insistence on regime change save more lives. However, they may hurt the idealists' sense of self-righteousness and also prevent or delay the achievement of other goals such as the 'democratisation of the wider Middle East' or securing control over energy resources.

In that respect parallels with the recognition of the independence of Kosovo, which we considered above, are appropriate. It is not unusual at all that wobbly and self-serving interpretations of various concepts of international law later come to haunt the authors of such interpretations. Even if made in good faith, and having at heart only altruistic and noble aims (which in world politics are always suspicious), it is better to study in detail all possible uses and abuses of one's preferred concepts. Sergei Karaganov writes: 'In international affairs, the old geopolitics and *Realpolitik* based on sheer interest and a balance of power are verbally rejected. The supremacy of human rights and human values and a renunciation of the spheres of influence are proclaimed. But practical policymaking appears to be in sharp contrast to what is being said. A fight for the spheres of influence, slightly disguised in the parables about democracy, is clearly underway'.[83] This comment, certainly applies not only to countries with which Russia has problems, but also to the Russian policies in the Caucasus and elsewhere.

Russia's overreaction to Georgia's attack in August 2008 in South Ossetia should be seen not as something idiosyncratic, but as a feature common to great powers generally. Their responses are often meant to not only adequately and proportionally react to the wrongs done, or perceived to be done, against them; rather, since they feel that their prestige and pride have been hurt, they have to send an

82 A. de Waal, 'How to End Mass Atrocities', *The New York Times*, 9 March, 2009.

83 S. Karaganov, 'Revolutionary Chaos of the New World', *Russia in Global Affairs*, 28 December 2011 (http://eng.globalaffairs.ru/pubcol/A-revolutionary-chaos-of-the-new-world-15415).

'unmistakable message', as they put it, to their opponents. Today, such messages are often sent in the form of missiles, drones attacks or aerial bombardments. As Dean Acheson, a distinguished American diplomat and lawyer, put it after the Cuban missile crisis: 'The power, position and prestige of the United States had been challenged by another state; and law simply does not deal with such questions of ultimate power–power that comes close to sources of sovereignty'.[84] Certainly, politics plays an immense, even central role in most international issues. Not only is international law always made in the cauldron of political processes, but in many areas its content is also highly political. However, this does not mean that there should not be or that there cannot be any laws governing such sensitive issues.

I understand that the impression my lines of argument have so far offered is that the use of military force for humanitarian purposes is basically counterproductive, and in the absence of the Security Council's authorisation it is also unlawful. This is indeed what I have intended to convey. And as a general proposition, this corresponds to political realities, existing legal norms, and maybe most importantly, it is even morally sound, notwithstanding a noble aim in the use of force – the protection of human rights in cases of their massive violation. The important point to be made is that any use of military force, even one genuinely carried out for the sake of saving human lives, contains in itself a significant potential for an even greater loss of life, the infliction of grievous bodily harm on a massive scale, the loss of property and the infringement of other values, which are protected as fundamental human rights.

Of course, the same may be said about the use of force in exercising one's inherent right to self-defence 'if an armed attack occurs', as confirmed in Article 51 of the UN Charter. However, wars of self-defence (though this right is often abused) are by their very nature wars of necessity – they are never wars of choice if we discount surrendering as an acceptable moral choice (it may also be a choice but then there is no use of force). Yet, the use of force by state A with humanitarian purposes against state B, in a case where B does not threaten A's security, can never be a war of necessity in the same

---

[84] *Proceedings of the American Society of International Law*, 1963, p. 14.

sense (both in a physical and moral sense) as wars of self-defence are (though a humanitarian crisis in neighbouring country C may constitute a security threat for A due, for instance, to refugee flows, but this is a different issue to be addressed separately). However, one may ask: can there not be any circumstances in which the use of force by state A in the territory of and against state B, in case of a severe humanitarian crisis in the latter, even if the crisis does not constitute a security threat to A, may be considered a 'war of necessity', if not in the physical sense (in that respect there is always a choice: intervene militarily or not) as wars of self-defence are, but in a moral sense, which wars of self-defence also are? We believe that in certain circumstances it would be possible to give a positive answer to this question. In situations where the use of military force is the only means of preventing or stopping massive human rights violations such as genocide or crimes against humanity, the absolute prohibition to use force would deprive these prohibitions of their enforceability even in principle, and in such a case these prohibitions cannot be considered as valid human rights norms. Therefore the use of military force in certain extreme circumstances may have the characteristics of a 'war of necessity' – a war of moral necessity. For example, both the world community of states and individual states that had the necessary capacities, first to prevent and then stop genocide in Rwanda (this would have clearly been a lesser evil than allowing the foreseeable and preventable genocide to happen and once started to stop it), failed in their duty both collectively and individually. Their's was a moral surrender similar to the behaviour of those nations who surrender without even attempting to fight when attacked by an enemy, resisting whom is not foreseeably a lost cause.

Moral justification for the use of military force for the sake of the protection of human rights in a foreign country can be best based on ideas developed by British political and legal philosopher Lord Raymond Plant. As human rights are real only in the case of their enforceability (at least in principle though not always in practice, but this is another, though no less important, matter which belongs more to the realm of practical politics and law than moral philosophy), their unenforceability, even in principle, deprives them of their quality as human rights. Lord Plant writes:

> Our responsibility for the rights of others is therefore not confined to *non-interference* in those rights, but also has to involve responsibility for doing what we can to secure those *enforceability* conditions, just because these are part of having a right and therefore must be involved in what respecting rights means. This seems to me to be the best way of linking a concern for rights and the possibility of intervention in a particular country, which may not be securing the enforcement conditions.[85]

If there are circumstances when the use of military force is the only means of protecting rights, and the resort to such an extreme measure, which in itself is wrought with the danger of massive violations of most fundamental human rights, is proportionate to the seriousness of the human rights violations (genocide, crimes against humanity and systemic massive violations of international humanitarian law), then the use of military force may be morally justified as a necessary condition of these rights being rights. The most important general guiding principle in such a situation should be that extreme human suffering, which one attempts to stop or prevent, has to be significantly and foreseeably higher than the human suffering that inevitably results from the use of force to end the suffering. And always, the objective should be to stop or prevent extreme human suffering and not to effect regime change, though this might occur as an inevitable or even necessary corollary of the intervention.

From these arguments of moral philosophy it is possible to move to the legal justification of the use of military force for the sake of the protection of human rights.

The UN Security Council's authorization would make interventions on humanitarian grounds both lawful under international law and legitimate in the eyes of most people, and though even they may, in principle, do more harm than good, in such cases there is less chance that hasty decisions, dictated by narrow self-interest and facilitated by an ignorance of the risks that any military operation involves, are made. However, in extreme circumstances, we believe there may not only be a moral-philosophical, but also a legal justification (therefore, there would not be any need to put it in the

[85] R. Plant, 'Rights, Rules and World Order' in *Global Governance: Ethics and Economics of the World Order* (M. Desai, P. Redfern eds.), Pinter, 1995, p. 207.

form: 'illegal but legitimate') for intervention on humanitarian grounds, even without the Security Council's authorisation. We would emphasise, first, the importance of the words 'in extreme circumstances' since any use of military force, as we have just discussed, inevitably leads to a serious loss of life, i.e. it always creates circumstances conducive to massive violations of the right to life – the most basic human right without which the enjoyment of all other rights becomes meaningless and impossible. Nevertheless, there may be circumstances when the use of military force may be justified not only on moral but also on legal grounds.

First, let us deal with a preliminary point. It is often said that if there were a right to use military force, states would constantly abuse it. It may well be the case, and in some military interventions allegedly carried out for humanitarian purposes, such justifications have been used to conceal other aims. However, so far states have more often referred to the right to self-defence when using force aggressively, i.e. they abuse this inherent right. Moreover, the fact that the use of military force with the purported aim of protecting human rights in cases of their gross and massive violation is often abused, should not in itself serve as an absolute obstacle on the road to human rights protection even by means of force, if other means have proven to be, or would clearly be, inadequate, and it is also one of those rare situations when the use of force foreseeably does less harm than its abstention. Almost every right, almost every good may be open to abuse. As the former President of the International Court of Justice Dame Rosalyn Higgins has written, 'we must face the reality that we live in a decentralised international legal order, where claims may be made either in good faith or abusively'.[86] The fact that claims over some values or rights are made abusively should not mean that these values or rights thereby become less valuable. Humans have enough intelligence and flexibility to not only confuse and mislead, but also to differentiate between use and abuse, sincerity and deception.[87]

---

[86] R. Higgins, *Problems and Process: International Law and How We Use It*, Clarendon Press, 1944, p. 247.

[87] Nicholas Wade opines that religion coevolved with the emergence of language as a safeguard against deception that came possible through the use of

Now, there comes the main, in our opinion, argument in favour of both the legality and legitimacy of the use of force for humanitarian purposes. There is no doubt, as we have discussed above, that the principle of the prohibition of the use of force is one of the fundamental principles of international law. The United Nations International Law Commission, in its various reports dealing with the issue of peremptory norms in international law (*jus cogens* norms), from which states cannot deviate or derogate even with the consent of other states, has always given as an example of such norms the norm prohibiting the use of military force.[88] As we saw above, this norm has not lost its fundamental importance notwithstanding its all too frequent violation. On the contrary, its significance is only enhanced by such breaches; the reason being that if a norm protects something that people continue to value highly (peace in this case) then violations of such a norm indicate that it is necessary to strengthen the norm instead of discarding it. In legal terms, we may say that in such cases strong *opinio juris* compensates for a less than perfect observance of the norm in practice. However, the prohibition of the use of force is not the only fundamental principle of international law. The principle of respect for and protection of human rights has acquired the same status. In its Draft Articles on Responsibility of States the International Law Commission emphasises not only the importance of the non-use of force principle as a peremptory norm of international law but also the same character of certain human rights norms, such as the prohibition of genocide, slavery and torture.[89]

In cases of gross and massive violation of such a fundamental human right as the right to life, which are always accompanied by egregious violations of many other rights, the prohibition of the use of military force may yield to the obligation to respect and protect human rights. In such cases we have two equally important and

language: 'With the advent of language, freeloaders gained a great weapon, the power to deceive. Religion could have evolved as a means of defence against freeloading' (N. Wade, *Before the Dawn. Recovering the Lost History of Our Ancestors*, The Penguin Press, 2007, p. 165).

[88] See, e.g., Draft Articles on Responsibility of States for Internationally Wrongful Acts, with commentaries, 2001, Yearbook of the International Law Commission, 2001, vol. II, Part Two, p. 112.

[89] Ibid., pp. 112–113.

weighty principles of international law that cannot be observed at the same time and in the same context; one has to give way. Such potential for collision is enshrined in the very nature of the principles of international law. As one of the greatest twentieth century international lawyers, Oscar Schachter, wrote, 'principles, in contrast [to rules], lack the element of definiteness, they are "open-textured", leaving room for various interpretations'.[90] And he emphasises that 'particular situations are covered by more than one principle. … They point to different legal conclusions. Indeed, it has often been observed that principles like proverbs can be paired off into opposites'.[91] In particular situations the prohibition to commit acts of genocide or crimes against humanity, and even more importantly, the obligation to prevent such acts being committed,[92] may outweigh the prohibition to use military force. In such extreme situations the use of force for humanitarian purposes, even without the Security Council's authorisation, may be both legitimate and lawful.

8. *INTERVENTION IN CIVIL WARS AND INTERNAL DISTURBANCES AND REGIME CHANGE*

International law has traditionally allowed so-called 'interventions by invitation', which the *Institut de Droit International* in its 2011 resolution has more correctly characterised as 'military assistance on request',[93] in 'situations of internal disturbances and tensions, such as riots, isolated and sporadic acts of violence and

---

[90] O. Schachter, *International Law in Theory and Practice. General Course in Public International Law*, Recueille des Cours de l'Academie de Droit International, 1982, vol. V, p. 43.

[91] Ibid.

[92] Article 1 of the Convention on the Prevention and Punishment of the Crime of Genocide provides that 'The Contracting Parties confirm that genocide, whether committed in time of peace or in time of war, is a crime under international law which they undertake to prevent and to punish'. (http://www2.ohchr.org/english/law/genocide.htm). As we emphasised above and it is not superfluous to reiterate this here, crimes against humanity and systemic war crimes are often not less grave than acts of genocide. Crimes against humanity are, by definition, 'widespread and systematic', while war crimes, if not individual excesses, but state policy (or policy of other organised groups), are always massive and heinous.

[93] http://www.idi-iil.org/idiE/resolutionsE/2011_rhodes_10_C_en.pdf.

other acts of similar nature, including acts of terrorism'. Such an invitation has to come from the lawful government. However, the *Institut*, when confirming the right of foreign military assistance at the request of governments, didn't review its 1975 Resolution 'The principle of non-interference in civil wars'[94] thereby explicitly excluding from the scope of permitted military assistance on request situations of non-international armed conflicts, i.e. in civil wars. This means that there should not be any intervention in civil wars even if the legitimate government gives its consent or asks for help. The reason for this is that interventions on the side of the government (it goes without saying that any military intervention on the invitation of the opposition is illegal) in civil war situations may undermine peoples' right to self-determination, as well as lead to other breaches of fundamental human rights. Of course, even in cases of internal disturbances and tensions, where military assistance to the incumbent government by its request is permitted, may enter into conflict with the principle of self-determination of people. For example, Saudi Arabia's military assistance at the request of Bahrain's King Hamad bin Isa al-Khalifa in March 2011 to put down a popular revolt against the Monarchy is clearly the case;[95] similarly, in the case of the conflict in Syria, if arming rebels is clearly illegal under international law, Russia's continued sending of weapons to the Assad government, even if in implementation of previous agreements, was also illegal, first, because these weapons were used, *inter alia*, against a civilian population, and secondly, because arming one side of the conflict violates the principle of self-determination of peoples. Therefore the *Institut*'s Resolution of 2011 prohibits direct military assistance to foreign governments by the sending of armed forces in cases where such assistance violates the right of peoples to self-determination or 'generally accepted standards of human rights and in particular when its object is to support an established government against its own population'.

If intervention in civil war situations which may well end up in humanitarian catastrophes may be necessary on humanitarian

---

[94] http://www.idi-iil.org/idiE/resolutionsE/1975_wies_03_en.pdf.

[95] E. Bronner, M. Slackman, 'Saudi Troops Enter Bahrain to Help Put Down Unrest', *The International Herald Tribune*, 14 March, 2011.

grounds, the Security Council's authorisation is needed. In such cases, if the targets of a UN sanctioned intervention are governmental forces, which are in the process of suppressing a popular revolt, regime change may indeed result. However, it should never be the *raison d'être* of the intervention. Which government will govern after the intervention has ended has to be decided by the people without any external interference. It seems that external assistance to domestically initiated regime change should be welcome in situations when the means and methods used by the government to govern, to stay in power and to put down rebellions against it grossly violate basic human rights. In extreme circumstances, when crimes against humanity or acts of genocide are committed in a country, and when the seriousness of such human rights violations outweighs the prohibition to use military force (a Rwanda 1994 type situation), even a non-Security Council sanctioned intervention may be justified. However, any intervention in civil wars, even if authorised by the Security Council is wrought with many dangers, and one of them is that the intervener may be forced to take sides and fight alongside one of the parties in an internal conflict. This is what has often happened. However, as we continue to reiterate, any changes to existing political regimes, economic structures and civil society institutions, if necessary, should be the matter left for the people themselves to resolve.

9. DETERMINANTS OF SUCCESS OF EXTERNAL INTERFERENCE: EFFORTS OF INTERVENERS OR CHARACTERISTICS OF THE TARGET SOCIETY?

Rory Stewart and Klaus Knaus make a succinct, precise, to the point and profound observation in writing that 'people who cannot name four cities in Libya can deploy four arguments against or for an intervention there. These are the same arguments that crippled our response to Bosnia and Rwanda, emboldened us in Kosovo, and drew us deeper into the indignities of Iraq and Afghanistan'.[96] The gist of

[96] R. Stewart, G. Knaus, *Can Intervention Work?, Amnesty International Global Ethic Series*, W.W. Norton & Company, 2011 (Kindle version), loc. 86.

this observation by these two persons who intimately knew the countries where foreign interventions took place (Afghanistan and Bosnia-Herzegovina), is that those who make decisions as to whether to intervene or not are usually high level politicians in Washington or sometimes in other Western capitals who know only their own country, judge other nations on the basis of that knowledge, and often do not even consider it necessary to understand other peoples. They extrapolate their knowledge of their own country, their own interests and values to other societies. Such a fallacy is characteristic not only of politicians but also of quite a few experts. James Dobbins at RAND, for example, concluded that the single most important variable to the success of nation-building efforts in foreign countries 'is the level of efforts the United States and the international community put into their democratic transformations. ... The higher level of input accounts in significant measure for the higher level of output measured in the development of democratic institutions and economic growth'.[97] James Pattison, similarly, makes the mistake all too common for many US politicians and experts; they believe that the success of external intervention, military or otherwise, depends mainly on the efforts of interveners, not the characteristics of the society intervened. Writing about factors central to intervention's success, he, for example, observes: 'These factors include the military and non-military resources of the interveners, a suitable strategy on their part, their commitment to stay the course, local and global support for the intervention (sic! local support should be considered as the most crucial single factor in the success of any intervention), and the intervener's fidelity to the principles of *jus in bello*'.[98] However, less abstract and more detailed studies show that it is not so much the nature of external efforts, but the various characteristics of the target society that determine the success or failure of interventions, including those of the expansion of democracy or nation building. Stewart and Knaus argue that '... foreigners who comprise "the international community" are usually much weaker

---

[97] J. Dobbins et al., *America's Role in Nation-Building: From Germany to Iraq*, RAND, 2003, xix.

[98] J. Pattison, 'The Ethics of Humanitarian Intervention in Libya', *Ethics & International Affairs*, 2011, Vol. 25, No. 3, p. 275.

than they imagine. They are inevitably isolated from local society, ignorant of local culture and context, and prey to misleading abstract theories'.[99] The United States Secretary of Defence during the Vietnam War, Robert McNamara, drawing lessons from that war, wrote later: 'We viewed the people and leaders of South Vietnam in terms of our own experience. We do not have the God-given right to shape every nation in our own image or as we choose. We did not recognize that neither our people nor our leaders are omniscient. We exaggerated the dangers to the United States'.[100] There is something significant in the fact that politicians or military leaders often happen to be wiser when in retirement. It seems that they become free of the herd mentality that affects their thought and action when in office. Gerald Knaus well summarises the main problem with interventions by Western nations in far-away countries:

> The red thread that runs through these recent policy debates on intervention is the reassuring notion that all fundamental problems have solutions. It is the belief that lessons learned in one place can be transferred to any other, and that what works in one intervention is likely to work elsewhere. It is the conviction that in the end everything depends mainly on good management, resources (troops, money), and political will, and that *the key to success lies with the intervener* (my emphasis RM): with the nature of the domestic political debate in the West and with the wisdom of military and civilian leadership.[101]

This excerpt deserves to be hanged on the walls of some world capitals. Such an attitude, even worldview, has its roots, as we discussed earlier, in the Judeo-Christian and Enlightenment's belief in universal history and a progress leading towards some final end, as well as a mixture of determinism and voluntarism. Both the West's achievements and failures rest on this worldview. The greatest wisdom would probably be the ability to recognise when one's worldview is apt and when it may pave the way to disaster, though this may be too much to ask. At the same time, the less philosophical, more routine roots of a belief in the ability of an intervener to radically change the

---

99 Stewart, Knaus, loc. 265.

100 R. McNamara, In Retrospect: *The Tragedy and Lessons of Vietnam*, Random House, 1995, p. 353.

101 Stewart, Knaus, Can Intervention Work, loc. 2187.

fundamentals of foreign societies lie in the ignorance of the complexities and diversity of the world.

Those Western experts who are intimately familiar with the non-Western world, where interventions usually take place, emphasise the importance of the characteristics of societies as the main determinants of the success or failure of such missions. So, Alexander Downes and Jonathan Monten write: 'We find that states that are relatively wealthy or ethnically homogeneous experience significant democratic gains after experiencing a FIRC (foreign-imposed regime change) by a democratic intervener, whereas states that are relatively poor or heterogeneous become less democratic (sic!)'.[102]

However, there may be a different danger. Sometimes those who know the country of potential intervention quite well and may have even been born and brought up there, may be the strongest advocates of intervention. This is what may be called the 'Chalabi phenomenon' after Ahmad Chalabi,[103] an Iraqi politician in exile in the US and a fierce opponent of Saddam Hussein, whose obsession with ousting of Saddam, personal political ambitions and outright lies contributed to the decision of the Bush Administration to invade Iraq in March 2003. Although even without Ahmad Chalabi's efforts the 2003 intervention would have taken place, since the Bush's Administration's foreign policy was guided by an interventionist ideology of remaking the wider Middle East in accordance with a liberal democratic blueprint. Therefore the Administration as a whole (the only prominent exception being the then Secretary of State Colin Powell) was only happy to be misled.

Sometimes the democratisations of Germany and Japan after World War II are given as examples of successful efforts to externally enforce democratisation. So, President George W. Bush stated in February 2003, just before the invasion of Iraq and the ousting of Saddam Hussein (this being one of the justifications of invasion): 'America has made and kept this kind of commitment before – in

---

102 A.B. Downes, J. Monten, 'FIRCed to be Free: Foreign-Imposed Regime Change and Democratization', http://www.duke.edu/~downes/FIRCed%20TO%20BE%20FREE_MAY28.pdf.

103 A. Roston, *The Man Who Pushed America to War: The Extraordinary Life, Adventures, And Obsessions of Ahmad Chalabi*, Nation Books, 2008.

the peace that followed the world war. After defeating enemies, we did not leave behind occupying armies, we left constitutions and parliaments. ... In societies that once bred fascism and militarism, liberty found a permanent home. There was a time when many said that the cultures of Japan and Germany were incapable of sustaining democratic values. Well, they were wrong. Some say the same of Iraq today. They are mistaken'.[104]

Germany certainly is not and never was comparable to, for example, Afghanistan. Although German society possessed seeds that helped grow German militarism and led to the First World War and the fascism that caused WW II and the Holocaust (such seeds were, of course, also present in other European societies), before and after WW I, and until Hitler came to power, Germany was not much different from other European countries. It was wealthy, industrially highly developed, stable, relatively homogeneous country with a highly educated population. If it were not for the onerous retributions imposed on Germany after it had lost the war it had started in 1914, and the 1929–1933 world economic crisis, it could well have been that Hitler and his NSDAP (the National Socialist German Workers' Party) would have never come to power in Germany. In that case, there would not have been any need for FIRC (foreign-imposed regime change) at all in that country. One of the important differences, besides other significant factors such as levels of economic development and historical and cultural traditions between Germany and Japan on the one hand, and Afghanistan, Iraq and many other countries where externally induced or supported regime changes are taking place on the other, was the relatively high level of religious and ethnic homogeneity of Germany and Japan. And as we emphasised above, the median age of the population is also a factor that either facilitates or hinders democratic changes.

What the defeats, occupations and following democratisations of Germany and Japan show is that even after the use of military force, democratisation may be possible (but never forget at what cost in human lives, suffering as well as in material devastations). What the

---

104 G.W. Bush, 'President Discusses Future of Iraq', White House Press Release, February 26, 2003, D 10.

cases of Germany and Japan confirm is that the success or failure of externally imposed democratisation depends less on what the external actors do and much more on the characteristics of the target society.

Stewart and Knaus conclude:

> Finally – and this is the most difficult truth for the international policy-makers to accept – intervention cannot always offer an end to suffering. A modern intervener does not have the power, the knowledge, or the legitimacy to "eliminate all the root causes of conflict", let alone fundamentally reshape the structures and cultural identity of a foreign land. Instead, intervention should aim to provide protection and relief at a specific time and place. And even such limited ambitions can often be defeated by a situation, which is intrinsically unpredictable. No crisis is fixed or permanent. But there are crises that "the international community" cannot address. Failure – however horrible – will always be a possibility: an option.[105]

The last point – failure may be an option – needs to be emphasised, since all too often politicians and military leaders use the mantra that failure is not an option until said failure has materialised, in the process sacrificing more lives and resources.

Today's attempts at regime change manifest a new tendency which, depending on where one stands, maybe seen either as promising or as worrying. With the emergence of politics and statehood, and up to the emergence of the possibility of a peaceful transition of governments through the ballot-box (sic!), there have always been those who have revolted against the authorities, be they slaves in the Ancient Rome, peasants in China, Russia and medieval Europe or the American, French and Russian revolutions. There isn't anything hitherto unheard of in outside assistance either for governments' efforts to quell rebellions (e.g., Vladimir Lenin called Czarist Russia 'the gendarme of Europe' for its military assistance to conservative European governments in the middle of the nineteenth century) or of giving a helping hand to rebels (as France did when the British colonies in America rebelled against the Brits). However, post-UN Charter international law prohibits interference in the internal affairs of states, and therefore any assistance to rebels would be in

105 Stewart, Knaus, loc. 339.

breach of international law. Today even assistance to governments to help them quell rebellions may be contrary to international law, to its principle of self-determination of peoples. At the same time, the further development of international law has led to the emergence and rapid evolution of international human rights law, combined with the international criminalisation of not only war crimes but also acts of genocide and crimes against humanity, and the revival of the concept of humanitarian intervention.

In the context of current regime change attempts, we face a series of problems related to these tendencies. Peoples rise up against unrepresentative and oppressive governments, especially when the latter don't deliver; and more often than not they don't. In a globalised world, such rebellions have become contagious; they come in the form of chain reactions. One of the serious problems with such chains is that their links are very different, or rather, often not real at all; they are virtual, existing only on the level of Facebook or Twitter. If in one country rebels may relatively easily and with relatively small casualties succeed, in a different country the authorities may be able to suppress revolts against them. Every case is specific. The success or failure of rebellions depends on too many variables, the most important of which are endogenous, not exogenous. Outcomes stretch from virtually bloodless coups without any significant foreign involvement (Tunisia), to relatively short but bloody conflicts where only foreign intervention tips the scales in favour of the rebels (Libya). Often there is the potential for protracted bloody civil wars with an uncertain result (Syria). What is new is that outside assistance to rebels in one country encourages rebels or potential rebels in other countries. However, the problem is that outsiders are unable to assist all rebels, and even more importantly, as domestic circumstances differ from country to country, what works in one case may completely fail in another. At the same time, rebels, being encouraged by an outside support that is not strong enough to tip the scales in their favour, don't compromise, even when the authorities are ready for concessions. Their demands are uncompromising – nothing less that the change of the incumbent regime and the prosecution or murder of its leaders and their supporters would satisfy them. Sometimes it may work, in different circumstances it leads to protracted civil wars and more bloodshed.

In 1979, Jeane Kirkpatrick, the US Ambassador to the United Nations during the Reagan Administration, published her most famous article, one that deserves to be studied not so much in order to agree with what she wrote, but as to reflect upon various policies and their unintended consequences. She wrote:

> In each of these countries [in China before the fall of Chiang Kaishek, in Cuba before the triumph of Castro, in certain crucial periods of the Vietnamese war, and, more recently, in Angola] the American effort to impose liberalization and democratization on a government confronted with violent internal opposition not only failed, but actually assisted the coming to power of new regimes in which ordinary people enjoy fewer freedoms and less personal security than under the previous autocracy–regimes, moreover, hostile to American interests and policies.[106]

Of course, these were times quite different from todays, and Jeane Kirkpatrick advocated relying on authoritarian governments, allied to the United States in its rivalry with the Soviet Union and its allies. Today even this reason for buttressing dictators has gone. But Kirkpatrick's conclusion that undermining dictators or overthrowing them may lead to unintended consequences, and that under new regimes people may enjoy fewer freedoms and less personal security than under the previous autocracies, that new regimes may be more hostile to American interests and policies, rings true also today.

[106] J.J. Kirkpatrick, Dictatorships & Double Standards, *Commentary*, November 1979.

CONCLUSIONS

Let us finish with where we started: the world as a whole is slowly becoming more homogeneous, while most individual societies are becoming, though not as slowly, more heterogeneous. Professor Amitai Etzioni's comment that 'the world actually is moving towards a new synthesis between the West's great respects for individual rights and choices and the East's respect for social obligations (in a variety of ways, of course); between the West's preoccupation with autonomy and the East's preoccupation with social order; between Western legal and political egalitarianism and Eastern authoritarianism',[1] is well within this panorama and gives additional support to it. However, in most cases it would be counter-productive and dangerous to try to artificially accelerate a move towards greater homogeneity (be it a world of liberal democracies, an Islamic Caliphate or a Sino-centric international system). Equally, it would be unwise and almost impossible to try to stop these changes. What we, humankind, represented by states, international organisations, civil society groups, business leaders and individuals, can do is to manage these processes.

Today, it is not Orwell's 1984 and a Big Brother or Leviathan that, at least for the Western world, is the most realistic and immediate danger; in many parts of the world, as we are seeing today, it is the failure or total collapse of states, not their strength and stability, that has been the main cause of massive human suffering. The clear and present danger is, rather, the unfettered global (especially financial) market without any democratic control. It is becoming a 'big brother' whose interference with individual liberties, though more anonymous and less direct than that of the state, may prove equally or even more nefarious. One of the most important tasks of the state should be the management of global problems such as the globalised economy and finances, the prevention of environmental degradation, the maintenance of national and international security, and qualified, contingent and contextual promotion of democracy and

---

[1] A. Etzioni, *From Empire to Community. A New Approach to International Relations*, Palgrave, 2004, pp. 14–15.

human rights.[2] It is sometimes said that states are too big for small things and too small for big things. However, if there are entities ready to take over some of the smaller things, there is nothing yet available to resolve big things. The rise of China and other Asian countries, where the role of the state has been instrumental in guaranteeing this rise, is further evidence that it is too early to send the state into the dustbin of history, as Marxists dream of, or cut it down to the size of a mere 'night watchman' as libertarians or neo-liberals would like. Wang Hui is right when he observes that '[S]ome people have linked globalization to the decline of the nation-state, but I don't think that is necessarily accurate. Instead, what has occurred is a transformation of its function, not its decline – parts of it are in decline but others are also on the rise'.[3] Speaking, for example, of the changing role of the Chinese state, he writes that '[T]he Chinese government will correspondingly be required to shift from a development-oriented government to a social service oriented one, which will also transform the Chinese economy from being reliant on exports to being led by domestic needs'.[4] It may well be that some Western governments will have to start pursuing opposing economic policies, but the important point is that markets and economies are not self-contained, self-regulating phenomena that function on their own without governmental (or inter-governmental) interference in various forms. Neither markets nor globalisation work on their own, automatically. Without governments there would be chaos and anarchy. Joseph Stiglitz writes that '[T]he interconnectedness of peoples, countries, and economies around the globe is a development that can be used as effectively to promote prosperity as to spread greed and misery. The same is true of market economy: the power of market is enormous, but they have no inherent moral character. We have to decide how to manage them'.[5] So far, as Stiglitz

[2] See, R. Müllerson, *Democracy – a Destiny of Humankind? A Qualified, Contingent and Contextual Case for Democracy Promotion*, New York, NovaSciencePublishers, 2009.

[3] Wang Hui, *The End of the Revolution: China and the Limits of Modernity*, Verso, 2011, p. 87.

[4] Ibid., p. xxviii.

[5] J. Stiglitz, *The Price of Inequality: How Today's Divided Society Endangers Our Future*, W.W. Norton & Company, 2012, p. xii.

puts it, most governments, including liberal democratic ones, have managed them for the sake of the top 1% of the population.[6] As the slave-owning democracy of Ancient Greece could not be a model of democracy for the twentieth century, democracy 'by 1% and for 1%' should not be a model of democracy for the twenty first century.

As often is the case in various domains, there is a positive side in negative tendencies or developments and *vice versa*. Moreover, what is positive in negative and negative in positive usually depends on where one stands, and the latter is dependent on where one sits. In the age of empires, be it Alexander the Great, the Roman Empire, the empires of Chingiz Khan or Tamerlane, the strong did not care, and didn't feel the need to be seen to care, about the wellbeing of those over whom they exercised their domination. However, already by the times of Western European colonialism, colonial powers felt a need to use a veil of *mission civilisatrice* in order to dominate the rest of the world. Colonial domination should not to be seen as exclusively benefiting the strong. It had to also be seen to as being carried out for the sake of the weak, as a mission of bringing the fruits of civilization to uncivilized nations. Though there was a lot of hypocrisy and naivety in colonial expansion, the need to show that one was acting not only for the sake of one's particular interest, but also for the common interest of humankind, was in itself a sign of progressive evolution.

In the contemporary world, American dominance, without any doubt serving particular American interests as they are understood by the political and economic elites of the country, is even more clearly passed off as a common good, as something that is benefiting the whole world. Sometimes this may well be so. America's potential for good is great, and time and time again it has been used for the benefit of humankind. However, too often too many Americans believe that other peoples not only have the right, but even the obligation to enjoy the same political and personal liberties as the Americans do, and in a similar vein the benefits of free markets. And Washington is ready to assist those peoples, sometimes without even consulting them. The only condition is that they

---

6 J. Stiglitz, 'Of the 1 %, by the 1%, for the 1%', *Vanity Fair*, May 2011.

shouldn't disobey; they must not insist on their 'incorrect' ideologies and put their particular interests above the common interests of humankind, as defined by Washington (sometimes with consultation with allies). One is allowed to exercise, and is even aided in exercising freedoms so far as such exercise doesn't contradict the vital interests of the dominant power.

British diplomat and scholar Adam Watson, after studying various international systems over the past 2,500 years observed: 'Powers that find themselves able to lay down the law in a system in practice do so'.[7] This feature indeed seems to be one of the most constant imperatives of international relations. It has not depended on the internal characteristics of dominant states but on their relative power, be it economic, political or most importantly military. However, even this invariable is not immutable in its application. For the first time in history, there is a global world system and no single power is able to dominate the entire system. Attempts to do so lead to imperial overstretch and increasingly shorten relative dominance. Therefore, Anatol Lieven's prediction that 'rather than a future in which Chinese hegemony will replace that of the United States we seem to be rapidly entering a world in which no country will exercise anything resembling true world leadership,[8] seems to be rather insightful.

---

[7] A. Watson, *The Evolution of International Society*, Routledge, 1992, p. 291.

[8] A. Lieven, 'The Cold War and the Post-Cold War World. Reflections about World Leadership', *Russia in Global Affairs*, 29 December 2011.

INDEX

Abkhazia
  recognition of 192–194
Acemoglu, Daron 46–47, 97–101
Acheson, Dean 218
Afghanistan
  Afghan soldiers, Western troops killed by 52
  liberal democracies, effect of policies of 211
  liberation of 51
Africa
  post-conflict reconstruction, participation in 104–105
Allott, Philip 40
Andropov, Yuri 133
Annan, Kofi 181, 198, 214–215
Arab Spring
  discontent, causes of 1–2
  external interference in 51–52
  internal causes 51
  local, regional and global factors 206
  onset of 1
  regime change dubbed 51
  US policy towards 53–54
Arendt, Hannah 66
Armenia
  Azerbaijan, situation with 210
Asia
  regional concert of great powers, advocacy of 63
  rise of 31, 234
al-Assad, President Bashar 199, 204
Aust, Tony 186
Autocracy, states operating as 130
Autocrats in power 100–101
Azerbaijan
  Armenia, situation with 210

Babst, Dean 161
Bahrain
  revolt in 201, 224
Bakiyev, Kurmanbek 96
Ban Ki-Moon 201
Becker, Seymour 120
Beilin, Yossi 129
Bellamy, Alex 215
Berlin, Isaiah 2, 9
Blackburn, Simon 70
Blair, Tony 36–37, 187
Bozemann, Adda 19
Brautigan, Deborah 105
Bremmer, Ian 81–82, 88, 138
Brown, Donald 20
Brown, Gordon 75
Burt, Richard 39
Bush, George H. 71
Bush, George W. 37, 70, 168, 228
Butt, Yousaf 211
Buzan, Barry 26, 30, 116

Canada
  post-modern state, as 166
Capitalism
  authoritarian 76–77
  competing forms of 83
  crisis of 63
  democratic, problems of 56–72
  effectiveness of 75
  excesses, remedy to 72
  free market 82
    state compared 122
  liberal-democratic 76
  robber 122
  state 81–82
  Western model of 83
Carpenter, Ted Galen 79
Cassin, René 182
Cavalli-Sforza, Luigi Luca 16
Central Europe
  transformations in 1
Chalabi, Ahmad 209, 228
China
  African countries, participation in reconstruction in 104–105
  American strategy 85
  Asia, leadership of 115
  authoritarian capitalism 76–77
  changing balance of power 86–88
  characteristics 116

charm offensive 106
complex decisions, ability to make 61
democratic traits, acquiring 78
economic development, accelerating 104
economic institutions 98
Empire, no return to 116
extractive and inclusive institutions 98–99
foreign direct investment 105
foreign policy issues, requests from Washington 112
GDP 103
historical comparison of 31
human rights record 112, 148
human spirit, democratization of 89
instability, consequences of 90
military expenditure 104
modernization, model of 102
modernizing 88–93
open, becoming 116–117
people, issues decided by 117
political and economic reforms 102
political institutions 98–99, 101
political reforms 77–78
political system, changes in 44
politically open, becoming 91
power relative to United States, reaction to change in 106
reforms in 6, 97–104
regional power, as 169
revisionist power, as 114
rise of 86–88
role of state 234
social movement 92
society, compared with USSR 133
Soviet Union's reforms compared 132–133
state capitalism, results of 81
states as integral parts of 107
successful transition, example of 114
Syria, no special interests in 204
Taiwan, integration of 112
Tiananmen Square, events in 92, 97
today's and yesterday's compared 89
US, foreign policy, requests as to 112
world's largest economy, becoming 86
world's reaction to rise of 104–113

Christopher, Warren 126
Chua, Amy 29, 94, 95
Churchill, Winston 59, 119
Cincotta, Richard 206
Civil society
dictatorships, in 42
interdependence 45
Civil war
intervention in 223–225
Syria, in 202
Claude, Inis 9
Colour revolutions
combination of 1
former Soviet Union territories, in 51
Cook, Robin 189
Cooper, Robert 166–167
Crimes against humanity
government committing, no nation deserving 209
humanitarian concerns prevailing over state sovereignty 215
international law, responsibility under 213
massive human rights violations, as 208
protection of population against 207
Syria, in 202–203
Crooke, Alastair 36, 71
Cultures
common traits 19–20, 23–24
human universals, list of 20
interpenetration of 23
universalization of 25
Czarist Empire
dissolution of 5
history of countries in 2
Russification 5

d'Azeglio, Massimo Taparelli 60
de Waal, Alex 217
Democracy
Britain as 46
Churchill's view of 59

Cold War, emergence or maturation in 165
demand-induced, to be 171
Eastern drift to 84
emergence and development of 60
external problems of 61–62
free market, effect of global spread of 94
free markets, and 64
future of 67
globalized world, limits of choice in 72–75
intrinsic value of 69
liberty, and 66
means, not an end, as 68
Middle East, movements in 194
Middle or Far East, in 72
Mill's view of 59
money, correlation with 61
multicultural 60
nation-state, and 59
non-Western countries, promotion in 99–100
organisations guiding regimes to 49–50
other forms of government, arguments favouring over 69
peace as conducive to 172, 179
personal rights, protection of 46
political participation 67
promotion abroad 147
promotion, theories for 49
public opinion, manipulation of 173
societies, construction of 60
United States as protector of 165
war against each other, near misses 171
war-proneness of states 175–178
Washington's policy of advancing 141

Democratic peace theories
belief in 161
dark side 176
dyadic 163
emergence of 162
European context, in 164
foreign interventions, justification of 178
hegemonic leader, role of 165–170
liberal international relations theories, as part of 162
politics of 161–164
problems with 164–173
reliance on 177
statistical picture, confusion of 171
statistical studies proving 163
war, absence of 161

Deng Xiaoping 6, 71, 89, 102, 104, 113, 132–134, 207
reforms, Gorbachev's reforms compared 102

Dennett, Daniel 67–68

Determinism
voluntarism, versus 40

Deudney, Daniel 31, 38

Development
models of 76

Dictators
overthrow of 208
undermining or overthrowing, unintended consequences of 232

Dictatorships
civil society in 42
countries ready for 50
leaders, fall of 50–51
xenophobic 211

Dimbleby, Jonathan 140

Diversity
cultural 59
social, acceptance of 26

Dobrynin, Anatoly 128

Domestic affairs, interference in
prohibition 180–181

Donnelly, Jack 73, 91

Dunn, John 64–65

East Asian states
political leadership 30

Eastern Europe
transformations in 1

Egypt
democratically elected Parliament, dissolution of 127

Enlightenment
history of 34
legacy of 33, 36
liberating ideas 33
soft and hard faces of 34

Enquist, Per Olov 34

Equality
  value and abuse of 66
Erdogan, Recep Tayyip 78
Estonia
  Russia, attitude to 149–150
  Russian speakers in 151
Ethnic cleansing
  international law, responsibility under 213
  response to 216
Etzioni, Amitai 12, 54–55, 68, 233
Europe
  international system 167–168
  liberal democracies in 167
  Russia as part of 153–160
European Union
  democracy deficit 62
Europeans
  modernity, path to 26
Evans, Gareth 216–217
Executive powers
  issues of 172

Feng Yongping 114
Ferguson, Niall 22, 84
Force, use of
  abuse of right 221
  circumstances for allowing 213–215
  justifications for 184
  legality and legitimacy of for humanitarian reasons 222
  massive human rights violations, to prevent or stop 219
  prohibition in international relations 179–180
  protection of human rights, for 219–223
  Security Council, authorisation by 214–215, 218, 220–221
  self-defence, in 218–219, 221
Free markets
  democracy, and 64
  doctrine of 42
Friedberg, Aaron 85
Friedman, Thomas 50
Fukuyama, Francis 13–14, 22, 38, 45, 47–48, 58, 61
Fuller, Graham 107

Galbraith, John Kenneth 122
Gat, Azar 76, 78, 89
Gelbard, Robert 188
Genocide
  government committing, no nation deserving 209
  international law, responsibility under 213
  massive human rights violations, as 208
  protection of population against 207
  Rwanda, in 207
Georgia
  Russia, military conflict with 149, 151
    South Ossetia, attack on 216–218
Germany
  democratisation 228–230
  retributions imposed on 229
Geuss, Raymond 13
Ghosh, Bobby 54
Global market
  danger of 233
Globalisation
  civil and political rights, negativing 73
  dangers of 56–57
  economic and social rights, negativing 73
  economic growth due to 73
  effect of 36
  process of 25
  socioeconomic structures, impact on 58
Goldstein, Joshua 199
Gorbachev, Mikhail 6
  naivety 132
  policies, admiration of 122
  reforms,
    Deng's reforms compared 102
    opening up of Russia by 125
  unpopularity in Russia 132
Granet, Marcel 18
Gray, John 36
Gvosdev, Nikolas 53, 55

Ha-Joon Chang 64
Habermas, Jürgen 41–42, 69, 71, 170
Healthcare
  spending on 177
Held, David 67
Herman, Arthur 106
Higgins, Rosalyn 221

Hind, Dan 33, 58
History
  categories of factors, combination of 40
  historical determination 33–41
  impersonal *perpetuum mobile*, not 40
  stages, transitions between 48
  teleological approach to 75
  today's problems, related to 14
  universal 33–41
Horner, Charles 107
Hulsman, John 141
Human rights
  head of state, violations by 183
  internal affair of state, ceasing to be 182
  international law, development of 181
  international movement, post-WWII 182
  life, right to 222
  massive violations 208, 215, 219
  promotion abroad 147
  respect for and protection of, principle of 222
  universality of 15
  use of force for protection of 219–220
Human societies
  Eastern and Western 29–32
  Eastern, inventions originating in 30
  elements eliminated from 25
  heterogenisation of 27–29
  improvement of quality of life 24
  layers of 41–43
  nation-states, organisation into 41
  post-industrial, co-existence of 23
  social, political or economic arrangements, no final form of 39
  tolerance in 29
  violence, curbing 25
  Western European, democratization of 28–29
Humanitarian intervention
  advocates of 228
  characteristics of societies, importance of 228
  civil war, in 223–225
  criteria of legitimacy for 213
  decisions as to, persons making 226
  internal disturbances, in 223–225
  regime change, and 198–199, 207–212, 223–225
  responsibility to protect, and 212–223
  secessionist movements, encouraging 198
  Security Council, authorisation by 214–215, 218, 220–221
  successful, determinants of 225–232
  use of force, and 179–187
Humanity
  concept of 11
  linear progress 22
Humankind
  common characteristics 18
  dissimilation 21
  diversity 17
  East African Rift Valley, emergence from 16
  ex uno plures
    e pluribus unum, replacement by 21–27
    evolution, in 15–21
  homogenization 24, 27–29
  interaction 21
  movement from Africa 17
  social groups, changes in 17
  universal history of 18
Huntington, Samuel 78
Hussein, Saddam 50
Hutton, Will 88

Ignatius, Adi 134
Ikenberry, John 31, 38, 109
Indonesia
  development of 91
Inequality
  economic and political 64
Innocent, Majou 172
Innovations
  copying 21–22
Internal affairs
  non-interference, principle of 11
Internal conflict
  government intervention in 8
International Criminal Court
  establishment of 183
International criminal tribunals
  establishment of 182–183

International humanitarian law
  conflict, application in 202
International Labour Organisation
  creation 74
  effectiveness of 74
  mandate 74
International law
  different theories of 10
  extreme responses to extreme situations, provision for 183
  head of state, dealing with atrocities by 183
  human rights, of 181
International peace and security
  conflicts threatening 184
  humanitarian crisis, threat stemming from 186
International politics
  different theories of 10
  study, methods of 12
International relations
  democratisation of 63
  Realist theories of 8
  regime change, issues with 161
International society
  social system of 5
International system
  contemporary, nature of 10
Iraq
  Kurds, safe havens for 185
  liberal democracies, effect of policies of 211
  severe humanitarian crisis in 186
  stable dictatorship in 130

J-Curve 137–138
Jacques, Martin 30, 110
Japan
  democratisation 228–230
Jarvik, Laurence 146
Jews
  Nazi persecution, complaint before League of Nations 182

Kagan, Robert 39
Kaletsky, Anatole 108, 109
Kant, Immanuel 161, 173–175, 177–178
Kaplan, Lawrence 178
Kaplan, Robert 130
Karaganov, Sergei 76, 83, 139, 217
Karzai, Hamid 209
Keller, Gabriel 189
Khestanov, Ruslan 139
Kinzer, Stephen 120
Kirkpatrick, Jeane 232
Kleine-Ahlbrandt, Stephanie T. 112
Knaus, Klaus 225–227, 230
Koh, Harold Hongju 169
Kosovo 188–189
  Albanians, acts of 188–189
  independence, recognition of 191–194
  international community, manipulative administration by 191
  Kosovo Liberation Army, acts of 188–189, 198
  NATO action in 184–192
  Rambouillet Agreement 189–190
  Serbian side, reports of atrocities of 188
Krauthammer, Charles 39
Kristol, William 178
Krugman, Paul 65
Kupchan, Charles 54, 57, 83
Kuper, Leo 59
Kuperman, Alan 198
Kyrgyzstan
  colour revolution in 94
  conflict in 93–97
  market reforms and democratization, introduction of 94
  racketeering in 96
  southern, inter-ethnic clashes 95
  Uzbeks and Kyrgyz, differences in lifestyle 95

Landis, Joshua 206
Language
  independent evolution of 19
  translation, difficulty of 19
Lantos, Tom 195
Latvia
  Russia, attitude to 150
  Russian speakers in 151
Lavrov, Sergei 143, 193
Law
  role in society 41
Layne, Christopher 162, 167, 171, 209
League of Nations

competence, challenge by Nazis to 182
Leverett, Flynn 203
Levy, Jack 162
Liberal democracy
Europe, in 167
foreign policy 38
imperfections 70
periodic elections, shortcoming of 61
problems of 56–72
promoters of 37, 39
promotion, arguments for 161
shortcomings of 59
universal model, not 109
war-proneness of states 175–178
West, following in 76
whether good for everyone 71
Whig narrative 35
world, view of 35
Liberty
democracy, and 66
Libya
foreign intervention, impact of 231
intervention in, arguments for 225
NATO Operation Unified Protector 196–199
one-sided view of events in 197
opposition, aim of 197
Lieven, Anatol 135, 141, 236
Lithuania
Russia, attitude to 150
Russian speakers in 151
Litigation
Western preference for 30
Lucas, Edward 123, 151
Lukin, Vladimir 135
Lukyanov, Fyodor 145, 153, 154, 157, 160
Lynch, Allen 132–133

Mahbubani, Kishore 31, 89
Mandelson, Peter 111
Markets
world and national 72
Marxism
critics of 44
Enlightenment, as emanation of 34
redesign of world, plan of 34
socialist development 49
McFaul, Michael 145
McNamara, Robert 227
Mead, Walter Russell 35, 79
Mediation
Eastern preference for 30
Medvedev, Dmitry 145, 157
Merry. Robert W. 145–146
Middle Eastern countries
Islamisation 53
women, restrictions on freedom of 53
Migration
current 27–28
Miliband, Ed 186
Mill, John Stuart 59
Miller, Aaron David 198
Minorities
repression, international norm against 214
rights of 60
Moïsi, Dominique 115
Morris, Ian 28, 40, 48, 130
Moyo, Dambisa 105
Murphy, Sean 185
Muslim countries
Islamists, power obtained by 52–53
women, restrictions on freedom of 53

Nasr, Vali R. 205
Nation-state
democracy, and 59
organisation into 41
Nationalism
role of 60
Nations
cultivation 55
Nazis
competence of League of Nations, challenge to 182
domestic repression and external aggressiveness 210
Neo-conservatives
interventionist policies 39
Non-Western societies
non-traditional fault-lines in 54–55
Western model of development imposed on 71
Western societies, transformation to 3, 7
North Atlantic Treaty Organisation (NATO)
Kosovo, action in 184–192

Libya, operation in 196–199
Russia, relations with 157–159
Serbia, operation against 184–192

O'Donnell, Guillerme 4
Obama, Barack 23, 123, 172

Pagel, Mark 17
Palestine
democracy, lack of 129
Pattison, James 226
Peace
democracy, as conducive to 172, 179
democratic theories. *See* Democratic peace theories
perpetual, conditions for 173–175
Peerenboom, Randall 90
Peres, Simon 129
Philosophy
self-consistency 8
western social and political, dominant trend in 13–14
Physical universe
changing order of 41
Pillar, Paul 199
Pinker, Steven 19–20, 22, 25
Poland
Russia, suffering from 151
Political regime
definitions of 4–5
Political system
central aspect of 43
Popper, Karl 36, 64
Power, Samantha 39
Putin, Vladimir 125, 153
authoritarianism 135–138
internal domestic legitimacy, lacking 145
isolation, not wanting 144
London Olympics opening, not attending 156–157
Moscow's relations with neighbours, emphasising importance of 149
political reforms 135
popularity of 137
vertical of power, strengthening 136
al-Qaddafi, Muammar
overthrow of 195–196, 199

Ramadan, Tariq 42, 80, 197, 207
Ramos, Joshua Cooper 76
Rar, Alexander 191
Reagan, Ronald 128–129
Rebellion
assistance to quell, legality of 231
Regime change
colour revolutions 51
general context of 3
international relations, issues with 161
intervention in 223–225
non-peaceful 7
parties, media views of 173
problems of 231
social and political processes 3
today's attempts at 230
current attempts, nature of 45
current, socioeconomic and political problems 41–56
Western political and economic systems, import of 45
Religion
monotheistic 33
Responsibility to protect
humanitarian intervention in terms of 212–223
interpretations of 216–217
Rice, Condaleezza 193–194
Rieff, David 198
Roberts, General Frederick 52
Robinson, James 46–47, 97–101
Rodrik, Dani 56, 59
Romney, Mitt 159
Rorty, Richard 37, 69–70
Rudd, Kevin 116
Rule of law
Britain, in 46–47
Rummel, Rudolf 162
Rumsfeld, Donald 12, 151
Russell, Bertrand 8
Russett, Bruce 171
Russia
Abkhazia, recognition of 149
Anglo-Saxon development, image of 37
authoritarian capitalism 76–77
bandwaggoning, practice of 141–149
believing in 119–124
capitalists, Kremlin dominating 122
Caucasus, buffer zones in 149
close neighbours, relations with 149–153
colonialism, considerations 120

deformity, land of 123
democracy,
not lost to 138–141
prospects of 135
desire to enfeeble 131
disappointment in 123
dislike of 123
domestic and foreign policy, changes in 142–143
dread of 123
expansionism, considerations 120
foreign policy,
economy, and 121
independent 144
GDP 102
geopolitical foe of America, described as 159
Georgia, military conflict with 149, 152–153
human rights record 148
liberal reforms, introduction of 135
national interests, acting in accordance with 121–122
NATO, relations with 156–159
NATO transport going though 158
non-governmental organizations, Western support for 145–146
part of Europe, as 153–160
political and economic shock therapies 102
post-Soviet history, circular movement of 137
regional power, as 169
South Ossetia, recognition of 149
Syria, supply of arms to 204
understanding 119–124
weakening of 136
Westerners' attitude to 122
wider Europe, integration into 155
wrongs committed against 123
Rwanda
governmental genocide in 207

Sachs, Jeffrey 61
Sakwa, Richard 144
Sarkozy, President 199
Saunders, Paul 156
Schacter, Oscar 223
Scheunemann, Randy 39
Schmitt, Carl 11
Schmitter, Philippe 4
Segal, Gerald 26, 30
Self-defence
use of force in 218–219, 221
Sen, Amartya 69
Serbia
NATO operation against 184–192
Sharansky, Anatoly 128–129
Shea, Jamie 188
Simes, Dimitri 39, 156
Slaughter, Anne-Marie 39
Smith, Tony 165
Social development
comparative study of 40
future trends, predicting 177
Social diversity
issue of 15
Social groups
differences in 3
Societies
failure of 24
South Korea
military rule 91
South Ossetia
Georgian attack on 216–218
recognition of 149, 192–194
Sovereign equality
principle of 180
Soviet Union
alteration of system, use of force for 129
China's reforms compared 132
collapse of 1, 125–135
emergence of small states on 109
dissolution of 122
doubly artificial entity, as 125
educated population of 125
empire, as 6
former republics, corruption, mis-management and inter-ethnic tensions 2
socialist development 49
society, compared with China 132–133
successor states, transformation of 130
Spasskiy, Nikolay 154
Stahn, Carsten 216
Starr, Frederick 107
State sovereignty
Commission 213
repressions and violations prevailing over 214–215

Stewart, Rory 225–227, 230
Stiglitz, Joseph 58, 65, 99, 177, 234–235
Strauss-Kahn, Dominique 73
Streeck, Wolfgang 66
Sullivan, Andrew 177
Sweig, Julia 147
Syria
  arms, supply of 204
  army, use of heavy weaponry by 202
  civil war, declaration of 202
  critics of regime 201
  future democracy 206
  humanitarian catastrophe, geo-political context of 202
  intervention in 204
  mass media reports from 199
  median age of population 206
  multi-ethnic and multi-religious country, as 200
  people, rights and interests of 205
  protected civil war, potential for 231
  redistribution of power in 205
  regime change 201
    calls for 203
  repressive government, use of force by 200
  revolt against regime 200
  war crimes and crimes against humanity in 202–203

Tagliavini, Heidi 152
Taiwan
  integration with China 112
Takeyh, Ray 53
Taxation
  perpetual peace, as step to 173–174
  wars, financing 174–175
Terror, war on 66
Theories of democratic peace 8
Treisman, Daniel 122–123
Trenin, Dmitri 103, 104, 149, 157
Tunisia
  bloodless soup in 231
Turkey
  market development in 78–80
Tyranny
  yoke of 66
Tyutchev, Fyodor 119

United Kingdom
  financial sector 58
  industrial and manufacturing base, loss of 58
United Nations
  Charter prohibitions 179–181
  humanitarian catastrophes, jurisdiction over 184
  Millennium Development Goals 102–103
  Security Council
    authorisation of use of force by 214–215, 218, 220–221
    power of 62
United States
  Asia-Pacific region as priority of security policy 113
  Beijing consensus 142
  China's rise, accommodation of 115
  Chinese credit, dependence on 108
  democracies, as protector of 165
  dominance of 235–236
  dominance of 81
  economic and financial future, control of 106
  English speaking elite, dealing with 148
  foreign affairs, legislative and judicial supervision of 172
  hegemonic power, as 168
  money and democracy, correlation between 61
  motto 15
  nation-building 16
  other states, unsettling impact on 211
  power relative to China, reaction to change in 106
  promotion of democracy, aims 120
  Washington consensus 142
Universality
  emphasis on 15
  human rights, of 15
  human society, of 21
  humankind, of 18

Voluntarism
  determinism, versus 40

Wade, Nicholas 24
Walpole, Robert 46

Walzer, Michael 21
Wang Hui 67, 92, 93, 103, 126–134, 234
War
  jus ad bellum 202
  jus in bello 202
War crimes
  international law, responsibility under 213
  massive human rights violations, as 208
  Syria, in 202–203
Watson, Adam 236
Western, Jon 199
White, Hugh 63, 111
Whitehead, Laurence 4
Witt, John Fabian 169
Wolfowitz, Paul 39
Women
  freedom, restrictions on 53
Working conditions
  variations in 74
World economic power
  Goldman Sachs predictions 86–87
Wright, Erik Olin 34
Wright, Quincy 161

Xu Kuangdi 91–92

Yang Jiemian 113, 204
Yang Yao 90
Yeltsin, Boris
  liberal reforms, introduction of 134
  oligarchisation of society under 134
  policies, suspicion of 122
  Russian Parliament, shelling 127
  shock therapy, exercise of 126, 134
  voting in 126
Yessenin, Sergei 15

Zizek, Slavoj 38–39, 76
Zoellick, Robert 111

www.ingramcontent.com/pod-product-compliance
Lightning Source LLC
Chambersburg PA
CBHW061608180926
51615CB00006B/20